D1756306

University Centre at
Blackburn
College

RESISTING NEOLIBERALISM IN EDUCATION

Local, National and Transnational Perspectives

Edited by
Lyn Tett and Mary Hamilton

First published in Great Britain in 2019 by

Policy Press
University of Bristol
1-9 Old Park Hill
Bristol
BS2 8BB
UK
t: +44 (0)117 954 5940
pp-info@bristol.ac.uk
www.policypress.co.uk

North America office:
Policy Press
c/o The University of Chicago Press
1427 East 60th Street
Chicago, IL 60637, USA
t: +1 773 702 7700
f: +1 773-702-9756
sales@press.uchicago.edu
www.press.uchicago.edu

British Library Cataloguing in Publication Data
A catalogue record for this book is available from the British Library

Library of Congress Cataloging-in-Publication Data
A catalog record for this book has been requested

ISBN 978-1-4473-5005-7 hardcover
ISBN 978-1-4473-5020-0 ePub
ISBN 978-1-4473-5006-4 ePdf

Policy Press works to counter discrimination on grounds of gender, race, disability, age and sexuality.

Cover design by Clifford Hayes
Front cover image: www.alamy.com
Printed and bound in Great Britain by CPI Group (UK) Ltd, Croydon, CR0 4YY
Policy Press uses environmentally responsible print partners

This book is dedicated to the memory of
Sue Gardener (1941–2017), inspirational literacy
educator, publisher and community activist.

Contents

List of figures, tables and boxes

Figures

Table

Boxes

Notes on contributors

Gwyneth Allatt is a Senior Lecturer in the Department of Education and Professional Development at the University of Huddersfield, where her main teaching role is with students training to teach in the lifelong learning sector. After graduating with a degree in English from Lancaster University, Gwyneth worked as a college librarian for some years before becoming an English teacher in adult and community education and eventually a teacher educator. She has an MA in History from the University of Huddersfield. Her current research has a focus on adult literacy and the various ways in which the concept of literacy may be perceived and understood.

Jo Bates is a Lecturer in Information Politics and Policy at the University of Sheffield. Her research examines the socio-material factors that influence the production and use of data, and both enable and restrict the movement of data between different people and organisations. Jo has led an Arts and Humanities Research Council project (The Secret Life of a Weather Datum) that examined the sociocultural values, practices and public policies shaping the journey and form of meteorological data from their initial production through to being reused in different contexts, including climate science and financial markets.

Zhe Chen is an international student from China pursuing doctoral studies in Teaching and Curriculum at the University of Rochester. Her research interests focus on educational policy in New York and the US, where she has interviewed elected and appointed education officials, organisation leaders, social activists, and leaders of the opt-out movement. She holds two master's degrees, one in International Education from the University of North Carolina at Chapel Hill and the other in Education Policy from the University of Rochester.

Pia Cort is Associate Professor at the Department of Education Studies, Aarhus University, Denmark. Her research areas include the role of transnational organisations in education policy, especially: the European Union and processes of Europeanisation; the connections between education policy and practice; vocational education and training from a comparative perspective; and lifelong learning policy. In recent research, she has looked into the schism between public policy discourse about low-skilled workers and low-skilled workers' own working life narratives (see, for example, Mariager-Anderson, Cort and Thomsen, 'In reality I motivate myself', *British Journal of Guidance and Counselling*).

Elisabeth Davies is an Assistant Professor in the Faculty of Information and Media Studies, Western University, Canada. Her research interests include documents and temporality, literacies, and metadata management.

Shiv Desai is currently working with Albuquerque Public Schools in New Mexico on implementing ethnic studies in the classroom, with a focus on healing and wellness. His previous research focused on a Youth Participatory Action Research (YPAR) project with LOUD (Leaders Organizing 2 Unite & Decriminalize). LOUD members, comprised of system-involved and allied youth, utilised YPAR to inform new policies to shape a more humanising juvenile justice system. His other research interests include centring and privileging youth voices through spoken word poetry, hip hop and other forms of artistic expression. His research draws upon critical race theory, critical literacy and decolonising/indigenous methodologies.

Vicky Duckworth is Professor of Education at Edge Hill University, England. Vicky has developed considerable expertise as an educationalist and researcher in the field of adult literacy and education. She is deeply committed to challenging inequality through critical and emancipatory approaches to education, widening participation, inclusion, community action, and engaging in research with a strong social justice agenda. Presently, she is leading a Universities and Colleges Union-funded research project, with Dr Rob Smith, which aims to understand and provide evidence of how the further education sector is vital in transforming lives and communities in 21st-century Britain (see: http://transforminglives.web.ucu.org.uk/about-this-project/).

Fergal Finnegan is a Lecturer at the Department of Adult and Community Education, Maynooth University, Ireland, and is a co-director of the Doctorate in Higher and Adult Education programme. His research interests include social movements, biographical research, social class and equality and higher education. He has edited books for The Policy Press and Routledge and has recently co-authored a book, *Access and widening participation in Irish higher education*, for Palgrave Macmillan. Fergal is one of the Editors in Chief of the international *Journal of Transformative Education*. He has been active in

European Society for Research on the Education of Adults (ESREA) since 2010, and is currently a co-convenor of the network on Active Democratic Citizenship and Adult Learning and a member of the steering committee and current vice-chair of ESREA.

Lesley Hagger-Vaughan is an Assistant Professor in the School of Education, University of Nottingham. She has a long-standing professional interest in European education policy issues. She has been a Senior Curriculum Advisor for the Qualifications and Curriculum Development Agency, supporting the development and implementation of the National Curriculum and national language qualifications and has worked on several European-wide curriculum and teacher development programmes. Lesley was a member of the project team on the European Commission funded project 'Investing in education: Strengthening the involvement of teacher trade unions in the European Semester on education training'.

Mary Hamilton is Professor Emerita of Adult Learning and Literacy in the Department of Educational Research at Lancaster University. She is Associate Director of the Lancaster Literacy Research Centre and a founding member of the Research and Practice in Adult Literacy group. She has a long-standing interest in informal, vernacular learning and how communicative and learning resources are built across the lifespan. She has become increasingly involved with historical and interpretive policy analysis, exploring how international influences reach into local practice and the implications of this for tutor and student agency in literacy education. Her current research is in literacy policy and governance, socio-material theory, academic literacies, digital technologies, and change.

Rachel Heydon is a Professor in the Faculty of Education, Western University, Canada, where she specialises in early childhood, literacy, and intergenerational curricula. The goals of her work are to promote expansive literacy and identity options for people across the lifespan and to support educators in collaboratively realising these goals. Two of Rachel's current projects are acting as co-director of the Provincial Centre of Excellence for Early Years and Child Care and intergenerational multimodal curricula. Rachel is the Canadian editor of the forthcoming *Bloomsbury Education and Childhood Studies* series and executive editor of the *Journal of Curriculum Studies*.

David Hursh is a Professor of Education at the Warner School of Education, University of Rochester, New York. Most of his research has focused on how governments, philanthrocapitalists, non-governmental organisations, corporations and investors have supported neoliberal education policies promoting high-stakes testing, privatisation and new managerialism. He has also written about education for environmental sustainability. His most recent books are *The end of public schools: The corporate reform agenda to privatize education* (2016) and (co-edited with Joseph Henderson and David Greenwood) *Environmental education in a neoliberal climate* (2017), both published by Routledge. He is an associate editor of the *Journal of Education Policy* and *Policy Futures in Education.*

Anne Larson is Associate Professor at the Department of Educational Sociology, Aarhus University, Denmark. She holds a degree in political science and a PhD in educational sociology. She has done research related to adult education for more than 20 years, with a special focus on policy. She has, thus, not only knowledge about the recent history of adult education policy through her research, but has also experienced it first-hand. Among her interests is the relationship between transnational education policy and national policy and practice, including how transnational policy is translated into national policy and not just implemented.

Bob Lingard is currently a Professorial Research Fellow in the School of Education at the University of Queensland, Australia. He has published 25 books, both edited and authored, including, most recently, *Globalizing educational policy* (Routledge, 2010) (with Fazal Rizvi), *Politics, policies and pedagogies in education: The selected works of Bob Lingard* (Routledge, 2014), *Globalizing educational accountabilities* (Routledge, 2016) (with Wayne Martino, Goli Rezai-Rashti and Sam Sellar) and *The international handbook of global education policy* (Wiley, 2016) (co-edited with Karen Mundy, Andy Greene and Toni Verger). He has also published more than two hundred journal articles and book chapters on the sociology of education and educational policy studies.

Kathleen Lynch is a Full Professor (adjunct) in the University College Dublin School of Education and was the UCD Chair and Professor of Equality Studies from 2003-2018. She played a key role in founding the UCD Equality Studies Centre in 1990 and the UCD School of Social Justice in 2004/5. Kathleen has written extensively on equality and justice issues. Her co-authored books include *New managerialism in education: Commercialization, carelessness and gender* (2015), *Affective equality* (2009), *Equality: From theory to action* (2004) and *Equality and* *power in schools* (2002). She is currently working on a new book, *Conflicts between Care and Capitalism*.

Sarah McGinnis grew up in Ottawa, Ontario, and earned her bachelor's degree in Education from Houghton College, New York. She has completed her master's in Teaching and Curriculum at the University of Rochester. She has worked to gather research and stories around the opt-out movement in New York State. Sarah is currently working on creating more resources (movie/book) to inform educators and parents about not only the opt-out movement, but also the many different issues surrounding high-stakes standardised tests.

Lori McKee is an Assistant Professor in the Faculty of Education at St. Francis Xavier University in Nova Scotia, Canada. Her research interests include multimodal pedagogies, multimodal literacies and the ways in which teacher professional learning can support teachers to enact these within early childhood classrooms. Lori has published in a variety of early childhood and literacy research journals, including the *Reading Teacher*, *Journal of Early Childhood Literacy* and *Language and Education*.

Marcella Milana is Associate Professor at the University of Verona, Italy, and researches the politics, policy and governance of adult education and learning from comparative and global perspectives. She is currently involved in a European project (ENLIVEN) on policy interventions in adult education markets, co-convenes the ESREA Network on Policy Studies in Adult Education, and co-edits the *International Journal of Lifelong Education*. Her recent publications include: *Global networks, local actions: Rethinking adult education policy in the 21st century* (Routledge, 2017), and (with S. Webb, J. Holford, R. Waller and P. Jarvis) *The international handbook on adult and lifelong education and learning* (Palgrave Macmillan, 2018).

Alison Milner is a doctoral student (Economic and Social Research Council studentship) in the School of Education, University of Nottingham. Her doctoral studies provide a critical, interpretive study of teacher professionalism in England and Sweden. Her wide research interests relate to teacher professionalism, teachers' professional identities, free schools, education policy, comparative education, European education systems, narrative inquiry and discourse analysis. Alison was a member of the project team on the European

Commission-funded project 'Investing in education: Strengthening the involvement of teacher trade unions in the European Semester on education training'.

Pamela Osmond has worked in the field of adult basic education in Australia since the 1970s. She has taught in a range of contexts and occupied a number of management and curriculum support roles in technical and further education (TAFE) colleges in the state of New South Wales (NSW). She has been employed as a teacher educator at the University of Technology Sydney and at TAFE NSW, and is the author of a wide range of teaching and learning resources, including *So you want to teach an adult to read…?* and *Literacy face to face*. Pamela has researched the history of adult basic education in NSW.

Katherine Quinn is a PhD candidate in the Department of Sociology at the University of Warwick. Her PhD research is an ethnographic study of The Hive, a joint public–academic library at the University of Worcester, which is concerned with envisioning radical alternatives to the neoliberal discourse dominant in academic librarianship theory and practice. Prior to beginning her PhD in 2015, Katherine completed an MA in Librarianship at the University of Sheffield and became involved in the Radical Librarians Collective while there. In between studying, she has also worked professionally in sixth-form, university and research institute libraries.

Francesca Rapanà is a Post Doc Fellow at the University of Verona, Italy, where she is involved in the European project 'Encouraging Lifelong Learning for an Inclusive and Vibrant Europe' (ENLIVEN) on policy interventions in adult education markets. Her research interests cover citizenship education, intercultural education and adult education. Her publications include: 'Da pionieri a cittadini. Modelli di educazione alla cittadinanza in famiglie di origine straniera', in M. Tarozzi (ed) *Dall'intercultura alla giustizia sociale. Per un progetto pedagogico e politico di cittadinanza globale* (Franco Angeli, 2015); and (with M. Tarozzi and L. Ghirotto) 'Ambiguities of citizenship. Reframing the notion of citizenship education', *Ricerche di Pedagogia e Didattica- Journal of Theories and Research in Education*, 2018, 8(1).

Shawn Secatero (Canoncito Band of Navajo) is an Assistant Professor at the University of New Mexico's Teacher Education Educational Leadership Program and serves as an adjunct instructor at New Mexico State University Grants. His research focuses on indigenous well-being, leadership and K-12 education, and he coordinates the POLLEN Native School Principals programme, the Striking Eagle Native American Basketball Invitational Project and the Tohajiilee Community School Dual Enrollment Program. Furthermore, Dr Secatero's extensive educational background incorporates project-learning initiatives that include spiritual, mental, physical and social well-being attributes of leadership and learning.

Annmarie Sheahan holds a doctoral degree in Language, Literacy and Sociocultural Studies at the University of New Mexico and is an Assistant Professor in English Education and Young Adult Literature in the Department of English at Western Washington University.

Rob Smith is a Reader in Education at Birmingham City University, England. His body of work explores the impact of funding and marketisation on further education. He has researched and written extensively in collaboration with practitioners in further and higher education settings. His recent research with Dr Vicky Duckworth focuses on further education as a space for transformative learning. Other recent work uses a Lefebvrian theoretical frame to look at higher education and further education space and how new educational architecture conceptualises teaching and learning.

Mia Sosa-Provencio is Assistant Professor of Secondary Education in the Department of Teacher Education, Educational Leadership, and Policy at the University of New Mexico. Prior to earning a Curriculum and Instruction Doctorate from New Mexico State University, Mia taught 9th- to 12th-grade Language Arts at Rio Grande High School in Albuquerque's South Valley. Her research includes framing education as social justice and particularly building academically rigorous, culturally fortifying schooling spaces, especially for Latina/o, Mexican/Mexican-American youth and all marginalised youth. Born in Las Cruces, Mia has deep roots in both Northern and Southern New Mexico and Juárez, Mexico.

Howard Stevenson is Professor of Educational Leadership and Policy Studies in the School of Education, University of Nottingham. He has written extensively on education sector industrial relations, undertaking funded research for Education International, the European Trade Union Committee for Education and a number of individual education unions in different countries. He was the lead researcher on the European Commission-funded project 'Investing in education:

Strengthening the involvement of teacher trade unions in the European Semester on education training'.

Lyn Tett is Professor Emerita at the University of Edinburgh and Professor of Community Education at the University of Huddersfield, UK. She carries out research within the broad area of community education and lifelong learning, and in particular investigates the factors that can lead to the exclusion of adults from post-compulsory education and the action that might be taken to promote social inclusion. Lyn has a particular interest in the adult literacies sector and has been involved in many projects in this area.

Virginie Thériault is Professor of Adult Education at the Université du Québec à Montréal (UQAM) in Canada. Formerly, she was Lecturer in Informal Education in the School of Education at the University of Strathclyde. Her current research interests include literacy mediation, bureaucratic literacies, young people experiencing precarity and community education. She also has a particular interest in understanding the connections between the francophone and anglophone traditions of literacy research. Her recent publications appeared in the *Journal of Adolescent & Adult Literacy*, *Ethnography and Education* and *Language and Literacy*.

Pat Thomson and Christine Hall are Professors of Education in the School of Education at the University of Nottingham, and are members of the Centre for Research in Arts, Creativity and Literacies. They have written over 30 book chapters and journal articles about their shared research, as well as two books, *Place-based methods for researching schools* (Bloomsbury 2017) and *Inspiring school change: Transforming education through the creative arts* (Routledge, 2017). They are currently working together, with Tate and the Royal Shakespeare Company, on an Arts Council-funded longitudinal research project, 'Tracking arts learning and engagement' (see: researchtale.net), and an evaluation of a writing and illustration programme run by Popup Projects.

Carlos Vargas-Tamez is a sociologist of education who specialises on global education policy. His research and publications focus on the intersections between education, human rights, well-being and social justice. He has worked for universities, civil society, international organisations and local governments in Latin America and Europe. For the past three years, he has worked for the United Nations Educational, Scientific and Cultural Organization (UNESCO), first coordinating research on the social relevance and cultural pertinence of education in five continents and, currently, as Chief of the Teacher Development Unit at UNESCO's Regional Office for Education in Latin America and the Caribbean.

Emily Winchip recently completed her doctorate at the School of Education, University of Nottingham. Her doctoral studies focused on understanding the effects of privatisation through an analysis of for-profit international schools and, in particular, the experiences of teachers working in for-profit schools. Emily locates her work in a critical feminist tradition, where she uses mixed methodologies. She specialises in the use of measurement models, in particular, Mokken and Rasch analysis. Emily was a member of the project team on the European Commission-funded project 'Investing in education: Strengthening the involvement of teacher trade unions in the European Semester on education training'.

Keiko Yasukawa is a Lecturer in Education at the University of Technology, Sydney. For many years, she coordinated and taught in the adult education teacher education programmes. She researches in the areas of critical mathematics and numeracy practices, workplace learning, and the tensions between policy, practice and pedagogy in adult literacy and numeracy. She is the editor of *Literacy and Numeracy Studies: An International Journal in the Education and Training of Adults*.

George K. Zarifis is Professor of Continuing Education in the Faculty of Philosophy, Department of Education, at the Aristotle University of Thessaloniki, Greece. His research interests focus on adult educators' training and professionalisation, university continuing education, and the comparative examination of adult learning and vocational education and training policies and practices in South-Eastern Europe. He researches, publishes, edits and co-authors in the area of adult and continuing education, and participates in a large number of European-funded projects and studies in the same field.

Foreword: the imperative to resist

Kathleen Lynch

The myth of meritocracy fuels the misperception that wealth inequalities arise from natural genius and hard work, although empirical evidence proves the contrary: most wealth is inherited intergenerationally rather than earned (Piketty, 2014). Correlatively, the unrealisable dream that there can be equality of opportunity in economically and socially unequal societies is sold to children and teachers, incentivising them with false promises (Mijs, 2016): they imbibe the myth that there can be equality of opportunity without equality of condition, thereby undermining resistance to injustices that are endemic to education in an economically unequal society (Lynch, 2019). Yet, resistance is possible and education can and does play a central role in this.

As Althusser (1971) observed, there are three major institutions of ideology: the media, religion and education. While religion and the media are generally outside democratic control, this is not true of education. Education is a basic human right and is recognised as such in Article 26 of the Universal Declaration of Human Rights, Article 13 of the International Covenant on Economic, Social and Cultural Rights (ICESCR) and Article 2 of Protocol No. 1 of the European Convention on Human Rights. Moreover, it is recognised as a constitutional right in many countries.

While the status of education as a human right does not guarantee that it can operate as a site to resist injustices, it most certainly challenges it morally and enables it legally to do so. Education is a relatively autonomous field of social practice (Bourdieu, 1993) and, as many chapters in this book demonstrate, educationalists can and do exercise this autonomy in creative and imaginative ways, challenging the values and practices of neoliberalism in many different educational settings.

While the relative autonomy of education enables it to exercise resistance, there is also a moral imperative to do so. Education is, at its foundation, a distributive process: it opens up new ways of knowing the world, facilitating new forms of consciousness and giving access to knowledge (Naidoo, 2015). Given this, resistance to injustice is integral to the very purpose of education itself. Education is compelled to be proactive in defending its foundations as a public good, enabling the unnamed, unknown, unspoken and unthinkable to be thinkable and visible. This means that there is a moral obligation on educationalists to protect its epistemological and ontological foundations by resisting attempts to undermine it as a human right and public service. Without such resistance, education is in danger of being incorporated into the market as an instrument of capitalism and profiteering, a simple provider of human capital.

While resistance is a set of actions and opposition, it is more than this. Resistance to neoliberalism is a mindset: a set of dispositions, be these individual or collective, that challenges the social and educational injustices that neoliberalism promulgates and institutionalises. It is about challenging the anti-solidaristic and anti-redistributive values of competitive individualism, hierarchy and anti-democratic practices that are endemic to neoliberal capitalism (Lynch and Kalaitzake, 2018).

In that respect, engaging in resistance involves taking a moral position; it is about making political and educational decisions, be these personal or collective, to institutionalise respect for holistic, critical education in every educational space. It is about undermining the hegemony of the market-led perspective, where scholars are required to mutate from being persons with human rights to education to being sources of human capital.

As Mary Hamilton and Lyn Tett observe in their closing chapter in this book, resistance is about making hope happen through the proactive pursuit of ideals. In my own experience, it involved working since 1990 with colleagues to establish and maintain the Equality Studies Centre in University College Dublin (UCD) as a site of egalitarian teaching, action and research, and then to establish the UCD School of Social Justice in 2004 (Lynch, 1995; Crean and Lynch, 2011). It also involved and continues to involve managing the disappointments and challenges in between, including the amalgamation of the School of Social Justice into a larger and more conservative school in 2015. The process of resisting has no ending; there is no time of arrival, just a constant state of becoming.

The intellectual incorporation of dissent is probably the greatest challenge for educationalists who are trying to promote resistance; to address this, ongoing vigilance in the face of incorporation and subversion has to be routinised in research and teaching practices. The only way to ensure that this happens is to place collective (especially) and individual reflective resistance at the heart of education itself. The ability of neoliberal capitalism to capture language and reinvent meanings and institutions that are nominally socially just while using those very same institutions and languages to pursue profit and market interests (Boltanski and Chiapello, 2005; Holborow, 2015) is a global threat to social and educational security that cannot be underestimated.

In an age of neoliberalism, where everything and everyone is counted and measured, fear of not measuring up is always in danger of constraining resistance, not least because resistance takes time away from those measureable achievements that advance individual careers and statuses. Resistance is about taking risks, professionally and personally. It is about making individual careers and institutional projects a second-order priority. To have the moral courage to resist those forms of education that undermine us in our humanity is vital, and, as the chapters in this book show, moral courage is made durable when it is collectively sustained and embedded in the culture of curricula, pedagogy, research and action.

References

Althusser, L. (1971) 'Ideology and ideological state apparatuses', in L. Althusser, *Lenin philosophy and other essays* (trans by B. Brewster), London: New Left Books.

Boltanski, L. and Chiapello, E. (2005) *The new spirit of capitalism*, New York, NY: Verso.

Bourdieu, P. (1993) *The field of cultural production*, Cambridge: Polity Press.

Crean, M. and Lynch, K. (2011) 'Resistance, struggle and survival: The university as a site for transformative education', in A. O'Shea and M. O'Brien (eds) *Pedagogy, oppression and transformation in a 'post-critical' climate*, London: Continuum, pp 51–68.

Holborow, M. (2015) *Language and neoliberalism*, New York, NY: Routledge.

Lynch, K. (1995) 'Equality and resistance in higher education', *International Studies in Sociology of Education*, 5(1): 93–111.

Lynch, K. (2019) 'Inequality in education: What educators can and cannot do', in M. Connolly, D.H. Eddy-Spicer, C. James and S.D. Kruse (eds) *The SAGE handbook of school organization*, London: Sage, pp 301–17.

Lynch, K. and Kalaitzake, M. (2018) 'Affective and calculative solidarity: The impact of individualism and neoliberal capitalism', *European Journal of Social Theory*. Available at: https://doi.org/10.1177/1368431018786379

Mijs, J.J.B. (2016) 'The unfulfillable promise of meritocracy: Three lessons and their implications for justice in education', *Social Justice Research*, 29(1): 14–34.

Naidoo, L.A. (2015) 'The role of radical pedagogy in the South African Students Organisation and the Black Consciousness Movement in South Africa, 1968–1973', *Education as Change*, 19: 112–32.

Piketty, T. (2014) *Capital in the twenty-first century*, Cambridge, MA: Belknap Press of Harvard University Press.

Introduction: resisting neoliberalism in education

Lyn Tett and Mary Hamilton

Introduction

This book arose from a seminar presented at the European Conference on Educational Research (ECER) in September 2017. The seminar itself was prompted by a concern that although there was much discussion and many publications that critiqued neoliberalism, very few actually suggested how its impacts might be resisted. The seminar generated a lot of interest and so we felt that it was important to bring together ideas from across the spectrum of education into a book.

In one of his last books, *Pedagogy of indignation*, Freire (2004:110) argues that neoliberalism is a deeply fatalistic discourse that 'speaks about the death of dreams and utopia and deproblematizes the future'. He reminds us that one of the key roles of critical intellectuals is to re-problematise the social reality of the present and to foster critical awareness of alternatives (see Roberts, 2005). Our aim here, therefore, is to offer positive examples of resistance to neoliberal education from across sectors and geographical contexts, and to show how these enable neoliberalism to be challenged and changed. In this introduction, we discuss what we mean by 'neoliberalism' and 'resistance', and go on to show how this book can provide 'resources of hope' (Williams, 1989) in troubled times.

Neoliberalism in education

We understand the defining features of neoliberalism to be a system within an institutional framework characterised by strong private property rights, free markets and free trade that involves deregulation, privatisation and the withdrawal of the state from many areas of social provision (Harvey, 2005). In education, this leads to a competitive market approach within which educational goods (such as qualifications, curricula, institutional reputation, expert labour) are branded and exchanged in an international arena (Rizvi and Lingard, 2010). This approach prioritises individualisation of achievement and competition rather than collaboration among practitioners and among students. It creates a low-trust environment where professionals (and students) have to be monitored and assessed by external yardsticks. The result is that efficiency and monetised values are prioritised over other pedagogical and social values, such as diversity, equity, well-being and care. Under neoliberalism, education systems have been mandated to develop efficient, creative and problem-solving learners and workers for a globally competitive economy, leading to the neglect of its social and developmental responsibilities (Olssen, 2009). These institutionalised practices have been partially accomplished by persuading each individual teacher and learner to treat the effects of neoliberalism as personal rather than structural, which therefore become accepted by individuals as normal rather than as in need of critique and transformation. A key way in which this acceptance happens is through the use of a plethora of metrics such as the Programme for International Student Assessment (OECD, 2016). These assessments are used to measure performativity through a focus on market considerations, which do not necessarily reflect the core values of the work, that is, the quality of the teaching, inclusion and relationships (Lynch, 2006).

Our contention is that such a system is in fundamental tension with more holistic and inclusive approaches to education, and is therefore challenging for all those participating in it. However, as Foucault (1998: 95) has argued, 'where there is power there is resistance' because resistance involves recognising and questioning socialised norms and constraints through discourse. While discourse 'reinforces [power], it also undermines and exposes it, renders it fragile and makes it possible to thwart' (Foucault, 1998: 101). Drawing on Foucault provides a way of thinking about resistance that focuses on the role of subjectivity and transgression in refusing to accept the neoliberal practices of performativity (Ball and Olmedo, 2013). This book is an exploration of how people in different positions within neoliberal education are responding to it and where they find resources and strategies to manage the tensions and contradictions that they encounter.

Resistance

When we envisage *resistance*, we often think of it as a collective, public and political activity; however, there are many types of resistance. In this book, we argue that the concept has two central dimensions: resistance must involve *action* (physical, material or symbolic) and be *oppositional*, in that actors challenge or subvert dominant discourses and practices in some way. Resistance also needs to be intentional, although some actions may be hidden from the view of powerful authorities, such as when practitioners avoid using reporting mechanisms that they consider unfair to the people they work with. Resistance is also interactional because it is 'defined not only by resisters' perceptions of their own behaviour but also by their targets' recognition of, and reaction to, this behaviour' (Hollander and Einwohner, 2004: 548). The possible resources and strategies will differ from context to context but a sense of action and of opposition holds these expressions of resistance together.

The different forms of resistance identified by Hollander and Einwohner are usefully integrated within a strand of literature dealing with 'everyday resistance'. These are less visible forms of resistance that Scott (1990) links to the notion of 'transcripts' (hidden and public), which are established ways of behaving and speaking that fit particular actors in particular social settings, whether dominant or oppressed. Resistance is a subtle form of contesting 'public transcripts' by making use of prescribed roles and language to resist the abuse of power – including things like 'rumour, gossip, disguises, linguistic tricks, metaphors, euphemisms, folktales, ritual gestures, anonymity' (Scott, 1990: 137). Scott (1985: 136) argues that 'most of the political life of subordinate groups is to be found neither in the overt collective defiance of power holders nor in complete hegemonic compliance, but in the vast territory between these two polar opposites'. Johansson and Vinthagen (2016: 421) add to this framework the term 'repertoire of resistance', which they argue is 'a combined result of the interplay between social structures and power relations, as well as activists' creative experimentation with tactics and experiences of earlier attempts to practise resistance, together with the situational circumstances in which the resistance is played out'. This means that groups develop a collection of ways of resisting that they understand and are able to handle, which are embedded in relationships and processes of interaction between the resisters and their targets. These repertoires are organised in specific contexts according to the historical and current power configurations, time, space, and relationships in which they are embedded.

Resistance is, however, more complicated than a simple 'us-and-them' analysis and requires a critically reflexive approach to identify and question the existing assumptions that underlie our actions and the context for that action. As actors, we have to make informed choices about our activism through asking critical questions of the self and thinking through the entire situation. Archer (2007: 4) argues that people have to 'consider themselves in relation to their (social) context and vice versa', where 'critical reflexivity acts as a mediating influence between the social context, structure and human agency' (Dyke et al,

2012: 835). This means that we need to acknowledge that we are all implicated in many ways in the neoliberal turn and so have to find ways of bringing in new perspectives that challenge the basis of our decisions and actions. Dialogic spaces that take account of different perspectives can help us do that. These spaces can be created through working together with congruent colleagues from across the wider social arena to question dominant epistemologies, or by having our assumptions exposed through an outsider view, such as when artists challenge teachers to create different pedagogic approaches. As we are products of multiple systems, critical reflexivity is an important stance that enables us to push back against the dominant culture through acts of 'everyday resistance'.

Resources of hope

Lilja and colleagues (2017) have demonstrated the link between these forms of 'everyday' resistance and more organised civil-society-based resistance. They point out that the latter 'can encourage and create yet other forms of everyday resistance through being inspired or provoked into new resistant identities' (Lilja et al, 2017: 52). They also show, however, that if resistance is unsuccessful, it eventually discourages action and people put their innovative energies into more productive issues. Our aim, therefore, is to encourage action by providing resources in this book that are designed to help us find innovative and productive ways of challenging inequalities in education. In particular, we present those that subvert and challenge narrow curricula and pedagogies that privilege the dominant culture. We agree with Williams (1989: 15) that we need to have an education system that is redesigned so that it provides full 'human relevance and control … [and] emphasises not the ladder but the common highway', because every person's 'ignorance diminishes me, and every [person]'s skill is a common gain of breath'.

Getting to this point, though, means that we have to engage with a variety of ways of challenging the dominant culture of neoliberalism. Williams (1977) suggests that such challenges occur not only through struggle and action, but also through changes in deep structures of feeling and imagination. In particular, he argues that dominant discourses 'select from and consequently exclude the full range of human practice [yet some] experiences, meanings, and values are nevertheless lived and practised on the basis of some residue – cultural as well as social – of some previous social and cultural institution or formation' (Williams, 1977: 125). These *residual* resources were formed in the past but are still 'active in the cultural process … as an effective element of the present' (Williams, 1977: 123) through people's 'practical consciousness'. In addition to these resources, there is '*emergent*' culture, which carries new meanings and values, and 'depends crucially on finding new forms or adaptions of forms' (Williams, 1977: 126). Throughout this book, there are illustrations of the use of both these forms of culture as resources with which to challenge and change neoliberalism so that the full range of knowledge can be expressed within education. For example, Chapters 2, 4 and 13 all emphasise the residual resources that come from historical traditions of policy and practice, whereas Chapters 7 and 15 concentrate on the emergent culture that arises from finding new spaces in which to do things differently. Chapters 8, 9 and 11, on the other hand, show the importance of drawing on both types of resources to elaborate new visions of resistance to neoliberalism.

Of course, this is just one of many possible theoretical frameworks that can be used to conceptualise resistance, and in the next section, we outline some of the rich variety of resources, contexts and frameworks that the authors have brought to bear on understanding and implementing resistance.

The structure of the book

In this book, voices are heard that subscribe to a variety of positions. The themes that they raise and the conceptual resources deployed reflect a range of perspectives that have the common aim of addressing questions of how the power of the neoliberal discourse might be resisted in education. Following this Introduction, the book is organised in five parts. The first three parts are focused on local contexts of resistance because this is where the 'wild profusion of practice' (Ball, 1994: 10) is most evident, and we illustrate how it is enacted in the fields of adult, school and higher education.

We begin with adult education because this is the area that often has enough flexibility to offer a variety of 'resources of hope' for democratic renewal. Within this part, the opening chapter by Virginie Thériault provides the most local example of 'dynamic resistance' from workers in two community-based organisations for young people in Québec, where practitioners find themselves in a situation of 'conflictual cooperation' in which they receive funding from the state but also maintain a critical stance towards it. Resourcefulness, awareness and creativity are identified as the key elements that enabled youth workers to navigate neoliberal practices and adapt them so that they would be meaningful to the young people with whom they were working. Next,

Vicky Duckworth and Rob Smith explore transformative learning that can overturn negative and stigmatising classificatory education within adult and further education in England. This chapter discusses the place of research in affirming localised understandings of education that cut across the grain of contemporary educational reform. In the context of the dominance of a 'skills' discourse in further education in England, they argue that literacy education can offer a differential space that is emancipatory for many learners at the local level of the family and community. The final chapter, from Gwyneth Allatt and Lyn Tett, examines how official policies are translated and enacted within and across a range of literacy programmes based in the North of England and Scotland. They show that despite the stress on performativity, the professional culture of literacy practitioners has enabled them to assert their agency to support literacy that is based in rich and meaningful practices, mainly through various acts of everyday resistance. These included 'workarounds', where they used their discretion to subvert policies that were seen to be unworkable in practice, as well as creating spaces that enabled them to continue to work in the ways that they valued.

The next part focuses on school education and again starts from the most local context, where Lori McKee, Rachel Heydon and Elisabeth Davies show how supporting the development of multimodal pedagogies in an early-years classroom in Ontario, Canada, helped to create more connected literacies, joyful engagement in learning and new relationships between children, teachers, materials and meaning-making. The chapter argues that professional learning spaces where teachers can exercise professional discernment and focus on children as pedagogical informants prompted teachers to reconsider their understandings of existing and dominant print-centric pedagogies, as well as of the children's capabilities as meaning-makers. Pat Thomson and Christine Hall's chapter points out that because schooling is dominated by the requirement to produce good test, exam and inspection results that can be reduced to statistical data, pedagogies have become dull and routinised. In order to resist that requirement, the chapter provides examples from across a range of English secondary schools of the collaborative work of teachers and artists, as well as partnerships between schools and arts organisations, that are able to disrupt these pedagogies. David Hursh, Sarah McGinnis, Zhe Chen and Bob Lingard are also concerned with testing regimes, and their chapter charts parents' resistance in New York State to neoliberal and corporate reform agendas. It has a particular focus on the opt-out movement against testing policies because parents identified these policies' negative impact on the quality of schooling. The authors also consider how this example of local action has national implications for resistance to the extension of the corporate reform agenda of public schooling. In the final chapter in this part, Shiv Desai, Shawn Secatero, Mia Sosa-Provencio and Annmarie Sheahan emphasis the role of subjectivity when they outline a pedagogical framework for use across teacher education and schools that utilises Chicana feminist and indigenous epistemologies. They argue that the neoliberal corporate 'reform' agenda contributes to destabilising communities and separates educators, children and families from the power that education holds to unlock inquiry, creativity, connectedness and agency towards resistance. Instead, they demonstrate how a 'Body-Soul Rooted Pedagogy' advances a theory and practice of schooling as medicine, healing and hope to embolden youth and educators across cultures and enact education as a corporeal, soulful practice whose lifeblood is students' untapped knowing, critical consciousness and artistic, performative, civically engaged selves.

The final local context is higher education, and we begin with Katherine Quinn and Jo Bates's examination of the political position of academic librarianship in England, exploring how critical knowledge production and dissemination can offer radical educational possibilities. They use a case study of the Radical Librarians Collective (RLC) to illustrate how it provides space for discussion and mutual aid between like-minded library workers. The everyday workplace practices of resistance that it provides includes resisting restrictions of access rights for students and members of the public and local community, both physically (gated spaces) and financially (paywalls, open access journals and so on). Mary Hamilton's chapter focuses on examples of different kinds of resistant acts that have taken place in recent years within the changing higher education workplace in England. Evidence is provided of resistance at the micro-interactional level and of workarounds, sabotage, subversive uses of language and 'hacking the system', most of which reflect strongly held principles that are not rewarded by the neoliberal university. She argues that the framework of 'everyday resistance' can help us to understand this evidence in the context of more recent political action and how it reflects high levels of discomfort and wider frustration with the directions in which universities are moving. The final chapter, from Fergal Finnegan, has the widest lens as it begins with a brief review of the overall impact of neoliberalisation on social and educational inequalities in Irish higher education. It documents and analyses everyday and political resistance to neoliberal higher education by staff, by students and through social movement campaigns. It explores higher education as a 'contradictory' space where neoliberalism is an incomplete project in which residues of other rationalities and practices are drawn upon. He argues that a new vision of the university needs to be developed that builds on the ideas of the 'knowledge commons' and the non-commodifiable nature of education to imagine new forms of higher education altogether.

Part IV is organised so that we move from the most specific illustrations of national policy to those that offer the most general perspective. Therefore, we begin with the interplay between policymaking that occurs within the European Union (EU), the Italian republic and one of its autonomous provinces in the chapter by Marcella Milana and Francesca Rapanà. The chapter critically examines how the cultural, economic and normative frames of reference that result from international–national–local policy interactions are locally appropriated (and [re]interpreted) using a public provider of popular adult education, the *Università della Terza Età e del Tempo Disponibile* (University of the Third Age and Free Time) (UTETD), as an illustrative case. The next chapter, from Pia Cort and Anne Larson, takes a historical perspective to trace Danish adult education policy from the 1960s, with its intertwining of popular and adult education, to the current focus on the return of investment in adult education. They argue that documenting the drift in adult education policy is a resistant act because political solutions tend to be naturalised as 'obvious' answers to societal problems; therefore, the Danish tradition of popular education, with its emphasis on dialogue and empowerment through participation, holds a potential to counterbalance the hegemonic discourse of 'qualification for the labour market' and contribute to a debate about common values and the 'good life' of Danish citizens. Keiko Yasukawa and Pamela Osmond, in the final chapter of this part, analyse the hegemonic discourse impacting upon the Australian adult literacy and numeracy field, where practitioners have experienced the imposition of externally produced and pedagogically alien tools and instruments for practice. Aspects are identified of the activity system that needs to be disturbed in order to provoke a radical transformation of the field through local and international practitioners exercising 'everyday resistance'. They argue that a new strand of resistance may grow and weaken the foundations of the neoliberal hold on adult education and civil society when organisations in the wider social arena, whose interests are congruent with practitioners' interests, work in conjunction with academic researchers in critically reinterpreting aspects of the dominant discourse.

The final part focuses on how, even at the transnational level, it is possible to disrupt the neoliberal discourse. It offers three different perspectives that again move from the more specific to more general examples of resistance. The first chapter, by Howard Stevenson, Alison Milner, Emily Winchip and Lesley Hagger-Vaughan, takes a little-known aspect of the EU's policy architecture, the European Semester, as an example of a 'policy space' in which social policy objectives are becoming increasingly significant. The authors identify a number of strategies available to social partner and civil society organisations that offer the possibility of 'opening up' the European Semester as a democratic space in which the case for high-quality public education can be made. The next chapter, from George K. Zarifis, is also concerned with EU policy but the focus here is on active citizenship in programmes for socially and economically at-risk adults. The author argues that adult education must resist the governing policy language and prevent the regurgitation of the messages of a dominant political culture that despite its value-filled rhetoric, professes to develop value-free practices. The priority should be to achieve active participatory citizenship education rather than seeing education as a panacea for ensuring national unity within the nation state. Adult education for active participatory citizenship can operate as a platform towards organising programmes that will operate as resistance agents to neoliberal callings. The final contribution to the book, from Carlos Vargas-Tamez, has the wide goal of 'bringing equity and inclusion back into education'. It explores how neoliberal understandings of equity in education are limited and may lead to the reproduction of disadvantage and marginalisation. It therefore proposes that equity and inclusion should be conceptualised under a notion of social justice so as to deconstruct inequality and subvert dominant utilitarian discourses. Finally, the chapter asserts that the 2030 Agenda for Sustainable Development and the education goal (SDG 4 - Education 2030) represent an invaluable opportunity to counter neoliberalism in education and to ideate different resistance practices. At the end of the book, Mary Hamilton and Lyn Tett gather together the ideas and strategies offered by contributors into an afterword – 'Resources for hope' – that can be drawn on by educationalists and used in their own contexts.

References

Archer, M. (2007) *Making our way through the world*, Cambridge: Cambridge University Press.

Ball, S.J. (1994) *Education reform: A critical and post-structuralist approach*, Buckingham: Routledge.

Ball, S.J. and Olmedo, A. (2013) 'Care of the self, resistance and subjectivity under neoliberal governmentalities', *Critical Studies in Education*, 54(1): 85–96.

Dyke, M., Johnston, B. and Fuller, A. (2012) 'Approaches to reflexivity: Navigating educational and career pathways', *British Journal of Sociology of Education*, 33(6): 831–48.

Foucault, M. (1998) *The history of sexuality: The will to knowledge*, London: Penguin.

Freire, P. (2004) *Pedagogy of indignation*, Boulder, CO, and London: Paradigm.

Harvey, D. (2005) *Neoliberalism: A brief history*, Oxford: Oxford University Press.

Hollander, J.A. and Einwohner, R.L. (2004) 'Conceptualizing resistance', *Sociological Forum*, 19(4): 533–54.

Johansson, A. and Vinthagen, S. (2016) 'Dimensions of everyday resistance: An analytical framework', *Critical Sociology*, 42(3): 417–35.

Lilja, M., Baaz, M., Schulz, M. and Vinthagen, S. (2017) 'How resistance encourages resistance: Theorizing the nexus between power, organised resistance and everyday resistance', *Journal of Political Power*, 10(1): 40–54.

Lynch, K. (2006) 'Neo-liberalism and marketisation: The implications for higher education', *European Educational Research Journal* 5 (1): 1–17.

OECD (Organisation for Economic Co-operation and Development) (2016) *PISA 2015 results, volume 1*, Paris: OECD. Available at: www.oecd.org/education/pisa-2015-results-volume-i-9789264266490-en.htm

Olssen, M. (2009) 'Neoliberalism, education, and the rise of a global common good', in M. Simons, M. Olssen and M.A. Peters (eds) *Re-reading education policy: A handbook studying the policy agenda of the 21st century*, Rotterdam: Sense Publishers, pp 433–57.

Rizvi, F. and Lingard, B. (2010) *Globalizing education policy*, London: Routledge.

Roberts, P. (2005) 'Review essay: Pedagogy, politics and intellectual life: Freire in the age of the market, pedagogy of indignation', *Policy Futures in Education*, 3(4): 446–58.

Scott, J.C. (1985) *Weapons of the weak: Everyday forms of resistance*, London: Yale University Press.

Scott, J.C. (1990) *Domination and the arts of resistance: Hidden transcripts*, London: Yale University Press.

Williams, R. (1977) *Marxism and literature*, Oxford: Oxford University Press.

Williams, R. (1989) *Resources of hope*, London: Verso.

PART I

Adult education

1

Accountability literacies and conflictual cooperation in community-based organisations for young people in Québec

Virginie Thériault

Introduction

In recent years, there has been an increasing interest in the rise of neoliberal practices and their effects on third sector organisations such as community-based organisations (Bradford and Cullen, 2014; Darby, 2016), which include the professionalisation of the sector and the use of monitoring and accountability systems. Bradford and Cullen describe how youth work, as a field, went through major changes in England, especially from the 1960s and 1970s until today, describing a shift from humanist perspectives to a focus on neoliberal and 'value for money' approaches. Community-based organisations have to demonstrate their value for money and therefore compete with each other to obtain limited financial resources (Darby, 2016). They have to engage with a wide range of literacy practices (for example, form filling) to obtain funding, as well as in order to justify it (for example, accountability reports). These can be described as accountability literacies: 'the reading and, particularly, writing practices associated with accountability systems' (Tusting, 2012: 121). In this chapter, literacies are considered as social practices rather than technical skills (Barton and Hamilton, 2012).

Since the beginning of the 1990s, the Québec government has increased its involvement with community-based organisations such as Le Bercail and L'Envol partly because of their potential economic benefits for society and the state. These organisations received more recognition but were also increasingly seen as the state's services providers (Savard and Proulx, 2012). As in other countries, this led to the rise of an accountability regime that focuses on standardisation and monitoring systems (Ade-Ojo and Duckworth, 2015). In the Québec context, Duval and her colleagues (2005: 23) describe the complex relationship between community-based organisations and the state as the paradoxical position of 'conflictual cooperation': the organisations receive funding from the state but also maintain a critical stance towards the state in order to defend and advocate for the people attending their activities. Conflictual cooperation therefore implies a complex amalgam of resistance and collaboration.

The aim of this chapter is to understand how youth workers at Le Bercail and L'Envol managed to navigate this accountability regime and its literacies. The chapter asks the following specific questions: what kinds of accountability literacies were present at Le Bercail and L'Envol; and what are the potential affordances of these literacies for resistance and conflictual cooperation?

Literacy studies and accountability literacies

This chapter draws on the perspective of the New Literacy Studies (NLS), which considers that literacies cannot be defined as the simple ability to read and write, but rather need to be understood as social practices situated in specific social and historical contexts (Barton and Hamilton, 2012). Tusting (2012) investigated accountability literacies in two different settings – a further education (FE) college and an early-years centre – and examined how practitioners learned these literacies. She mentions that a major difficulty in the FE college was that practitioners were accountable to various sources of funding that had different expectations and paperwork formats. For the early-years practitioners, paperwork was seen as an integral part of their professional identity (they had to do it in order to be good at their job), but this feeling was not shared by the FE practitioners (Tusting, 2012). This is in line with the idea that professionalisation is closely related to the rise of neoliberal practices such as accountability literacies in the third sector (Bradford and Cullen, 2014).

Literacy practices, such as case notes, can be an integral part of practitioners' professional identity and might also be sanctioned by their professional organisation. In her study about case notes in professional social work in England, Lillis (2017) notes that case notes usually include an account of the person's difficulties, the context of their general situation and the social worker's level of involvement. These notes can be used as evidence in a number of cases, including to conduct an investigation, to monitor someone's work and to make managerial decisions.

Case notes are increasingly recorded electronically and this links up with another important phenomenon in relation to accountability literacies and the third sector: the rise of electronic information systems. These systems are large computer-based databases in which practitioners record information about the people they work with and details about their involvement with them. Governments around the world are increasingly investing in such system because they believe that these databases make social services more 'transparent and visible' (Devlieghere et al, 2017: 2).

This brief overview sheds light on the complexity and power dynamics that accountability literacies might involve. This form of literacies can shape practitioners' professional identity, their practices and their relationships with agents of power such as the state.

Understanding conflictual cooperation

As the term 'conflictual cooperation' has never been theorised, the following sections provide an overview of key concepts that, altogether, contribute to explain this paradoxical position: moral and procedural accountabilities, everyday resistance, and dynamic resistance. Based on her analysis of the term 'civil society' and of its different constitutive elements, Kaldor (2003) explores how different groups (social movements, non-governmental organisations, social organisations and nationalist and religious groups) balance their work between conflicting demands. According to Kaldor (2003), third sector organisations embody the neoliberal strand of civil society. She asserts that because the state has minimised its involvement in offering social services, these organisations have taken over this responsibility and consequently contributed to a neoliberal economy by, for instance, supporting employability measures and an economic agenda. Kaldor explains that third sector organisations are accountable to the people they serve (that is, moral accountability), as well as to their funders and internal structure (that is, procedural accountability), where they must show that they are delivering what they were paid to do. While very valuable, the concepts of moral and procedural accountabilities only offer a binary vision of the complexity at play.

As mentioned earlier, conflictual cooperation implies both resistance and collaboration. Despite the wide-ranging use of the term 'resistance', it is generally understood as involving: resisters (for example, individuals or groups of people initiating resistance), their targets (for example, individuals, groups of people and institutions as agents of power) and observers (for example, interested bystanders such as researchers and other actors) (Hollander and Einwohner, 2004). Resistance can take subtle forms and might hardly be visible; such a form of resistance is called 'everyday resistance' (Scott, 1985). This can involve subverting everyday practices in order to resist agents of power (for example, employers or funders). To do so, resisters rely on what Johansson and Vinthagen (2016: 422) call a repertoire: 'a collection of ways or methods of resistance that people are familiar with, know of, understand and are able to handle'. Resistance is a situated practice rather than a desired product or intention (Johansson and Vinthagen, 2016). Therefore, resistance in the third sector is likely to include practices with which practitioners already engage on a day-to-day basis, such as accountability literacies.

Darby's (2016) empirical study in a third sector organisation called Oblong, a grass-roots community centre, in Leeds (England) sheds more light on the intricate dimensions of conflictual cooperation. Her study indicates that despite Oblong having values that were diametrically opposed to capitalism, the organisation had to engage with a range of neoliberal practices, such as obtaining a loan and grant funding and dealing with accountability practices. Based on her empirical work, Darby suggests a framework called 'dynamic resistance' to describe the different ways in which third sector organisations challenge neoliberalism and its practices. She explains that 'dynamic resistance' includes four elements: rejection, resilience, resourcefulness and reflexive practice. Rejection is the recognition of a problem and of the idea that it cannot be changed. Resilience represents the urge to do something about the problem identified. The third aspect is resourcefulness, which implies that an organisation: '(1) finds, challenges, and creates ways of accessing resources; (2) develops its skills; (3) builds or strengthens its foundational narratives; and (4) demands or consolidates its recognition and legitimacy' (Darby, 2016: 983). Reflexive practice implies that an organisation must reflect on itself and question its positions, practices, values and future goals. According to Darby (2016), organisations could engage with this process in a more or less systematic way in order to prevent issues such as mission drift or the feeling of being hijacked by a neoliberal logic.

Overall, the paradox or tensions present in conflictual cooperation can be explained by community-based organisations' moral and procedural accountabilities. Beyond this dualistic representation, everyday resistance emphasises how day-to-day practices can be subverted, and consequently how resistance is inextricably embedded in context. Finally, dynamic resistance offers a more comprehensive model developed specifically for the third sector. Together, these concepts constitute the theoretical underpinning of my use and understanding of the concept of conflictual cooperation.

Overview of the study and its methodology

This chapter draws on an ethnographic and participatory study conducted in two community-based organisations – Le Bercail and L'Envol – for young people aged 16 to 30 who were experiencing precarity (Thériault, 2016). Pseudonyms are used to refer to the two community-based organisations and the research participants.

Le Bercail and L'Envol were located in the same mid-sized city in the province of Québec. Their services included (either at one or both organisations) a youth shelter for runaways, supervised flats (affordable accommodation with regular follow-up by a youth worker), structured workshops (including topics such as, cooking, gardening, photography, computing, arts, theatre and so on) and counselling services.

The study extended over three phases: (1) intensive participant observation sessions and interviews (April and May 2012); (2) participatory analysis workshops (April 2013); and (3) dissemination and knowledge-exchange activities (October and November 2015). The overarching aim of the study was to understand the literacy practices used in community-based organisations and their relations to those of the young people attending their activities. During the first phase, 27 people took part in the participant observation sessions. In addition, 21 participants were interviewed: 14 young people and seven youth workers. This chapter only focuses on the data related to accountability literacies and therefore mainly concentrates on the youth workers' accounts. All the interviews with the youth workers were conducted in French; translations are therefore used in this article.

Specific questions were asked about accountability literacies at the end of the research interviews in 2012. I asked the youth workers to describe the kind of accountability literacies that they were expected to do as part of their job, and how these might affect their work with the young people. A content analysis was performed on the following data: transcripts of seven interviews (phase one); audio recordings of three focus groups with eight youth workers (phase two); and observation notes (phases one and two). The data selected for this chapter were analysed with the software NVivo following a content analysis approach (Gibbs, 2008).

The employees at Le Bercail and L'Envol described their positions in the organisations differently, but to facilitate the readability of this chapter, I will refer to them all as youth workers. When asked about the number of hours usually spent on accountability literacies, the youth workers' answers varied from two hours to ten hours per week (average of 35-hour working week). It is important to mention that because of their different roles, some youth workers had more to do in terms of accountability literacies.

Accountability literacies at Le Bercail and L'Envol

Five main sets of accountability literacies were identified at Le Bercail and L'Envol: (1) grant applications; (2) reports; (3) annual general meetings (henceforth, AGMs); (4) statistics and electronic information systems; and (5) recording and case notes. These categories overlap with one another, signifying that in order to complete one literacy demand (for example, fill in a grant application form), youth workers had to rely on the other types of literacies (for example, reports or case notes). In the following sections, I shall discuss these accountability literacies and highlight their potential affordances for conflictual cooperation.

Grant applications

Not all the youth workers who took part in the study had to prepare grant applications. Tommy, who had a coordinating role at Le Bercail, was involved with such literacy practices but his colleagues were not. At L'Envol, grant applications were a sensitive topic. Élise said that grant applications were not "part of our remit, but we still do a little bit". She explained that she would write up sections of a grant that described the activities they were doing with the young people. Once finished, she would send these to the director of the organisation. Similarly, Carl at L'Envol mentioned that he was not "technically" supposed to be involved in preparing grant applications, but, in reality, he often had to write them up himself.

Catherine and Carl at L'Envol expressed concerns regarding the lack of funding for some of their activities. The difficulties expressed by the youth workers resonate with Darby's (2016) idea that neoliberalism can install a climate of competition between community-based organisations (and even between services within the same organisation) as they must bid against each other for the same money. Based on the data, it seems that grant applications did not offer room for resistance at Le Bercail and L'Envol. The youth workers recognised that there was a problem, which parallels 'rejection' in Darby's (2016) model, but the findings also suggest that they felt powerless with regard to this form of literacy, which they perceived as involving high stakes.

Reports

If they obtain funding, the community-based organisations become accountable and are required to produce monthly, trimestral, mid-year and/or annual reports depending on the funders' requirements. Some of the services offered at Le Bercail and L'Envol were funded by multiple sources, including charities, foundations and private companies, but primarily by government bodies (federal, provincial and/or municipal).

Similar to Tusting's (2012) findings, the various formats required by the different funders, as well as the nature and pace of changes, were perceived as confusing by some of the youth workers. For instance, Élise could not remember the exact name of the Canadian government funding scheme that financed some of L'Envol's activities since it had been rebranded a few times. Also, Carl explained that his position at L'Envol was funded by four different funders that required him to produce different reports in different formats. Even for the smallest grant, for instance, CAN$300 (about £170), Tommy at Le Bercail had to produce a report.

The main funder at both L'Envol and Le Bercail was the Canadian government, through its agency called Service Canada and its programme Skills Link. As explained by the youth workers, this programme aims at the development of skills so that young people experiencing precarity can take part in the labour market. One of the youth workers at Le Bercail (who I prefer not to name as this was a sensitive issue for them) said, off the record, that they had to be very careful with the way they were describing their activities to the funding body and the public in general. They could not mention "learning and education" and had to use the terms "training and skills development" instead. In other words, they were pressured to use vocabulary associated with employability rather than education. This could be explained by the fact that education in Canada is a provincial responsibility, not a federal one. Yet, it could also be interpreted as a sign of a shift in adult education and community education towards a skill-focused and employability approach (Ade-Ojo and Duckworth,

2015). Although the youth workers demonstrated some forms of 'resourcefulness' (Darby, 2016) while collaboratively writing reports, this form of accountability literacy did not offer many affordances for resistance.

AGMs

Under the Companies Act (Québec), incorporated non-profit organisations such as Le Bercail and L'Envol are required to hold an AGM. A specific procedure must be followed and a set of documents must be made available to the public before the meeting, which includes a report on the activities of the organisation, a financial statement and budget forecast, an external auditor's report, and the minutes of the previous AGM (Gouvernement du Québec, 2017).

During the first phase of the study, I observed the preparations of the AGM at Le Bercail and L'Envol. I also attended L'Envol's AGM (25 April 2012), which took place in a large room where the organisation would normally hold community dinners and sometimes music shows. The audience was composed of L'Envol's staff, employees of other community-based organisations, funding bodies' representatives, young people attending activities at L'Envol and family and friends. The event was punctuated by PowerPoint presentations summarising the documents mentioned earlier, various speeches by the director, coordinators and youth workers, and short sketches prepared by the young people. With the support of the youth workers, the young people prepared short texts to introduce each service offered at L'Envol. They also presented some of the statistics reported in the annual report.

Involving youth participants in the AGM seems to be a common practice for community-based organisations for young people (based on my observations and discussions). A similar practice was also observed at Le Bercail. Tommy suggested that the young people could prepare a video for the AGM in which they would present what they were doing at Le Bercail. The group instead decided to recite a slam poem – poetic texts that are usually performed as part of an oral poetry competition:

> The project [Mobili-T]
> Project in employability
> To develop our aptitudes,
> Put in place healthy attitudes
> Stabilising ourselves, experimenting, progressing
> Elaborating and actualising…

> Then, after six months
> With self-knowledge,
> self-confidence, and self-esteem
> I will find a job
> Or I go back to education
> With all my worries
> Left behind. (Slam poem for the AGM at Le Bercail, my translation)

The language used in the slam poem suggests that the young people were aware (or had been made aware) of the programme's expected outcomes and funders' requirements (return to education or employment). Yet, the poem also included information about the young people's everyday routine on the programme and what they considered important work. The poem's last section reflects their situation of precarity and hopes for the future – information that might not be included in a regular accountability report.

These examples of participation suggest that the AGMs were an opportunity for the young people to make their voices heard during an important event attended by funding bodies' representatives. They were putting words and faces on the statistics and other information presented in the accountability reports. Such practices relate to Darby's (2016) framework of 'dynamic resistance' and, more specifically, its element of resourcefulness. The staff at Le Bercail and L'Envol organised their AGMs so that they could also serve as a platform to foster young people's voice and learning (speak in public, write/perform a skit, recite poetry and so on). It therefore strengthened its foundational narratives and values, which focus primarily on helping young people experiencing precarity.

Statistics and electronic information systems

The reports produced by the youth workers at Le Bercail and L'Envol drew on a wide range of evidence collected throughout the year. The main source of evidence was the statistics produced by electronic information systems. Youth workers at Le Bercail and L'Envol used electronic information systems to compile quantitative information about the young people. Sometimes, the software was provided by the employer (for example, Ève-Lyne and Frédérique) but others had to create a bespoke database (for example, Catherine, Élise and Carl).

Carl created his very own database where he kept a record of his involvement with young people and descriptions of each participant's needs and situation. With just "a few clicks", Carl spent around four to five minutes after each meeting to complete a participant's file. An employee of the local school board helped him to create this database (the school board partially funded Carl's job). Carl's database included detailed information about the young people (for example, gender, age, language[s] spoken, immigration status and so on), as well as the services that they had received at L'Envol. This allowed Carl to analyse the current state of the services offered to young people. According to Carl, the tables and statistics that he was able to produce with this database allowed him to concretely prove the "credibility, the relevance" and value for money of his work for society.

As illustrated in Darby's (2016) study, community-based organisations must often adopt neoliberal practices in order to achieve their mission and survive. Carl's example illustrates this paradoxical position and emphasises the resourcefulness and creativity that youth workers need to carefully navigate these complex accountability literacies. With the help of a colleague, Carl was able to create a database that allowed him to fulfil the funders' requirements but also show the impact of his work on young people's lives and on society as a whole without absorbing substantial amounts of his weekly work time.

The service for which Carl was employed at L'Envol initially recognised two possible outcomes: returning to education or obtaining employment. Carl had to "push" the funders to also include another possible outcome, which he described as "back to a healthy life" ("*retour à la santé*"). With the addition of this outcome, Carl was able to include accounts for the work that he was doing helping young people with their social lives, mental health and addiction problems. Carl felt that it was important to include this dimension because it was impossible to help a young person to return to education or find a job without first addressing these personal issues. As explained by Kaldor (2003), third sector organisations are more flexible and innovative, and may 'call to account' and bring specific problems to the attention of the state. In this example, Carl's concerns were heard and he was able to make important changes to the services offered. He was able to prioritise moral accountability over the procedural one (Kaldor, 2003), resisting a more functional approach to youth work.

Recording and case notes

Similarly to the social workers in Lillis's (2017) study, the youth workers at Le Bercail and L'Envol wrote case notes that offer a qualitative account of the young people's current life, difficulties, social network and progress, as well as their participation in the organisation's activities and type of support provided. The case notes were sometimes handwritten or typed into a Word document, or kept electronically in a database.

Even though these notes are viewed as time-consuming by some youth workers, all of them acknowledged the fact that they were useful for a variety of reasons. As a new employee, Olivier read the case notes in order to get an overview of the young people attending the activities at L'Envol prior to participating in them himself. Catherine, also at L'Envol, said that writing case notes "forces you to reformulate your thoughts" and to question your initial assumptions about the young people. As a more experienced youth worker at L'Envol, Élise used the case notes to keep track of what was going on in the participants' lives. Based on the data, it appears that case notes can sometimes encourage reflexivity and critical thinking. This could relate to what Darby (2016) calls 'reflexive practice', which requires practitioners to question their practice and values.

Charles, Élise and Catherine explained that case notes were also part of their professional identity, distinguishing their work from other forms of youth work such as street-based youth work or youth clubs, where case notes were generally not taken. This echoes Tusting's (2012) study, which indicates that the degree to which accountability literacies were 'integrated with people's professional identities' can affect their learning and mastery of such literacies. As mentioned earlier, professionalisation of the third sector has been closely associated with neoliberalism (Bradford and Cullen, 2014). Considering that community-based organisations are, to some extent, in competition with each other (Darby, 2016), adopting such accountability practices might put Le Bercail and L'Envol in a more advantageous position and boost their credibility with regard to future funders.

The data also suggest that some young people understood that youth workers were keeping a record of their lives and participation at L'Envol and Le Bercail. Catherine and Charles observed that these forms of accountability literacies sometimes had an impact on their relationships with the young people. According to Catherine, some young people at L'Envol had had negative experiences with the state and its institutions in the past, and case notes were perceived as being "nebulous and actually very scary". With this knowledge, Charles at Le Bercail avoided writing case notes in front of the young people because of the negative impact that it could have on his relationship with them. Charles and Catherine wanted to be on good terms with the young people in order to best support them but they were also asked to be 'overseers' for the funders, who wanted results for their investment.

Some youth workers were aware of the tensions that might arise from their contradictory responsibilities towards a funding body and the young people – or their moral and procedural accountabilities (Kaldor, 2003). It is interesting to note that youth workers at L'Envol had organised a meeting to clarify their 'dual roles'; defending young people's rights but also making sure that they would respect the rules of the funders. This awareness could be linked to the elements of rejection, resilience and resourcefulness identified by Darby (2016) in her framework of dynamic resistance.

Conclusion

The main goal of this chapter was to understand how a group of youth workers in Québec managed to navigate an accountability regime and its literacies. Five main sets of accountability literacies were identified at Le Bercail and L'Envol: grant applications; reports; AGMs; statistics and electronic information systems; and recording and case notes. The analysis also reaffirmed the relevance of the concept of conflictual cooperation, as defined by combining moral and procedural accountabilities, everyday resistance, and dynamic resistance.

It was possible to identify connections between the accountability literacies present at Le Bercail and L'Envol and the concept of conflictual cooperation. Yet, some forms of accountability literacies offered more affordances for resistance than others. For example, the youth workers in both organisations recognised that there was a general issue with a lack of funding but felt disempowered with regard to grant applications and report writing. The findings suggest that the youth workers were more familiar with the literacies associated with the AGM, electronic information systems and case notes, and were consequently able to partially take ownership of them and to subvert their original purposes, which thus resulted in a form of everyday resistance.

Darby's (2016) concept of 'dynamic resistance' has proven particularly helpful in understanding the potential affordances of accountability literacies for resistance and conflictual cooperation. Dynamic resistance's four constitutive elements (rejection, resilience, resourcefulness and reflexive practice) were identifiable in the ways in which youth workers dealt with accountability literacies at Le Bercail and L'Envol.

Similar to Darby's (2016) findings, practitioners at Le Bercail and L'Envol were forced to engage with neoliberal practices, but they also found ways of adapting them so that they would be meaningful to their work and the young people with whom they were working. The data suggest that some youth workers were aware that their work was located in a paradoxical position of 'conflictual cooperation'; some demonstrated a clear understanding of the duality embedded in their roles. The increased focus on employability also seemed to have silenced the organisations' contributions to young people's education. The more experienced youth workers seemed more sensitive to these issues.

The findings suggest that practitioners could benefit from having a deeper understanding of the effects of neoliberalism on their work and the literacy practices that it produces. A better awareness of this would allow them to identify opportunities for resistance and to pursue their fundamental mission. Youth workers, such as those working at Le Bercail and L'Envol, are well placed to make suggestions about future programmes and funding allocations, providing that enough flexibility is granted. Multiplying the opportunities for young people to make their voices heard by agents of power is also an important way forward. Such practice should be encouraged and further developed in community-based organisations.

References

Ade-Ojo, G. and Duckworth, V. (2015) *Adult literacy policy and practice: From intrinsic values to instrumentalism*, London: Palgrave Macmillan.

Barton, D. and Hamilton, M. (2012) *Local literacies: Reading and writing in one community* (2nd edn), London and New York, NY: Routledge.

Bradford, S. and Cullen, F. (2014) 'Positive for youth work? Contested terrains of professional youth work in austerity England', *International Journal of Adolescence and Youth*, 19(1): 93–106.

Darby, S. (2016) 'Dynamic resistance: Third-sector processes for transforming neoliberalization', *Antipode*, 48(4): 977–99.

Devlieghere, J., Bradt, L. and Roose, R. (2017) 'Creating transparency through electronic information systems: Opportunities and pitfalls', *The British Journal of Social Work*, OnlineFirst: 1–17.

Duval, M., Fontaine, A., Fournier, D., Garon, S. and René, J.-F. (2005) *Les organismes communautaires au Québec: Pratiques et enjeux* [*Community-based organisations in Québec: Practices and issues*], Montréal: Gaëtan Morin.

Gibbs, G.R. (2008) *Analysing qualitative data*, London: Sage.

Gouvernement du Québec (2017) *Loi sur les companies, Chapitre C-38* [*Companies Act, chapter C-38*], Québec: Gouvernement du Québec.

Hollander, J.A. and Einwohner, R.L. (2004) 'Conceptualizing resistance', *Sociological Forum*, 19(4): 533–54.

Johansson, A. and Vinthagen, S. (2016) 'Dimensions of everyday resistance: An analytical framework', *Critical Sociology*, 42(3): 417–35.

Kaldor, M. (2003) 'Civil society and accountability', *Journal of Human Development*, 4(1): 5–27.

Lillis, T. (2017) 'Imagined, prescribed and actual text trajectories: The "problem" with case notes in contemporary social work', *Text & Talk*, 37(4): 485–508.

Savard, S. and Proulx, J. (2012) 'Les organismes communautaires au Québec: De la coexistence à la supplémentarité' ['Community-based organisations in Québec: From coexistence to supplementarity'], *Canadian Journal of Nonprofit and Social Economy Research*, 3(2): 24–42.

Scott, J.C. (1985) *Weapons of the weak: Everyday forms of peasant resistance*, New Haven, CT: Yale University Press.

Thériault, V. (2016) 'Literacy mediation as a form of powerful literacies in community-based organisations working with young people in a situation of precarity', *Ethnography and Education*, 11(2): 158–73.

Tusting, K. (2012) 'Learning accountability literacies in educational workplaces: Situated learning and processes of commodification', *Language and Education*, 26(2): 121–38.

2

Research, adult literacy and criticality: catalysing hope and dialogic caring

Vicky Duckworth and Rob Smith

Positioning literacy and hope

In the UK and internationally, the current discourse around literacy is driven by international surveys that have become increasingly important over the last 25 years (for example, those produced for the Programme of International Assessment of Adult Competencies [PIAAC]). Produced and promoted by a range of agencies, including the Organisation for Economic Co-operation and Development (OECD), the United Nations Educational, Scientific and Cultural Organization (UNESCO) and the European Union, national governments commit considerable funding to these surveys and countries then compare themselves against one another using the results.

When literacy is conceptualised as a singular 'autonomous' (Street, 1995) skill to be acquired and tested through competency assessment, it can become a vehicle for bringing about the symbolic domination of institutionalised literacies that derive from notions of human capital, economic investment and returns (Becker, 1993). Framed by these human capital discourses, at the level of the individual, literacy becomes a technology for stratifying human beings as embodied labour power. In many ways, this 'economisation' of literacy serves to depoliticise it. This is consistent with a neoliberal hegemonic view that typically attempts to neutralise politics through a common-sense assumption that economic considerations are sovereign (Davies, 2014).

Challenging this, we argue that literacy needs to be positioned within a discourse of transformation that includes re-imagining it as a catalyst for hope, whereby learners, their families and their communities are positioned positively in relation to possible life-course trajectories and other new possibilities that they can imagine for themselves. Here, we are drawing on the thinking of Ernst Bloch, who writes powerfully about the connection between hope and agency. For Bloch (1986: 443), hope:

> is indestructibly grounded in the human drive for happiness and … has always been too clearly the motor of history … when the will had learnt both through mistakes and in fact through hope as well, and when reality did not stand in too harsh a contradiction to it, [it] reformed a bit of the world; that is: an initial fiction was made real.

This positive orientation towards the future and to the idea that agency can bring about change in the world inhabited by the individual is viewed by Bloch as an inherent 'drive' in people, which is, however, characteristically thwarted by current economic and political discourses and conditions. As such, 'Hope has to be learned.... It does not just come about automatically but is the produce of experience, failure and resistance to an everyday acceptance of reality.... Hope therefore learns but it also teaches as well as constitutes its own conditions' (Thompson, 2013: 7).

A pedagogy of transformation engaged through literacy learning, which embeds hope, care and solidarity, can be driven by dialogue with and between learners and their teachers about their world picture, barriers and interests. Here, literacy is linked to the self and 'rooted in conceptions of knowledge, identity and being' (Street, 2003: 77–8). In practical terms, transformative literacy teaching and learning creates ideological spaces that recognise and draw on learners' experiences and existing knowledge as a starting point in the curriculum (Ade-Ojo and Duckworth, 2016). Such a curriculum offers space to explore the attitudes, beliefs and experiences that learners bring into the classroom, and the ways in which structural inequality, including class, gender and ethnicity, shape them. This exemplifies an epistemological resistance to neoliberal orthodoxy and instrumentalist views of education that marginalise and stratify people (Duckworth and Smith, 2018b). In transformative pedagogy, literacy becomes a lever for agency where bodies are not static, but have the ability resist inequality across the personal and public domains travelled.

Methodology

The project utilised a methodological approach with roots in critical pedagogy (Freire, 1995; Breunig, 2005). Interviews were framed informally to foster a sense of equality between participants. Research conversations (we reject the term 'interviews' because of the connotations it carries of an unequal and unidirectional exchange and distribution of power) were also reciprocal and dialogical as stories were exchanged and opinions and feelings shared. These conversations sought to affirm the positive learning identities that participants have grown during their studies.

The methodological approach also sought to endorse newly established learning identities and to share in a collective imagining of future plans. Underpinning this was a sense of research as a social practice (Herndl and Nahrwold, 2000), that is, not divorced from everyday relations or having any 'mystique' that might in any way make participants feel like 'subjects'.

In dissemination, the methodology used video as a medium for foregrounding participants' voices. The narratives as they were spoken by participants in the videos are an attempt to stay true to the affective and situated dimensions of participants' experiences as articulated by them. The sharing of stories that digital media and a website make possible connects these local stories with national and international audiences. In that sense, the project contributes to the creation of cultural capital (Bourdieu and Passeron, 1977), which can foster networks of collective resistance in the field of adult literacy and education that cross local and national boundaries.

Transformative teaching and learning and differential space

In our analysis, we drew on the theories about space and time developed by Henri Lefebvre (1991). Lefebvre (1991: 49) saw abstract space as 'dominated' and often oppressive, and defined it as 'the urban spaces of state regulated neo-capitalism characterised by their commodified exchange value and their tendency to homogenisation'. 'Differential space', on the other hand, offers a counterpart to abstract space, which arises from its contradictions and the inherent possibilities that are constrained within it. Differential space 'privileges inclusiveness and use value rather than the exchange value of abstract space. It is often transitory space which can arise from the inherent vulnerabilities of abstract space' (Leary-Owhin, 2015: 4).

An alternative view of literacy education that offers resistance to the neoliberal economised form of literacy connects to the tradition of critical pedagogy that can be traced back to Freire (1995). This alternative provides a setting for the emergence of differential space and for teaching and learning practices that are resistant. Adult literacy classes provide and realise this resistant and differential space in three significant ways: first, by engaging with learners' educational biographies while critiquing the dominant utilitarian view of education; second, by providing an affirmative and confidence-building environment for the development of learners' aspirations; and, third, by embedding a consciousness-raising dimension that focuses on a reorientation to possible life-course trajectories in the future.

The picture of transformative teaching and learning that emerged from our research data has strong resonances with the Body-Soul Rooted Pedagogy outlined by Sosa-Provencio and others (2018) inasmuch as it seeks to address stigmatised and spoilt learning identities, to enhance learners' agency and empowerment through a recognition of the value of their personal, cultural and locally situated knowledge bases and values, and to provide hope.

In our conceptualisation, teaching and learning interact to produce transformative educational experiences. Our research participants' experiences of transformative teaching and learning constituted resistance in Hollander and Einwohner's (2004) terms inasmuch as their re-engagement with education originated in a personal decision to act against the negative impact of earlier educational experiences and to salvage hope from assigned 'failure' and the loss of hope. Our findings illuminate how students often internalise a deep belief in their intrinsic deficits and that this provides a starting point for transformative pedagogies. In this case, the resistance involves repositioning the learner away from being a commodified and objectified subject, and instead reclaiming education from neoliberalism in order to reassert its purpose as a social and human process oriented towards the flourishing of individuals and the fostering of positive benefits for families, communities *and* society as a whole. It is in this sense that transformative pedagogies are an enactment of differential space as 'politicised-democratic space' (Leary-Owhin, 2016). In the next section, we will focus on the narratives of three project participants to illustrate some of the project's findings.

The ripple effect of transformative teaching and learning

Anita returned to education as a mature student. Regarded as a failure at school because of her dyslexia, she developed a skill set as a parent and in the community. Further education harnessed these skills and she began to study to become a social worker:

> 'In 18 months, I'll be a qualified social worker. My tutors are the ones that got me here.... They never once doubted me. They made me grow. Through that, I've been able to inspire my kids. One's at Manchester University ... he's in his final year. My daughter wants to go to Oxford to do medicine. My oldest one has gone into the building trade and is doing fantastically well.... He would never have done that, but he saw that I could do it: "If mum can do it, I can do it".'

The initial barrier that adult education helped Anita to overcome was the constriction of the label of being 'thick'/dyslexic that marked her out at school as a failure according to the dominant model of 'autonomous' literacy. A key emergent theme in this passage is the notion of the ripple effect of transformative learning. In a sector of education in England dominated and governed by metrics that are linked to funding (Smith, 2015), the notion of the ripple effect contributes to a discourse of resistance; it is a *counter-metric* – an unmeasured and therefore widely unrecognised social benefit that falls outside a neoliberal purview but nevertheless has a significant positive (economic) impact beyond the achievement of a qualification by a single individual. Anita's transformation can be described as her consciously harnessing a trajectory that moves away from 'dead-end jobs' towards a career with significant organisational and administrative responsibility and challenging literacy demands. Her tutors' affirmation and encouragement are signalled as key ingredients in her learning experience. Her aspiration to have fulfilling employment has, in turn, brought about transformation in the dynamics of her family. Consequent on a rebirth of hope and the construction of a positive learning identity, a material change in Anita's social positioning inside her family, her community and then in society were able to take place.

Anita's narrative illustrates how when mothers' confidence and expertise is repositioned as valued knowledge, they can develop new literacies, advocate for their children and contribute to their literacy progress. Anita's transformation is grounded in a conscious resistance against the identity imposed on her during her years of schooling. In that sense, Anita's learning identity has become a site for struggle in itself. In shrugging off the deficit-based, spoilt identity of a failed learner, she is resisting the label assigned to her but also, implicitly, the educational process that imposed it. This aspect of the resistance resides in her agency as a learner in the transformative teaching and learning experience. It is through a refashioning of herself as a learner and 'subject' that Anita's resistance is realised. This is perhaps best understood by remembering how, as subjects, in Zizek's (1994) terms, we are never outside ideology, but, rather, embody it and live through it. To the extent that, as subjects, we are inserted into the symbolic/social order that shapes what we do and who we are, ideology is the terrain that makes identity possible. The adult literacy classroom, here operating as differential space, consolidates a new resistant identity for Anita.

Jade is a mother who attends adult literacy classes run by a local charitable trust in a town with high levels of unemployment and social deprivation. Her literacy classes have given her aspirations for her future and to be the best possible role model for her son:

> '[My improved literacy] gives me confidence.... It makes me feel more like I can go and get what I need to achieve and ... be who I want to be. I just want to be like ... someone with a job, have money. I want to be able to treat my son. I used to get holidays when I was younger and ... I want to be able to treat my son to stuff like that. At the moment, I can't really do that and it's making me feel like I can do it. I can do it. I'm gonna do it.... I want to give him the best childhood that he could have and that's by me doing what I want to do as well.... I've been through times of depression but I've always tried to stay positive.... I've been at the lowest place in life.... My son brought me out of it. Children look up to their parents and I want him to look up to me.... It's all about him really. What he's had in his life up to now is crap. He deserves a lot more. Kids are innocent and pure, and they are the way they are taught.'

This passage illustrates the centrality of motherhood as a motivational force for Jade as an adult learner. The passage also echoes Tenet Six of Sosa-Provencio and other's (2018: 10–11) Body-Soul Rooted Pedagogy in that Jade's learning has impacted strongly on her hope and well-being while allowing her to heal herself and others. The affective dimension of her learning experience is a key to understanding it. Bourdieu's (2002) concept of habitus is useful here. The meanings of habit and habituation that habitus carries within it may be connected to established social patterns of being and acting in the world, but they are also bodily, they involve feelings of acceptance and resignation or the possibility of resistance and rekindled agency. This is what is (re)activated in the adult literacy classroom as 'differential space'. Jade's account communicated strongly a habitus associated with poverty and unemployment. For Jade, resistance was founded upon action and the rejection of despair, in breaking free of the determinism of her habitus up to that point.

Emotional capital may be viewed as being essential for opening up possibilities for educational success (Reay, 1998, 2000). Emotional capital includes that need to be a good mother, which includes caring for children; this includes educational care (O'Brien, 2007), such as the support offered by Jade and Anita. Reay (1998, 2000) suggests that an investment of emotional energy in education by working-class mothers depletes their own emotional well-being. However, in Jade's and Anita's cases, we see motherhood acting as a catalyst to the women empowering themselves, returning to education and finding satisfaction in helping their children to succeed.

Another participant, Marie, is a staff nurse. She grew up in a large family on an estate in a town with high levels of socio-economic deprivation. In our conversation with her, she talked about how she went back into education after a negative experience of school. Adult education brought about a turning point in her life when she became 'hooked' after starting a course at a local college rather than taking up another low-paid job opportunity. Key in this was her experience of a learning environment in which *affirmative regard* replaced the *judgemental pedagogical gaze* that she had experienced at school. By this, we mean the tendency of schooling environments to label and judge learners on the basis of their background in a way that *fixes* them and obstructs their ability to achieve and find themselves in their learning. The displacement of this by affirmation and confidence-building learning relationships brought about a big change in the opportunities and the educational and life-course trajectories of her family. As she stated:

> 'I don't care if [my son] stays in education till he's 30 years old. I want him educated because education gives you power and that's what I want my children to have. I want them to be able to make choices. Definitely, I want them to be able to … you know … say, "Well, actually, I don't want to do that, I want to do that. And I want to go and live there, I don't want to stay there and live there. And I want to have a car and I want to do this". Just choices.… I want them to be able to go to Costa and get a coffee. Something I could never do … that's what education will give him: choices.'

Biesta articulates three purposes of education: qualification, subjectification and socialisation. By socialisation, he means:

> Through education we … represent and initiate children and young people in traditions and ways of being and doing, such as cultural, professional, political, religious traditions.… [A]s research in the sociology of education has shown, [(socialisation)] also works behind the backs of students and teachers, for example in the ways in which education reproduces existing social structures, divisions and inequalities. (Biesta, 2015: 77)

In one sense, then, Marie's resistance is resistance to the socialisation (implicit or otherwise) of her schooling and (potentially) the schooling of her children. Marie places a great emphasis on the range of opportunities that she wants for her children through education. This contrasts with her own experience of schooling as institutionalised socialisation that limited her potential on the basis of judgements made about her social class background. Looking to the future as a mother, she is determined to actively resist any similar educational effect on her children. Her transformative education experience has rekindled her sense of agency to act in and on the world. As Bloch (1986: 198) states:

> No thing could be altered in accordance with wishes if the world were closed full of fixed, even perfected facts. Instead of these there are simply processes, i.e. dynamic relationships in the Become has not completely triumphed, The Real is process: the latter is the … mediation between present, unfinished past, and, above all: possible future.

There are echoes in the renewed perspective on life and the world in Marie's narrative and Bloch's view of the way in which wishes (as expressions of hope) interact with the world. Key in this is the idea that the world is not fixed, but in an ongoing process of becoming; in other words, retaining hope is an important aspect of our ability to act on the world, to resist and change our circumstances.

It is important to note that for Marie, transformative learning experiences included seeing the world in new critical and politicised ways. Marie described having her eyes opened to the systematic inequality of our society and the wider world: "I used to think doctors and police were all good and that people like that never lied. Now I know different.… I used to think people were better than me. But no one's better than anyone: we're all equal". The unseen literacy at work here is connected to social and cultural capital, as defined by Bourdieu, but moves beyond that to a newly established 'informed' position within the field of social relations. Through her engagement with learning, Marie has developed a broad-based *critical social literacy* – a facility for reading social relations in her workplace but also in society more widely. This social literacy provides Marie with a vantage point from which not only to understand her own position within society, but also to begin to come to grips with the bigger structural forces that shape her life and the lives of others. This social literacy is deeply imbued with criticality as Marie's transformative educational experience involved mobilising her resistance to the socialising impact of her experience of schooling – the educational processes and judgements that labelled her and positioned her as from a specific background and limited *by* that background. Her resistance is deliberate, active and oppositional, but is oriented towards resisting the purposes of educational experience and the structures underpinning those rather than being explicitly directed at individuals or specific institutions.

Acquiring social literacy is about being able to navigate the complexities of different social groups and settings. We might call it wholeness or confidence but it is not a façade or a mask. Rather, it comes from a deep understanding of the self as subject: our sense of who we are in society. To that extent, it is also intensely political.

The role of teachers in facilitating dialogic care

According to our research data, teachers play a vital role in creating the social conditions in which transformative teaching and learning takes place (Duckworth and Smith, 2016, 2018). These teachers understand that, in some cases, it has taken enormous courage on the part of some would-be adult learners to cross the threshold onto college premises. An initial focus of their work is to create a safe learning environment, establish trust and build confidence. In a region marked by historically high levels of unemployment and job losses, one of the teacher participants, Judith, was conscious of the importance of her teaching work:

> 'For me, transformational teaching is teaching that makes a difference.... People have come in and they've been very quiet and haven't had much confidence. You'll see them five or ten years later and they'll say "I'm a primary school teacher now", or "I'm a social worker", or "I'm doing

> my master's degree".... And you think: "Wow what a difference!".'

What is interesting about the description is that Judith does not regard the transformation as something directed by her. Instead, the transformative potential is immanent in the learners and her role is to enable it. Judith sees this transformative process as a collective phenomenon and as having social as well as individual origins:

> 'People feel once they get to their 20s or 30s, "Oh, I didn't stick in at school", or "I'm not clever enough", or "I'm never going to do anything". And it only takes one person in a friendship group to go and do something like an Access Course and go on and do well and then their friends want to come on as well.... We have to break the cycle of low aspirations in the North-East because we've got whole generations now who don't work.'

Judith's understanding of her role is deeply rooted in the location of the college and in the communities that the college serves. In this case, her role involves addressing the legacy of the industrial strategies of the 1980s, when the large-scale industries of motor manufacturing and coal and steel production faced privatisation and decline. Judith identifies some important ingredients in the formation of dialogic caring relationships with the learners. Among these is the respect that she has for them as people. Once more, the egalitarian nature of transformative teaching and learning comes across powerfully:

> 'We try to get to know the students as people and be part of their journey.... A lot of people think they're not academic when, actually, they are.... They're so used to thinking of all the things they can't do.... By the time they finish, they realise that they can do the same as those people they thought were better than them because they had a degree or they are a doctor. I've had people say to me ... "I've learned how to phone up and complain if I'm not happy about something. I've learnt to say, I disagree with that". At the end of the day, they are empowered.'

The emphasis in this is very much on the self-discovery by learners of already-there potential: a process that makes *becoming* a realisation of immanence and that unlocks the door to a previously remote and unattainable future. The role of the teacher here constitutes resistance to further education as a project that seeks, through the attainment of symbolic qualifications, to objectify students and circumscribe their potential, and to cast this only or mainly as contributing to an economic 'skills' narrative. Judith also highlights how transformative teaching and learning reaffirms agency, allowing students to assert themselves in social situations and to resist meanings that might undermine this agency. The teacher's role is one of convening the educational experience and opening up the learning dialogue with individuals.

Discussion: dialogic caring and hope

The ideological coupling of choices and opportunities for all has been colonised by neoliberal discourse that champions meritocracy and signally fails to address the structural causes of social inequality (see, for example, Angus, 2013). Through emphasising essentialist notions such as 'talent' (an ideological and mystical quality like IQ), this version of meritocracy implies an affirmation of a system that produces 'failure' and a condemnation of the lifestyle, culture and choices of the poor and marginalised (Duckworth and Smith, 2018a). Alternatively, literacy education that is holistic and culturally sensitive has the potential to transform students, teachers and researchers to become writers of their own educational stories and, moreover, authors of their own lives. The telling and sharing of the stories (including through the research) was a way for the participants to make connections with others with similar experiences. Offering a democratic and 'differential' space, both in the classroom and through the project website, facilitated a dialogical sharing of stories that constitutes *resistance capital*: a collective and dynamic resource for meaning-making and resistance to inspire and offer hope to teachers and learners.

Conclusions

While a focus on 'self-improvement' and the development of individual income potential is a version of transformation that coheres with neoliberal precepts, a key distinction of transformative teaching and learning identified in this research that sets it apart in this respect is that transformation extends beyond the individual into the family and the community, and includes the development of a personalised critique and understanding of social inequality and the student's positionality within this. For Anita, Jade and Marie, adult literacy classes acted a first step in a transformative journey. Through their educational journeys, these women and their teachers challenge and subvert dominant discourses and existing hierarchies. Their narratives show them making sense of the complexities of their lives and of their structural positioning as literacy learners in a society based on inequality of opportunity and choice. They overturn the monopoly on hope that is reified by existing social inequalities and the employment and income structures that support this.

Our research revealed how teachers, even when constrained by performative curricula, can open up a space for critical reflection and dialogue that facilitates learners to challenge notions of what literacies are. In this space, through action and opposition, they offer resistance to passivising, knowledge-transmission approaches to education, instead catalysing hope, overturning the negative impact of a classificatory education system and allowing students to rearticulate the relationship between their education and their futures.

References

Ade-Ojo, G. and Duckworth, V. (2016) 'Of cultural dissonance: The UK's adult literacy policies and the creation of democratic learning spaces', *International Journal of Lifelong Education*. Available at: www.tandfonline.com/doi/abs/10.1080/02601370.2016.1250232

Angus, L. (2013) 'School choice: Neoliberal education policy and imagined futures', *British Journal of Sociology of Education*, 36(3): 395–441.

Becker , G.S. (1993) *Human capital: A theoretical and empirical analysis with special reference to education*, London: University of Chicago Press.

Biesta, G. (2015) 'What is education for? On good education, teacher judgement and educational professionalism', *European Journal of Education*, 50(1): 75–87.

Bloch, E. (1986) *The principle of hope. Volume 1*, Cambridge, MA: MIT Press.

Bourdieu, P. (2002) 'Habitus', in J. Hillier and E. Rooksby (eds) *Habitus: A sense of place*, Aldershot: Ashgate.

Bourdieu, P. and Passeron, J. (1977) *Reproduction in education, society and culture*, London: Sage.

Breunig, M. (2005) 'Turning experiential education and critical pedagogy theory into praxis', *Journal of Experiential Education*, 28(2): 106–22.

Davies, W. (2014) *The limits of neoliberalism*, London: Sage.

Duckworth, V. and Smith, R. (2016) 'Further education in England – Transforming lives and communities: Interim Report', UCU. Available at: https://www.ucu.org.uk/media/8461/FE-in-England-transforming-lives-and-communities-interim-report-Jan17/pdf/Transforming_lives_FE_report_Jan17.pdf (accessed 30 July 2017).

Duckworth, V. and Smith, R. (2018a) 'Transformative learning in English further education', in C. Borg, P. Mayo and R. Sultana (eds) *Skills for sustainable human development of the international handbook on vocational education and training for changing the world of work*, Switzerland: Springer International, Springer Nature.

Freire, P. (1995) *The pedagogy of the oppressed*, New York, NY: Continuum.

Herndl, C. and Nahrwold , C. (2000) 'Research as social practice', *Written Communication*, 17(2): 258–96.

Hollander, J.A. and Einwohner, R.L. (2004) *Sociological Forum*, 19 (4): 533-54.

Lefebvre, H. (1991) *The production of space*, Oxford: Blackwell.

Leary-Owhin, M. (2015) 'A fresh look at Lefebvre's spatial triad and differential space: A central place in planning theory', draft revision of a paper presented at the 2nd Planning Theory Conference, University of the West of England 21-22 June 2012. Available at: https://www.academia.edu/17161563/A_Fresh_Look_at_Lefebvre_s_Spatial_Triad_and__Differential Space_A_Central_Place_in_Planning_Theory (accessed 13 May 2019).

Leary-Owhin, M.E. (2016) *Exploring the production of urban space: Differential space in three post-industrial cities,* Bristol: Policy Press.

O'Brien, M. (2007) 'Mothers' emotional care work in education and its moral imperative', *Gender and Education*, 19 (2): 159–78.

Reay, D. (1998) '"Always knowing" and "never being sure": Institutional and familial habituses and higher education choice', *Journal of Education Policy*, 13(4): 519–29.

Reay, D. (2000) '"Dim dross": Marginalised women both inside and outside the academy', *Women's Studies International Forum*, 23(1): 13–21.

Smith, R. (2015) 'College re-culturing, marketisation and knowledge: The meaning of incorporation', *Journal of Educational Administration and History*, 47(1): 18–39.

Sosa-Provencio, M.A., Sheahan, A, Desai S. and Secatero, S. (2018) 'Tenets of *Body-Soul Rooted Pedagogy*: Teaching for critical consciousness, nourished resistance, and healing', *Critical Studies in Education*, DOI: 10.1080/17508487.2018.1445653

Street, B. (1995) *Social literacies: Critical approaches to literacy in development, ethnography and education*, London: Longman.
Street, B. (2003) 'What's "new" in New Literacy Studies? Critical approaches to literacy in theory and practice', *Current Issues in Comparative Education*, 5(2): 77–91.
Thompson, P. (2013) 'Introduction: The privatisation of hope and the crisis of negation', in P. Thompson and S. Zizek (eds) *The privatisation of hope*, Durham, NC: Duke University Press, pp 1–20.
Žižek, S. (ed) (1994) *Mapping ideology*, London: Verso.

3

The employability skills discourse and literacy practitioners

Gwyneth Allatt and Lyn Tett

Introduction

In this chapter, we draw on our study of adult literacy practitioners (Allatt and Tett, 2018) to explore the ways in which the human capital (HC) model of knowledge impacts at the transnational, national and local levels on literacy programmes. This model claims that there is a universal relationship between economic development, individual prosperity and vocational achievement. HC was defined by Becker (1975: 16) as 'any stock of knowledge or characteristics the worker has (either innate or acquired) that contributes to his or her productivity'. This focus on productivity came at the expense of other forms of knowledge that lead to the development of an individual's potential, greater well-being and so on; yet, it has become universally accepted in transnational policy documents from the European Union (EU) and the Organisation for Economic Co-operation and Development (OECD) (for example, OECD, 2013; EUR-Lex, 2015). When the HC model is applied to literacy learning, it prioritises skills-focused education and reduces the person 'merely to "human capital", not as a life to be lived, but as mere economic potential to be exploited' (Gillies, 2011: 225).

The HC perspective, which regards countries and their citizens as competitors in a global marketplace, also gets translated into measurable indicators, such as those used in the Programme for the International Assessment of Adult Competencies (PIAAC), which aims to 'measure the key cognitive and workplace skills needed … for economies to prosper' (OECD, 2016: 1). These powerful standards then become taken for granted in our everyday practices, meaning that the focus of education is on the national productivity agendas that are in the interests of industry, often at the expense of the needs of employees, who are treated as an investment rather than as social and cultural beings (Rizvi and Lingard, 2010). In addition, the narrow domains of skills-focused knowledge perpetuated by these interests become accepted as normal and so are difficult to challenge (Gorur, 2014).

At the national level too, policy documents in the UK similarly prioritise HC over social capital outcomes in adult literacy programmes. For example, Scottish policy states that 'if an individual has a weakness in [literacies] skills, they are less likely to make an effective contribution to Scotland's economy.... This is potentially a drag on Scotland's economic capacity' (Scottish Government, 2012: 1). Similarly, English policy highlights the benefits of literacy development to the 'wider economy' (Department for Business, Innovation and Skills, 2014: 2). The document acknowledges that 'labour market engagement, i.e. work, is the biggest driver of skills development' (Department for Business, Innovation and Skills, 2014: 4). Certain groups are identified as a priority within literacy education policy, including the unemployed and the 'inactive' in order to help them find sustainable jobs, and 'low-skilled parents' in order to equip them to 'get into work and contribute to the economy' (Department for Business, Innovation and Skills, 2014: 23).

As Hamilton (2012: 171) has argued, when the focus is on economic growth through increased productivity, 'formal learning is privileged over informal learning and standardised and measurable outcomes are preferred for demonstrating achievement', and this narrows the curriculum because the achievement of employability skills becomes the most important focus. This economistic discourse then tends to drive a curriculum that prioritises narrow employment skills-focused learning that neither respects learners' own goals nor values their life experiences. Yet, as Ball (1994: 10) notes, 'policies are always incomplete in so far as they relate to or map onto the "wild profusion of local practice"', so we examine how employability-focused policies are implemented at the local level based on research with experienced literacies practitioners.

We are interested in the *practices* that literacies staff engage in at the local level that enable them to counter some of the negative impacts of an employment skills-focused curriculum through what Johansson and Vinthagen (2016) termed 'everyday resistance' . This type of resistance is 'informal and non-organised ... [and] is heterogeneous and contingent due to changing contexts and situations' (Johansson and Vinthagen, 2016: 418). In order to do this, we investigate a variety of literacies programmes and detail how these practitioners justify the resistant practices they develop.

Methodology

The data on which we draw are derived from two areas of the UK: Scotland's central belt and the North of England. The Scottish sample comprised 20 people from community-based projects in Scotland's four major cities and six other local authority areas. In each of these areas, a literacy practitioner and the person who had overall responsibility for literacies were interviewed. Experienced people were interviewed because they were able to reflect on changes over time. Their experience ranged from 20 years of service to nearly six years, with the median being 12 years. The interviews lasted around an hour and discussed how the opportunities and constraints of employability-focused programmes had influenced their approaches to learners.

The English sample involved teachers of adult literacy from a range of organisations, including colleges and training providers in the northern English counties of West and South Yorkshire. Telephone interviews of approximately 20 minutes were held with 17 teachers, with experience ranging from one to 20 years, to identify their perceptions of literacy. Additional face-to-face interviews lasting between 40 minutes and one hour were held with four of these practitioners who represented different contexts (further education colleges, local education authority and private training providers) to explore their views in greater depth. The relationship between literacy and employability and economic concerns was an emerging theme in both telephone and face-to-face interviews. The interviewees' characteristics are detailed in Table 3.1.

The conversations were recorded and transcribed, and then the transcriptions were analysed thematically (Braun and Clarke, 2006). To do this, we first identified themes from the literature on teaching and learning in adult literacy (for example, Smythe, 2015) and then set out to find instances of these in the interview transcripts, paying attention to new themes that arose and that were important to each of the cohorts as a whole. This means that in the analysis, themes were checked against each other and back to the literature. This method has the advantage of giving a holistic picture rather than a fragmented view of individual variables. The names used in the quotes are pseudonyms.

Although practitioners from Scotland and England were working in somewhat different contexts, they were all responding to the changes in welfare benefits that were implemented across the UK. Therefore, we report on these changes in the outcomes that they were expected to deliver mainly using examples from both samples. Where they differ, as in the local authority literacies services in Scotland, we detail the different possibilities available.

Table 3.1: Interviewees' characteristics

Name (pseudonym)	Location	Type of organisation	Years of experience
Alan	Scotland	Homelessness non-governmental organisation (NGO)	18
Ann	Scotland	Local authority (LA) Community Learning Service (CLS)	17
Brian	Scotland	LA CLS	18
Callum	Scotland	LA CLS	13
Carol	North England	Further education college (FEC)	12
Catherine	North England	FEC	1
Clare	North England	Training provider	4
David	Scotland	LA CLS	7
Debbie	North England	FEC	5
Denise	Scotland	LA CLS	12
Donna	North England	Adult education college	11
Emma	Scotland	Family learning NGO	16
Faye	North England	Training provider	1
Felicity	North England	Adult education college	8
Garry	Scotland	Youth-focused NGO	12
Heather	North England	FEC	9
Jane	North England	Training provider	2
Jim	Scotland	Youth-focused NGO	15
Jo	Scotland	LA CLS	11
Joe	North England	Training provider	4
John	North England	Training provider	11
Judith	Scotland	LA CLS	16
Karen	Scotland	LA CLS	20
Kathy	Scotland	LA CLS	10
Lorna	Scotland	LA CLS	5.75
Louise	Scotland	LA CLS	14
Lucy	North England	FEC	20
Margaret	Scotland	LA CLS	9
Mary	North England	Training provider	12
Moira	North England	FEC	12

Table 3.1: (continued)

Name (pseudonym)	Location	Type of organisation	Years of experience
Pauline	North England	Training provider	20
Pete	Scotland	LA CLS	17
Sarah	North England	Training provider	5
Sheila	Scotland	LA CLS	19
Sian	Scotland	Family learning NGO	8
Sonia	North England	Training provider	1
Sue	Scotland	LA CLS	20

Source: Taken from Allatt and Tett (2018: 8).

Practitioners' views

All the respondents reported that there had been changes in how they organised and approached literacies programmes. These changes were driven by two main issues: new approaches to welfare provision (DWP, 2011, 2012) that caused differences in learners' participation; and funding reductions in local authority and non-governmental organisation (NGO) budgets that led to involvement in externally funded projects. Emerging out of these changes was another challenge: the impact on the values that underpinned their practice.

Impact of the new welfare provision

Most people highlighted the greater demands now made on literacy learners due to the changes in the welfare system which meant that large numbers of people who had not accessed literacies services before were now being referred from Job Centres. These pressures arose from "Jobseekers having to use digital skills to actively seek employment" (Emma), with Sarah reporting that one learner, referred to a literacy class from the Job Centre, was sent there because he "was having trouble filling in online all the stuff he had to fill in – CVs, evidence that he was applying for jobs and so on". The changes in the welfare system had particularly impacted on people with mental health issues, who had previously been on long-term benefits but now had "to apply for jobs and this is adding to their stress and their ill health" (Denise). Another interviewee commented: "I feel that learners, particularly the longer-term unemployed … are pushed from pillar to post, from agency to agency, where boxes are ticked and statistics are generated to justify funding" (Jim).

Working with learners who were further from the labour market was also difficult because "there is also quite a lot of buck passing by the other sectors [such as further education and private providers], especially when individuals have mental health issues" (Margaret). There was a particular impact from private providers because they "tend to cherry-pick those learners that are nearest to achieving the specified outcomes so we can end up supporting the learners that are further away from being employment ready" (Sheila). There were also issues arising from other professionals who had a lack of belief in the possibility of improvement: "This leads to inward thinking along the lines of developing a CV, job search, digital skills, etc. All these are important but the emphasis needs to be more on building up people's confidence in themselves" (Pete).

Challenges of a different nature were also reported in the interviews, with Joe describing the effect on learners' motivation and conduct in the classroom when they were required by the Job Centre to attend literacy classes (or benefits payments would not be made) rather than attending by their own volition:

> 'The Job Centre – I would say that has had a massive effect because … suddenly we were having people who were being forced to come … and it feels completely different … almost like a crowd control type of situation because they are quite forthright in putting across how little they want to be there.'

A number of literacies services in Scotland had set up systems so that this new group of learners could be more appropriately accommodated. For example: "we have been providing training to our front-line staff … on how anti-social behaviour issues can be effectively defused … and also awareness-raising sessions so that they can be more sympathetic to people in very distressed states" (Karen). Others were working more closely with colleagues, including "the financial services staff, who do sessions in libraries to help with benefits" (Ann). Finally, a number had "established pathways that enable staff to understand who to refer learners to, as well as signposting the implications of the rules for claimants" (Brian).

External funding

The participants all considered that their practice was more constrained because "funding cuts mean that more of our resources are being targeted at employability skills" (Pete). "A lot of our workshops are based on getting people to see how to write an email for a job and how to write a letter, how to write a job advert" (Faye); "I teach functional skills and the main aim is to get our students ready for the world of work" (Debbie). Another practitioner described employability as "Forcing our hand to look at ways of doing things". External funders required different types of outcomes, so "depending on the funding stream, courses can be very prescriptive in content and expect learners to achieve accreditation, so there are fewer opportunities for learners to develop more personal interests that usually enable them to be more engaged in learning" (David). Other teachers experienced similar restrictions:

> 'I'm expected to be demonstrating progress and taking students through to the appropriate level of exam.... There's not really much room in terms of our funding and our policy for having people who just come along because they want to learn a bit.' (Jane)

Practitioners such as Lucy also had concerns about the effects on learners:

> 'Obviously for people to get on the right course and to achieve is all important but I think there is perhaps a more learner-focused developmental approach that I think may be lost in the drive to improve performance in the target-driven culture.'

Capturing employability outcomes was difficult, especially where the criteria for success were the numbers moving onto other courses, or gaining a qualification or employment. This was because many participants "were far away from the job market and although many gained 'soft skills' such as increased confidence, they could not be accredited and were not easy to record" (Sue). Other funders were a bit more flexible and so "any improvement in literacies or ESOL [English for Speakers of Other Languages] communication skills or digital skills to being able to demonstrate that people can write a CV ... or that they have moved onto accredited courses" (Pete) could be included.

A number of interviewees had found more creative ways of delivering outcomes, including making "use of impact statements from learners that include gains in self-confidence that are powerful ways of explaining the whole-life impact that they experience" (Ann). Staff also had to be careful about how they described their provision, as one of the managers said: "I was anxious we might lose our family learning provision, so I pitched this as parental engagement for employability.... Crucially, this still allows us to deliver some of the initial work that is so valuable" (Karen). Another interviewee described how some of the courses offered within her organisation had to be titled 'Communication for Employment' rather than 'English' or 'Literacy'; "It's jargon basically to get the funding" (Sonia). For some, external funding had made it possible to develop more 'critical literacy' programmes that "developed communication and numeracy skills at the same time as involving the participants fully" (Sue). However, such temporary funding could generate a huge administrative burden that "took skilled staff away from the 'front line' and meant that their ability to innovate was lost" (Sue).

The focus on employability had also brought opportunities because "we are able to offer a greater range of courses in response to the learners, many of who see employability as their key goal" (Callum). Many practitioners reported that they were now "attracting greater numbers of learners" (Sian) but one worried that "we aren't as focused on the people that are more difficult to reach because of the demand from those that are more aware of the opportunities we offer" (Judith).

Another issue that managers had to be clear about was what could be achieved. Brian explained that "for the work with young people, we get an initial starting payment but if they don't complete a training course or move onto a positive destination, then we get nothing, so we have to plan accordingly". This meant that external funding had to be thought through carefully so that it did not compromise "the values about what good practice should look like" (Lorna).

Underpinning values

So, being clear about values was crucial, and for nearly all of the interviewees, good practice meant "ensuring that the learners' goals are at the centre of our provision" (Kathy). A key value was "being focused on the assets that learners bring rather than their deficits" (Jo), and many practitioners showed how they operationalised these values. For example, Gary said: "rather than writing CVs, we build the curriculum around what the young people are interested in. That way, they do end up developing their literacies skills but in ways that arise from their own interests". Many operated from 'a funds of knowledge' approach (González et al, 2005), where participants are actively involved in developing their lived experiences, which become validated as legitimate sources of knowledge. For example, Alan, working in a project for homeless people, started off by:

> 'Asking them about their housing issues or how they have dealt with social work so that we can use their experience. We get to deliver our outputs about being "employment ready" but we start from their knowledge rather than telling them what to do and it's so much more effective.'

Similarly, Sian, who was based in a family learning project, said: "we always work from the strengths of our learners, so we start from what the parents know and ask them to share their knowledge with each other, so it's about changing attitudes … learning how to see themselves positively again".

So, rather than seeing knowledge as an economic commodity, most of the interviewees were focused on knowledge as a way of expressing critical opinions about the world. For example:

> 'We discuss why they think they didn't get qualifications when they were at school and what they think could be done about it in ways … that put the emphasis back on the system failures. They then write about how they might change education and this helps to build up their skills, as well as improving their self-esteem.' (Louise)

Learners' creativity was also encouraged by practitioners trying to meet the requirements of funding and qualifications while still providing a positive learning experience. Carol, for example, explained her strategy as "strategic compliance – making space for things like creative writing as well as meeting regulations. It's not part of the curriculum, but learners often respond well to it using genres they are familiar with". Good practice also involved taking time to remove barriers to help people towards becoming more employable. This meant that 'although our overall aim is to move young people onto positive destinations, behind that is helping them to take small steps … so they gain the confidence in what they know" (Jim).

Working in these ways was not easy because of the time and commitment it took. In particular, staff were under pressure from the Job Centres to report on learners' attendance, but "we have made it clear that any referrals they make to our provision is on the basis that we will not monitor or report on learners' attendance because it would violate our principles" (Ann). Staff were helped to stick to their value base because of the " 'passion for the job that gives you the courage to work in this way because all your experience tells you that this is the right kind of approach that is going to help people to learn" (Emma). The practitioners also had the support of colleagues that they considered "shared their values" and so they trusted them "to make good judgements" (Sian). However, there was still "a big discrepancy between the rhetoric about the value of our work and the lack of funding for it at the local authority level" (Brian).

Constraints and frustration related to "the pressures of achievement and funding" (Mary) were a common feature of the interviews with practitioners, and the requirement for end examinations linked to course funding was another source of conflict with their personal and professional values:

> 'The big thing really is the funding … and being a post-19 provider, we are funded for less and less.… When I first started delivering here, we were able to put on courses that would help people to grow in their confidence and in themselves. It didn't matter so much if you didn't have a formal exam, whereas now, all our learners have to achieve a formal exam.' (Pauline)

Interview participants explained how they had adopted a variety of ways in which to maintain their own values in relation to literacy learning in the face of policy requirements and the employability agenda. One interviewee, for example, described how she incorporated literature and creative writing into her literacy classes so that "It's not just about an exam … I feel we're in danger of losing the love of literature, the love of writing … we are having to just drill it in" (Felicity). Another of the literacy teachers from the English sample had changed her role in the time between the telephone interview and the face-to-face meeting. She explained how her frustration at the restricted view of literacy resulting from funding constraints and assessment processes at her previous organisation had inspired her to leave her job and work freelance, offering literacy classes that were more tailored to learners' individual needs and interests and developed their literacy through creative writing, project work and reading poetry and fiction: "Literacy is not just about filling in a form" (Sarah). Donna, meanwhile, echoed the other practitioners in questioning the constraints of the employability agenda: "Should people be trained up just to do the jobs they do?".

Some practitioners appear to resist the constraints of an employability-focused curriculum by recognising that learners often had different reasons for attending literacy classes:

> 'A lot of people come here because they have to. Sometimes, pressure from the Job Centre and so on … but I think it's more about being amongst people who are in a similar position to them socially, as well as to do with being literate and about gaining confidence generally through developing these skills, particularly in speaking and listening. It empowers them. They might then feel more able to go out into the wider world, whether it's to get a job or progress onto a college course … I'm not sure that when they joined the class, that could have been their aspiration.' (Sarah)

In some cases, this recognition of learners' varying motivations and success involved valuing and celebrating their progress in non-work-based contexts. The ways in which learners use their literacy to support their children with schoolwork, for instance, was a commonly recurring theme in the North of England interviews, as was their increased involvement in their communities as a result of their literacy development. One participant was particularly proud of her learners' achievements, one of whom had gained so much confidence that she had become a volunteer 'Reading Friend' at her child's school, listening to and encouraging pupils' reading, while one of her classmates, who had initially described herself as not being a reader, had "blossomed": "She was borrowing books and she was just eating them up and she said that in the evening, she no longer puts on the television because she would prefer to sit and read and that was lovely" (Sarah). Another learner from the class had recently had some of her creative writing published in the local newspaper. In a different organisation, a literacies teacher working with individuals recovering from drug and alcohol abuse praised them for their ability to engage and demonstrate commitment:

> 'A lot of the clients said that coming to classes actually helps them to commit to things. Because of the nature of their addiction and their recovery, they don't tend to stick to things.… Obviously, we have to be very engaged with them to get them to stay, but the majority of them do come back.' (Sonia)

Discussion and conclusion

In this chapter, we have argued that the policy context is dominated by the HC discourse at both the international level through the statistics and reports of the OECD and the EU and also at the level of the nation state. Underpinning this discourse is the assumption that work of any kind is the solution to poverty, despite a great deal of evidence to the contrary (for example, Rubenson, 2015). It is also assumed that people should invest in their own marketable skills and that failure to do so is their fault. These assumptions are reflected at the state level both through changes in welfare provision and through the focus on narrow skills for employability, leading to a deficit view of learners. At the heart of the discourse is a failure to acknowledge the structural inequalities that caused these problems.

Literacies workers have been able to resist this dominant discourse of deficit at the local level to some extent. A shared understanding of what is good practice and clear views of the underpinning value system have driven this alternative discourse. Staff have asserted their agency to support literacies that are based in rich and meaningful practices and have found ways to avoid reducing the curriculum to narrow employability-related competencies. The curriculum they have offered has instead been based on a 'funds of knowledge' approach (González et al, 2005). This approach has helped learners to develop the effective strategies and skills that they already use rather than being seen as having individual deficits that need to be corrected. As we have shown, the values that drove the practitioners' pedagogical practices included a focus on the learners' goals, and so the learning arose out of 'the inherently socially negotiated character of meaning ... in, with, and arising from the socially and culturally structured world' (Lave and Wenger, 1991: 51). The practitioners also emphasised the importance of using the individual's wider experience and operated from the position that the learners' experiences were a positive resource; thus, they used a 'learning curriculum' (Lave and Wenger, 1991). Moreover, by recognising that learners were competent, engaging in learning was more likely to give them 'an increasing sense of identity as a master practitioner' (Lave and Wenger, 1991: 111).

The ways in which these literacy practitioners operated to translate and enact policy texts (Ball et al, 2012) were mainly through various acts of everyday resistance. These included what Smythe (2015) has called 'workarounds': situations in which literacy educators seize, rather than seek, discretion when 'policies are seen to be unworkable in practice, or in conflict with professional and philosophical values' (Smythe, 2015: 6).

They also created spaces so that they could continue to work in the ways that they valued, and they have been helped in taking this stand by the strengths they derive from being part of a long tradition of literacies work that places the learner at its centre (Hamilton and Tett, 2012). This also shows how resistance is 'historically *entangled* with (everyday) power' (Johansson and Vinthagen, 2016: 418, emphasis in original) and has been enacted through resisting changing managerial discourses that no longer accept the importance of a learner-centred curriculum.

Yet, working in these ways requires a costly effort to simultaneously respect the learners' own knowledges while satisfying the requirements of funders in delivering the outcomes that they expect, and such costs 'are placed unfairly on the shoulders of these practitioners who face an on-going struggle to work in the ways they value' (Allatt and Tett, 2018: 15). We have shown how resourceful the practitioners were in finding creative solutions, so we can only hope that they will continue resisting the neoliberal discourse over the long term.

References

Allatt, G. and Tett, L. (2018) 'Adult literacy practitioners and employability skills: Resisting neoliberalism?', *Journal of Education Policy*, DOI: 10.1080/02680939.2018.1493144.

Ball, S. J. (1994) *Education reform: A critical and post-structuralist approach*, Buckingham: Routledge.

Ball, S.J., Maguire, M. and Braun, A. (2012) *How schools do policy: Policy enactments in secondary schools*, New York, NY: Routledge.

Becker, G. (1975) *Human capital: A theoretical and empirical analysis* (2nd edn), New York, NY: Columbia University Press.

Braun, V. and Clarke, V. (2006) 'Using thematic analysis in psychology', *Qualitative Research in Psychology*, 3(2): 77–101.

Department for Business, Innovation and Skills (2014) *Adult literacy and numeracy: Government response to the House of Commons Business, Innovation and Skills Select Committee. Fifth report of session. 2014–15*, London: BIS.

DWP (Department for Work and Pensions) (2011) 'The Work Programme'. Available at: www.gov.uk/government/uploads/system/uploads/attachment_data/file/49884/the-work-programme.pdf (accessed 28 February 2018).

DWP (2012) 'Explanatory memorandum to the Jobseeker's Allowance (Sanctions) (Amendment) Regulations 2012 No. 2568'. Available at: webarchive.nationalarchives.gov.uk/20130128102031/http://www.dwp.gov.uk/docs/jsa-sanctions-draft-regs-2012-memorandum.pdf (accessed 28 February 2018).

EUR-Lex (2015) 'New priorities for European cooperation in education and training', 2015/C 417/04. Available at: https://eur-lex.europa.eu/legal-content/EN/TXT/PDF/?uri=CELEX:52015XG1215(02)&from=EN (accessed 28 February 2018).

Gillies, D. (2011) 'State education as high-yield investment: Human capital theory in European policy discourse', *Journal of Pedagogy*, 2(2): 224–45.

González, N., Moll, L. and Amanti, C. (2005) *Funds of knowledge: Theorizing practices in households, communities, and classrooms*, New Jersey, NJ: Erlbaum.

Gorur, R. (2014) 'Towards a sociology of measurement in education policy', *European Educational Research Journal*, 13(1): 58–72.

Hamilton, M. (2012) 'The effects of the literacy policy environment on local sites of learning', *Language and Education*, 26(2): 169–82.

Hamilton, M. and Tett, L. (2012) 'More powerful literacies: The policy context', in L. Tett, M. Hamilton and J. Crowther (eds) *More powerful literacies*, Leicester: NIACE, pp 1–12.

Johansson, A. and Vinthagen, S. (2016) 'Dimensions of everyday resistance: An analytical framework', *Critical Sociology*, 42(3), 417–35.

Lave, J. and Wenger, E. (1991) *Situated learning: Legitimate peripheral participation*, Cambridge: Cambridge University Press.

OECD (Organisation for Economic Co-operation and Development) (2013) *Skills outlook 2013: First results from the survey of adult skills*, Paris: OECD Publishing. Available at: http://www.oecd.org/site/piaac/Skills%20volume%201%20%28eng%29–full%20v8– eBook%20%2801%2010%202013%29.pdf

OECD (2016) *The survey of adult skills: Reader's companion*, 2nd ed, Paris: OECD Publishing. doi:10.1787/9789264258075-en.

Rizvi, F. and Lingard, B. (2010) *Globalizing education policy*, Abingdon: Routledge.

Rubenson, S. (2015) 'Framing the adult learning and education policy discourse: The role of the OECD', in M. Milana and T. Nesbit (eds) *Global perspectives on adult education and learning policy*, Basingstoke: Palgrave Macmillan, pp 179–93.

Scottish Government (2012) *Improve the skill profile of the nation: Scotland performs*, Edinburgh: Scottish Government.

Smythe, S. (2015) 'Ten years of adult literacy policy and practice in Canada: Literacy policy tensions and workarounds', *Language and Literacy*, 17(2): 4–21.

PART II

School education

4

Making spaces in professional learning for democratic literacy education in the early years

Lori McKee, Rachel Heydon and Elisabeth Davies

Introduction

This chapter provides narrative illustrations from Ontario, Canada, of a case study of professional learning to support early primary teachers (that is, teachers of children aged 3.8–8 years) in designing and implementing multimodal pedagogies. We offer these illustrations as a *resource for hope* (Williams, 1966), or a way of thinking about teacher professional learning that can support rich, meaningful and democratic literacy education in an era when neoliberal discourses dominate. Specifically, we present the example of teacher-participant 'Esther's' first-grade classroom that was unruly and unfocused, and then transformed into a hive of innovative, multimodal pedagogies and practices.[1] We detail how the professional learning introduced new pedagogical repertoires, materials and ideas into the classroom, providing resistance to reductive literacy pedagogies. The changes promoted connected, purposeful literacies, joyful engagement in learning, and new relationships between children, teachers, materials and their meaning-making. We frame these findings within a view of professional learning that defies neoliberal approaches to professional development aimed at increasing test scores while deprofessionalising teachers.

Context of the study

The study took place in Ontario, Canada. Governance of education in Canada is a provincial/territorial responsibility. As the most populous province, Ontario is a potentially powerful influence in the country. In terms of literacy education, Ontario is also a global force, with Allan Luke identifying Ontario as an example of successful curricular reform (Literacy Research, 2018) and the British Broadcasting

Corporation naming Canada an 'education superpower', pointing to Ontario's 'strong base in literacy' as part of the reason for its potency (Coughlan, 2017).

There is evidence that Ontario's lauded literacy education is entangled in neoliberal discourses that limit spaces for teachers to privilege children in curriculum-making (Schwab, 1973), to support the expansion of children's literacy options (that is, the opportunities that children have to be active makers of meaning and curriculum through engagement with multiple modes, media and genres) (Heydon, 2013), to exercise their professional discernment in developing and enacting literacy-related pedagogies (Hibbert and Iannacci, 2005), and to participate in professional learning that supports teachers to enact these (Hibbert et al, 2013). We understand curriculum-making (Schwab, 1973) as the process of forging responses to questions such as what should be learned and how, and agree with the literature that centres children and teachers in this process (for example, Harste, 2003).

Curriculum research has identified that certain institutional policies and structures, including an outcomes-based curriculum and standardised assessments, can limit teachers' professional discernment and impede fulsome literacy learning opportunities for children. Ontario's programmatic literacy curriculum (for example, OME, 2006), the document that directs what happens in schools (Doyle, 1992), reflects a multidimensional view of literacy that includes 'listening and speaking, reading, writing, and viewing and representing' (OME, 2006: 4); however, specific curricular outcomes communicated as 'expectations' atomise literacy and reduce it to discrete skills (Loerts and Heydon, 2017) (for example, 'By the end of Grade 1, students will … spell some high frequency words correctly' [OME, 2006: 43]). Further, although the programmatic curriculum allows space for teachers to design pedagogies to reach outcomes, assessment measures can direct these pedagogies towards reductive literacies.

Administrated by the crown agency of the Education Quality and Accountability Office, Ontario's standardised literacy assessments are administered in grades 3, 6 and 10 (EQAO, 2007), with the grade 10 test, purported to 'demonstrate' a student's 'understanding of how to utilise certain literacy skills and participate in society once graduated' (Godin, 2017: 2). These assessments, the scores of which are publicly available, prioritise a narrow version of print literacy and position particular children (especially minoritised students) as deficient because the test identifies what children *cannot* do, rather than what they *can* (Kearns, 2016). The assessments promote wash-back in the form of directing teachers' pedagogies towards repetitive print literacy activities to promote literacy-related skills that might be on the test (Loerts and Heydon, 2017).

The assessments also wash back into professional learning activities for teachers. In Ontario, schools are mandated to design *school improvement plans* to 'improve the level of student achievement' (EIC, 2000: 6). As accountability measures, these plans often focus on curriculum outcomes, respond to the school's performance on standardised assessments and place some responsibility on teachers for realising goals for increased student and school achievement (EIC, 2000). The Ontario government identified the importance of teacher professional learning activities for helping schools reach literacy achievement goals, and recognised that collaborative models to professional learning can support plans for school improvement (OME, 2013). Thus, measures external to the classroom, including mandates, curricular outcomes and standardised assessment scores, often dictate the foci of professional learning, and teachers are mandated to participate as ways to address the deficiencies identified by these measures.

The tensions just discussed are not unique to Ontario. The literature is filled with examples of professional learning activities steeped within conversations about standardised student achievement measures (for example, Heineke, 2013), and focused on addressing student deficiencies through instructional practices that focus on literacy skills that can be easily measured (Brownell et al, 2014). This was the context of the professional learning in this study.

Rationale and theoretical framework for the study

Within the aforementioned context, this study focused on creating professional learning opportunities to support teachers in designing and implementing classroom literacy curricula that promoted expansive literacy options for children. Building on work by Flewitt et al (2015), which recognises the potential that digital technologies have for expanding literacy options, and Johnson et al (2016), which identifies that Canadian teachers request support in creatively using digital technologies, the study focused on supporting teachers to design literacy lessons that included digital tools. We understand that every classroom curriculum (that is, what actually happens in classrooms) (Doyle, 1992) is produced by a network of actors, which may be human (for example, teachers, students) and/or non-human (for example, literacy tools, assessments) (Heydon, 2013). These actors translate each other in various ways to produce particular effects; for instance, standardised assessments, given their weight in the network, tend to overpower programmatic curriculum expectations that might forward multimodal literacies, instead producing skills-oriented literacies. Changes to classroom curricula can thus be made by altering actors and the ways in which they interact.

Multimodal literacies and pedagogies

We view multimodal pedagogy as a way of promoting expansive meaning-making options for children. Multimodal pedagogy 'creates the potential for learning' (NLG, 1996: 9) by acknowledging the diverse ways that teachers and students can expand their literacy options as they combine and recombine multiple modes in meaning-making events (Cope and Kalantzis, 2000). Whereas traditional pedagogical models position teachers as sources of knowledge and focus on the transmission of information from teachers to students, multimodal pedagogies position teachers as 'designers of learning processes and environments' (NLG, 1996: 73). As a designer, the teacher creates learning events that are responsive to their particular students, and invites students to be active in meaning-making (for example, Cope and Kalantzis, 2009). Within the pedagogical design, the teacher has a responsibility to create opportunities for the students, as text designers, to select and combine different modes in meaning-making (Stein, 2008). Within this pedagogical design, teachers (McKee, 2017) and children (Gillen and Hall, 2013) are positioned as capable meaning-makers and co-creators of classroom curricula. This *asset-oriented* (Heydon and Iannacci, 2008) view of teachers and children as curriculum-makers and the focus on expanded understandings of literacies informed the professional learning design in the study.

Methodology

We highlight data from one case within an exploratory, multiple-case attempt to create professional learning opportunities to support early primary teachers to design and implement multimodal literacy pedagogies. Study questions concerned: the learning opportunities afforded to the teachers as they collaborated to design literacy lessons that included digital technologies; the ways in which the teachers configured their lessons to include print and digital resources; and the learning opportunities for the children as they participated in the lessons. This study was approved by the Research Ethics Board of Western University, Canada, and by the ethical review boards of the participating school districts.

Design of professional learning

We drew on a communities of practice (CoP) model (Wenger, 1998) as a collaborative, participatory structure to support teacher professional learning within the study. This model is commensurate with multimodal pedagogies given that it also positions teachers as knowledgeable meaning-makers (for example, Clandinin and Connelly, 1992) who draw on formalised content knowledge (Wenger, 1998) as well as practical knowledge in curriculum design (Clandinin, 1992), and whose learning is supported within relationships (Wenger, 1998). The CoP was comprised of teachers who elected to meet because they had an interest in designing and implementing literacy lessons that included digital technologies. The professional learning meetings provided a flexible structure for the teachers to collaboratively design these literacy lessons. Lori McKee, who is also a teacher, facilitated these meetings and collaborated with the teachers. Within this structure, a teacher identified a literacy learning goal for her/his students. The teachers collaborated to design a lesson that included digital technologies and responded to the identified goal, and the teacher then implemented the lesson and Lori documented. The teachers viewed images and artefacts of that lesson, reflected on the learning opportunities, and identified possibilities for follow-up lessons.

Participants

We share the example of Esther's first-grade classroom. The class of 18 students (ages six and seven) was located in a publicly funded Catholic elementary school in a small Ontario town. Esther participated in the professional learning with the other first-grade teacher in the school, 'Fireball'. Esther and Fireball both had almost a decade of teaching experience; however, they were new to teaching the first grade. Esther had previously taught secondary school while Fireball was an experienced elementary teacher. As such, Fireball had been assigned by the school to be Esther's mentor.

Study methods

Methods were ethnographic and narrative. Data sources included audio-recordings of lesson planning and implementation, photographs of Esther and her students as they participated in the lesson, audio-recordings of informal conversations with participants during the implemented lesson, semi-structured interviews with the teachers, and the researcher's reflexive journal. Data collection took place over three months in professional learning meetings as the educators collaborated to plan literacy lessons, as well as in the teachers' classrooms when the lessons were enacted.

Analysis focused on what was included in the network that produced the classroom curriculum, the literacy learning opportunities that were created, how the children responded to them and the relationship of the classroom curriculum to the professional learning (Heydon, 2013). Data from multiple sources were triangulated to identify areas of resonance and dissonance (Pahl, 2007). To promote trustworthiness, member checks were conducted with the teacher-participants.

Findings

Our findings concern Esther's participation in the professional learning, the changes that this participation brought into the classroom, the children's responses to these changes and Esther's response to all of this. The professional learning opened up possibilities for Esther to see herself and the children as active, literacy curriculum informants, and introduced this new perspective, as well as a new, dynamic relationship among materials, teacher and students, into the classroom curriculum.

An open, flexible, pedagogical design: "Have a play and see what happens" (Fireball)

The changes introduced into Esther's classroom curriculum were supported through the collaborative lesson design in the professional learning meetings. Following the methods outlined earlier, the teachers collaboratively planned a lesson for Fireball's class, he implemented it and the teachers reflected on artefacts and images of the lesson. As we reflected on Fireball's lesson, Esther became excited about the ways in which Fireball's students responded to the lesson, which invited the children to create stories using the Puppet Pals iPad application (Polished Play, 2016),[2] paper and pencil. As the teachers considered how Fireball's students combined digital and traditional resources and how the children's practices expanded their stories, Esther explained that she wanted to replicate Fireball's lesson design with her students:

Esther: 'I want you [Fireball] to come and teach my kids this, and show them this [images of Fireball's students creating stories]…'

Fireball: 'No.… If the kids were to see this, that would take away their creativity, right?'

Esther: 'Ohh!'
Fireball: 'Because that is the whole idea behind this. The kids were seeing what *they* could do.' (6 April 2017)

Fireball reminded Esther to trust her professional discernment and to orient her view to centre on the children's practices.

Following this guidance, the CoP collaboratively designed a lesson for Esther's classroom. Opening the pedagogy was gradual, with Esther hesitating at first, saying that her students had never used the digital application before. Fireball encouraged Esther to design the pedagogy to invite the children's exploration, saying "just see what [the children] come up with … have a play and see what happens … try out some different things" (6 April 2017). Fireball's suggestion for Esther to plan the lesson to support the playful exploration of literacies and technologies made space in the classroom for the unexpected.

Collaborative, unexpected and joyful: "He just jumped in!" (Esther)

Within the CoP, Esther planned her trial lesson with technology to fit with the existing literacy practices in her classroom. Each day, the children followed a literacy routine of reading levelled texts independently while Esther worked with a group of children to practise reading sight words. The classroom was defined by the sounds of young readers reading patterned texts aloud and calling out the sight words 'to, is, at, it, he, be' as Esther held up flash cards.

Following independent reading, Esther invited the children to the carpeted instruction area. Typically, this was a conflict-filled time that Esther struggled to control. Today, as the children moved to the carpet, they jostled with one another for preferred seats and argued, "No! I am staying here!", and Esther directed, "some of you are not listening … okay … go over there. Then he can see too". Another child complained, "He is laughing at me!" (6 April 2017). This kind of conflict was commonplace during classroom observations and Lori noted that Esther's class was "unsettled" and "unfocused" (23 March 2017). The teachers confirmed that Lori's observations were representative of typical classroom dynamics and explained that the class was working with a school district social worker to become more aware of their behaviour.

When the children had settled, Esther began her lesson by inviting the children's engagement and demonstrating how to use the Puppet Pals app (Polished Play, 2016) to create an animated story, saying: "I think that you are going to have some fun with this … we are going to create a story.… You don't have to write any words. We are just going to record our voices" (6 April 2017). Immediately, the children's demeanour changed as they intently watched Esther demonstrate how to use the app to create a story. As Esther began to create the story, she noticed Mike's eager anticipation and asked him to move a character in response to the story's emerging plot. Partway through the story, Esther paused as though she did not know what to say next and Mike spontaneously collaborated with her to create the animated story (see Figure 4.1):

Esther:	'It was a beautiful sunny day in the town. There was a beautiful red building, blue building, green building [long pause]…'
Mike:	'And he came in and tried to steal the colours … 'til it's black. Then he walked away to get more houses and a dragon came to live there … and he shooted fire…'
Esther:	'Shhhh [making fire-breathing sound]…'
Mike:	'You stop it right now, dragon!' (6 April 2017)

Figure 4.1: Mike collaborates with Esther to create a digital story

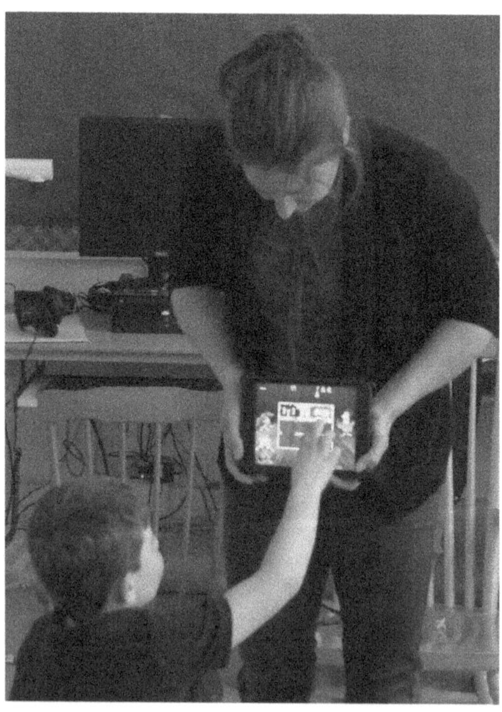

Esther revised the story plot in response to Mike's collaboration. Esther was excited about the way that Mike had co-authored the demonstration story and, in a later planning meeting, told Fireball: "I didn't even know what to say next and he just jumped in!" (13 April 2017).

As the children collaborated with each other and their teacher to create the story, the change in the classroom was palpable. In the field notes, Lori documented: 'What happened was so exciting.... [Esther and her students] constructed a playful story.... The kids leaned in to see and were so interested. The change in the spirit of the class was amazing. The kids were focused and relaxed' (6 April 2017) (see Figure 4.2). Following the demonstration story, the children's focused engagement continued as they had the choice of working in partners or independently to create digital stories.

Figure 4.2: Children engaged and focused as Mike and Esther create the demonstration story

"I didn't expect that!" (Esther)

The classroom was alive with sounds of excited children creating animated stories and Esther started noticing the children's literacy practices in new ways. Abby tucked herself behind a bookshelf and pushed against the bins of levelled texts to create a space for her iPad (see Figure 4.3). As Abby created her story, she jumped up and down excitedly while she changed the background scenes and moved her characters around the screen. Esther observed Abby's focused enthusiasm and the ways in which she used the technology to change the scenes to support her story plot, and expressed her surprise to Lori:

Esther:	'Did you see Abby?'
Lori:	'I know! It was really good.'
Esther:	'It was totally planned out…'
Lori:	'She knew exactly what she wanted! Three scenes!'
Esther:	'I didn't expect that!' (6 April 2017)

Esther was surprised by the way in which Abby created her story because previous assessments suggested that Abby understood little about story composing and had identified Abby as 'struggling' in

Figure 4.3: Abby pushes bins of books back to create space for her iPad and creates a story

learning to read and write. Further, Esther had not known that Abby could use the technology to change the story scenes because Esther had not demonstrated how to use this feature of the application. Finally, Abby's animated story was more fluent and expressive than what she had been able to communicate using print-based resources. The new lesson created through the professional learning introduced new literacy tools, new opportunities for composing and a new disposition in Esther to allow the children to play with literacies. Within the space created by the changes to the classroom curriculum, Abby repositioned herself as a capable meaning-maker.

The children used the technology to create collaborative stories, demonstrating joy through their laughter, giggles and engagement to complete the invitation to compose. In a classroom where they had quarrelled with each other about seating locations minutes before, the children were focused and engaged in collaborative, joyful, meaning-making activities. The children's joy overflowed as Anna was overcome with laughter as she collaborated with Lily to create the digital story (see Figure 4.4). Esther also recognised the significant shift in classroom practices from unsettled to joyful. In the field notes, Lori documented:

Figure 4.4: Anna and Lily laughing together as they create their story

> After our lesson, Esther [phoned] me … she said that she was so excited about the lesson that she wanted to call. She couldn't believe how Mike just jumped in with helping tell her story.… She commented on how happy Anna and Lily were and how there was just so much joy. (6 April 2017)

The children's responses to the teachers' open pedagogy that invited the children's explorations were a catalyst for the teachers' reflections.

"I am seeing the students in a different light" (Fireball)

In our planning meetings, the teachers reflected on the ways in which the children responded to the pedagogies. The children's joyful, collaborative literacy practices caused the teachers to reconsider the ways in which they viewed the children:

Fireball:	'Esther, seeing the pictures in *your* class, *I* am seeing the students in a different light … seeing how engaged they were with this, and then hearing the stories about what happened in the class…'
Esther:	'Oh yeah!… That was a shock!'

The teachers' reflections on the children's innovations further expanded the pedagogies as they reconsidered the capabilities of the children.

Discussion

We offer glimpses into Esther's classroom as *resources for hope* (Williams, 1966): illustrations of teachers' professional learning that can forward meaningful literacy education that invites children and teachers to be part of curriculum-making. We conceptualise this as democratic literacy education. These resources are forwarded at a time when neoliberal discourses are becoming instantiated in classroom curricula, guided by accountability measures like standardised assessment and curricular outcomes, producing collateral effects such as anaemic, skills-based literacies that undermine the promotion of children and teachers as active designers of literacies and curricula.

The changes in Esther's classroom promoted connected, purposeful literacies, joyful engagement in learning, and new relationships between children, teachers, materials and their meaning-making. The CoP created collaborative spaces for Esther to exercise professional discernment in identifying what kinds of learning opportunities could support her students, and envision new possibilities for her own classroom. Together, she and Fireball, joined by Lori, planned, viewed and reflected on literacy teaching, where rather than focusing their gaze on mandates or outcomes, they focused on children's literacy practices and their effects, and extended their pedagogies from there. Prompted to focus on the children, and creating space for playful exploration, Esther's pedagogical design became more open. Other actors that produced changes in the classroom curriculum included the iPads, app and focus on story composition. The changes were characterised as a move towards a more active, joyful classroom.

Resistance to literacy mandates is commonly conceptualised as occurring through teachers' active resistance (for example, Garan, 2002). However, this case demonstrates how the classroom curriculum changed not because the teacher decided to resist neoliberal literacy discourses, but because of the network of actors working together: Esther's support through the CoP to loosen her pedagogy; the iPads and app providing composition tools that were flexible, inherently multimodal and engaging; and the school district's interest in the professional learning project that supported 'digital literacy', thus backing Esther to experiment.

The digital tools were an apt place to begin supporting democratic literacies. They provided an entrée to the school district, but, more fundamentally, they created questions in the CoP about what literacy can be in schools. Just as Abby pushed against the levelled books to create space for her iPad, curricula need to be broadened to allow space for children to expand their literacy options. The digital tools in the study connect to Thibaut and Curwood's (2018: 49) hope for multiliteracies: 'supported by constantly evolving digital tools … we argue that multiliteracies can be used to close the gap between teacher-directed, individual, and assessment-driven learning, and authentic, shared, and purpose-driven learning'. They also argue that 'multiliteracies are crucial for understanding how teachers and students interact with each other, and with texts within blended spaces for learning' (Thibaut and Curwood, 2018: 50). Esther and the students, within the network, began to transact in the process of active composition in ways that were impossible in rhyming off sight words.

The moments in Esther's classroom that we share in this chapter are arguably not a wholesale change in the classroom curriculum that can revolutionise literacy education or the professional learning that is offered to teachers. They are, however, moments of hope. Participating in the CoP, even for a short time, provoked Esther to reroute from the traditional path of lesson composition identified in the literature, which focuses on outcomes and assessments, and fits into a larger discourse of school improvement. Instead, Esther was prompted to take a risk, play and be open to the children's practices. Taking up this invitation introduced new actors into the classroom curriculum, prompting new effects. The focus on composition, the tools for multimodal, digital composition, and the loosening of fossilised frameworks where children are word-callers (for example, the reading of sight words) and readers of levelled texts created spaces for the children's literacy practices to be generative and recognised by their teacher as innovative. Examples such as these promote a practice of hope that Simon (1992: 3) taught us years ago to be 'the acknowledgment of more openness in a situation than the situation easily reveals' and the ability to 'envisage … possibility' and act 'upon it … by loosening and refusing the hold that taken-for-granted realities and routines have over imagination'. This was a practice that Esther could perform and whose example might promote a new 'way of life' (Williams, 1966: 330) in classrooms, allowing teachers and children to commit 'to the future' to 'make the present' in classrooms during this neoliberal era 'inhabitable' (Solnit, 2016: 4).

The study communicates that resisting neoliberal discourses that deprofessionalise teachers, reduce literacies to autonomous skills and shut children out of informing the curriculum requires professional learning spaces that invite teachers to exercise professional discernment. As the teachers use their discernment, they turn their gaze towards the children to inform their pedagogical design rather than focusing on mandates or scores. This shift in gaze allows the teachers to see new possibilities.

Acknowledgements

This research was supported by the Social Sciences and Humanities Research Council of Canada.

Notes

1. All participant names are self-selected pseudonyms.
2. Puppet Pals (Polished Play, 2016), an iPad application, allows users to create animated stories.

References

Brownell, M.T., Lauterbach, A.A., Dingle, M.P., Boardman, A.G., Urbach, J.E., Leko, M.M. and Park, Y. (2014) 'Individual and contextual factors influencing special education teacher learning in literacy learning cohorts', *Learning Disability Quarterly*, 37(1): 31–44.

Clandinin, D.J. (1992) 'Narrative and story in teacher education', in T. Russell and H. Munby (eds) *Teachers and teaching: From classroom to reflection*, London: Falmer Press, pp 124–37.

Clandinin, D.J. and Connelly, F.M. (1992) 'Teacher as curriculum maker', in P.W. Jackson (ed) *Handbook of research on curriculum*, New York, NY: Macmillan, pp 486–516.

Cope, B. and Kalantzis, M. (2000) 'Introduction: Multiliteracies: The beginning of an idea', in B. Cope and M. Kalantzis (eds) *Multiliteracies: Literacy learning and the design of social futures*, New York, NY: Routledge, pp 3–8.

Cope, B. and Kalantzis, M. (2009) 'Multiliteracies: New literacies, new learning', *Pedagogies: An International Journal*, 4: 164–95.

Coughlan, S. (2017) 'How Canada became an education superpower', BBC News. Available at: www.bbc.com/news/business-40708421

Doyle, W. (1992) 'Curriculum and pedagogy', in P.W. Jackson (ed) *Handbook of research on curriculum*, New York, NY: Macmillan, pp 486–516.

EIC (Education Improvement Commission) (2000) 'School improvement planning: A handbook for principals, teacher and school councils'. Available at: www.edu.gov.on.ca/eng/document/reports/sihande.pdf

EQAO (Education Quality and Assessment Office) (2007) 'Framework: Ontario secondary school literacy test'. Available at: www.eqao.com/en/assessments/OSSLT/assessment-docs/framework-osslt.pdf

Flewitt, R., Messer, D. and Kucirkova, N. (2015) 'New directions for early literacy in a digital age: The iPad', *Journal of Early Childhood Literacy*, 15(3): 289–310.

Garan, E.M. (2002) *Resisting reading mandates: How to triumph with the truth*, Portsmouth, NH: Heinemann.

Gillen, J. and Hall, N. (2013) 'The emergence of early childhood literacy', in J. Larson and J. Marsh (eds) *The Sage handbook of early childhood literacy* (2nd edn), London: Sage, pp 3–17.

Godin, N. (2017) 'Understanding the power of literacy and Ontario's literacy education: A critical analysis of the EQAO and its definition of literacy practices', master's project, York University. Available at: http://hdl.handle.net/10315/34192

Harste, J. (2003) 'What do we mean by literacy now?', *Voices from the Middle*, 10: 8–12.

Heineke, S.F. (2013) 'Coaching discourse', *The Elementary School Journal*, 113(3): 409–33.

Heydon, R. (2013) 'Learning opportunities: A study of the production and practice of kindergarten literacy curricula', *Journal of Curriculum Studies*, 45(4): 481–510.

Heydon, R. and Iannacci, L. (2008) *Early childhood curricula and the de-pathologizing of childhood*, Toronto: University of Toronto Press.

Hibbert, K. and Iannacci, I. (2005) 'From dissemination to discernment: The commodification of literacy instruction and the fostering of "good teacher consumerism"', *The Reading Teacher*, 58(8): 716–27.

Hibbert, K., Rich, S., Scheffel, T.-L. and Heydon, R. (2013) 'Orchestrating expertise in reading and writing', *Education, 3–13*, 41(2): 125–37.

Johnson, M., Riel., R. and Froese-Germain, B. (2016) *Connected to learn: Teachers' experiences with networked technologies in the classroom*, Ottawa: MediaSmarts/Canadian Teachers' Federation.

Kearns, L.-L. (2016) 'The construction of "illiterate" and "literate" youth: The effects of high-stakes standardized literacy testing', *Race, Ethnicity and Education*, 19(1): 121–40.

Literacy Research (2018) 'LRA 2016 distinguished scholar lifetime achievement session Allan Luke', video, 8 January. Available at: https://youtu.be/s08Kr5N-_H8

Loerts, T. and Heydon, R. (2017) 'Multimodal literacy learning opportunities within a grade six classroom literacy curriculum: Constraints and enablers', *Education 3–13*, 45(4): 490–503.

McKee, L. (2017) 'Pedagogies of possibilities: (Re)Designing teacher professional learning to support the use of digital technologies in multimodal pedagogies', PhD dissertation, The University of Western Ontario, Electronic Thesis and Dissertation Repository, 5157. Available at: https://ir.lib.uwo.ca/etd/5157

NLG (New London Group) (1996) 'A pedagogy of multiliteracies: Designing social futures', *Harvard Educational Review*, 66(1): 60–92.

OME (Ontario Ministry of Education) (2006) 'The Ontario curriculum grades 1–8: Language (revised)'. Available at: www.edu.gov.on.ca/eng/curriculum/elementary/language18currb.pdf

OME (2013) 'School effectiveness framework'. Available at: http://edu.gov.on.ca/eng/literacynumeracy/SEF2013.pdf

Pahl, K. (2007) 'Timescales and ethnography: Understanding a child´s meaning-making across three sites, a home, a classroom and a family literacy class', *Ethnography and Education*, 2(2), 175–190.

Polished Play (2016) 'Puppet pals HD' (version number 1.9.1), mobile application software. Available at: https://itunes.apple.com/us/app/puppet-pals-hd/id342076546?mt=8/

Schwab, J.J. (1973) 'The practical 3: Translation into curriculum', *The School Review*, 81(4): 501–22.

Simon, R.I. (1992) *Teaching against the grain: Texts for a pedagogy of possibility*, Toronto: OISE Press.

Solnit, R. (2016) *Hope in the dark: Untold histories, wild possibilities* (3rd edn), Chicago, IL: Haymarket Books.

Stein, P. (2008) 'Multimodal instructional practices', in J. Coiro, M. Knobel, C. Lankshear and D.J. Leu (eds) *Handbook of research on new literacies*, New York, NY: Lawrence Erlbaum Associates, pp 871–98.

Thibaut, P. and Curwood, J.S. (2018) 'Multiliteracies in practice: Integrating multimodal production across the curriculum', *Theory Into Practice*, 57(1): 48–55.

Wenger, E. (1998) *Communities of practice: Learning, meaning, and identity*, Cambridge: Cambridge University Press.

Williams, R. (1966) *Resources of hope: Culture, democracy, socialism*, London: Verso.

5

Countering dull pedagogies: the power of teachers and artists working together

Pat Thomson and Christine Hall

Dull pedagogies

Pedagogy: a word with varying meanings. We take pedagogy to be more than the methods used by teachers, although this is how it is most usually used in Britain. We understand pedagogy as the totality of a learning experience: the ways in which relationships are developed and conversations are held; the practice used to sequence, pace and scaffold knowledge and skills; the use of time/space; the monitoring and formative and summative assessment of learning; the ethos of the classroom and school; and the ways in which the everyday lives of students are recognised, valued and used to connect them to what counts in schooling.

Dullness is not about teacher-directed learning. Dullness is situated in predictability and universality – the day after day of the same pedagogy regardless of what is to be learnt. Dullness is located in unadulterated textbook- or PowerPoint presentation-based learning that fails to connect with students' existing understandings and experiences. Dullness is located in remoteness – students unable to interpret material for themselves, inhibited by the constant administration of ritualised right/wrong questions-and-answer routines. Dullness is coverage prioritised over understanding. Dullness is material thinly presented – difficult material skated over so that students do not have time to get to grips with its key ideas and practices. Dullness is the refusal to allow feeling and bodies into the conversation. Sameness and monotony numbs students and teachers alike.

Ironically, dull pedagogies are often used with the intent of producing rich and deep learnings, though they frequently work counter to this aim. Dullness can be being asked to respond to half a book or an event in history taken out of context, or being asked to grapple with a contemporary crisis like climate change without having access to useful concepts and terminology. Dull pedagogies fail to ignite students' passion for a discipline, fail to spark new lines of thought and fail to kindle the desire to learn more, to dig deeper, to explore further.

Dullness matters. In England, default structures like the 'three-part lesson', introduced originally as improvement strategies for underperforming teachers, have become overused and decoupled from deep learning. Too many students and teachers feel trapped in pedagogic routines designed to service accountability goals and audit regimes (see, for example, Gillborn and Youdell, 2000; Ball et al, 2012; Kulz, 2017; Ward and Quennerstedt, 2018). In our own research, we have documented how the steady diet of dull pedagogies, designed to please inspectors, actively produces underachievement (Thomson et al, 2010a). However, in work supported by the Creative Partnerships (CP) programme, we have also witnessed an attempt by teachers in England to disrupt the default pedagogies embedded in the daily lives of their schools (Thomson et al, 2009; Hall and Thomson, 2017b), and it is this work that we discuss in this chapter.

There is, of course, no single right way to build knowledge, know-how and a habituated curiosity and desire to know more, and no single right way to avoid being dull. CP's approach was to fund artists to work on pedagogical reform with teachers, to develop pedagogies that challenged, provoked and invited students to go beyond what they imagined they could do.

Enter artists

For the last 15 years, we have been studying the collaborative work of teachers and artists, and the partnerships between schools and arts organisations. We have come to understand not only that there is a lot that teachers can learn from artists, and vice versa, but also that the two are not interchangeable (Hall et al, 2007; Thomson et al, 2012a).

When artists and teachers work together, the default pedagogies are changed. They often begin new teaching with some form of provocation or exploration. They are likely to mix some direct teaching of key concepts with self-directed inquiry, which uses a range of materials, genres, platforms and media. Artists often draw on their own expertise to teach in different ways. For example, performing artists draw on their knowledge of ensemble work, rehearsal room techniques, improvisation or verbatim approaches to offer new routes to explore, interrogate and build knowledge. Visual artists bring studio practices of idea generation, documentation and reflection, problem solving, and counter-thinking to offer different approaches to formative assessment. Writers bring finely honed observation and listening skills, combined with artisan practices of drafting, revising and editing, to offer expanded avenues for the production of texts. These, we argue, are the 'signature pedagogies' of artists, pedagogies that teachers experience and learn from in partnership teaching arrangements and can then use to develop their own pedagogical repertoires (Hall and Thomson, 2017a). Through partnership, artists and teachers can work together to create spaces and practices where, at least temporarily, dull, routinised pedagogies are disrupted. Sometimes, these alternative pedagogies are sustained. Sometimes, as we have witnessed, they spread throughout the school, changing it for the better, for teachers and students alike.

The benefits that artists bring to schools usually focus on practice – additional methods and skills. However, we argue that it is the artists' ontologies, epistemologies and relational-material practices that are equally, if not more, important. Without these underpinning ways of being, thinking and acting, what artists offer can be seen simply as techniques to be copied, as better ways to meet test and inspection requirements, as different ways to form neoliberal subjectivities (cf Galton, 2010).

An equitable ontological orientation

The artists that we have watched and worked with often shared an ontological position that we see as Rancièrian, that is, artists believed that all young people are equally capable of having worthy and interesting ideas and bringing them to fruition. They took the classroom to be a community of artists, which, as Rancière (1991: 71) puts it:

> would repudiate the division between those who know and those who don't, between those who possess or don't possess the property of intelligence. It would only know minds in action: people who do, who speak about what they are doing, and who thus transform all their works into ways of demonstrating the humanity that is in them as in everyone. Such people would know that no one is born with more intelligence than his [sic] neighbor, that the superiority that someone might manifest is only the fruit of as tenacious an application to working with words as another might show to working with tools.

This ontological standpoint does not deny that difference and inequality exist; rather, it suggests that any pedagogical approach that begins by assuming that there are hierarchies of talent, knowledge and skill in a classroom will not only work as if they exist, but also bring them into being (Rancière, 2004a). Rancière argues that teachers must start from a position of assumed equality – not sameness, but assuming that all students are equally capable, that they share the same potentials and possibilities. What would we do differently, he asks, if this were our starting point? (For a Rancièrian classroom narrative, see Box 5.1.)

Box 5.1: All children can imagine

'Story Lady' presented the Welsh legend of Gelert the dog to a diverse inner-city class. Gelert foils a wolf's attempt to steal his master's newborn baby. Returning home and seeing signs of a struggle, the master assumes that Gelert has attacked the baby and kills the dog. When he realises what has happened, the master is consumed with remorse.

Throughout the reading, Story Lady paused to ask the children to imagine details of the events – the colour of the curtains, how the sleeping baby looks, Gelert's breed and appearance, the sound of the fight between the dog and the wolf. These questions produced enthusiastic responses from the children. Story Lady kept order without being teacherly. She ensured that everyone who wanted to speak could do so. She used the story to introduce the idea of everyday courage and facilitated an equally enthusiastic conversation about courage in everyday life and who the children knew who was brave.

Later, in the staffroom, the class teacher apologised to Story Lady for the class's ill-mannered behaviour. She expressed concern about some of their 'silly ideas', such as that Gelert was a dachshund or a Jack Russell. Story Lady listened and then carefully responded to the implicit criticism of the discussion process that she had been using.

'Everyone can imagine their own Gelert', she said; 'It's important that each child can connect their lives to the story they are being told. Having pictures in your mind of what is happening is the way I allowed them to enter into the story in their own way. Everyone's Gelert is different, no one's Gelert is wrong.' (Based on Thomson and Hall, 2015)

In contrast to these artists, teachers almost invariably begin by thinking that students have varying interests, knowledges, needs and abilities, and will need different kinds of support. This is how teachers are trained to think in initial teacher education, policy documents and curriculum guidelines. The problem with this ontology is that – in the English context, at least – difference and diversity have been translated into policy and practices that serve to (re)produce hierarchies of outcome: a differentiated curriculum, an inequitable ladder of levels of attainment, a pecking order of sets used for student grouping and so on.

The artists' orientation – to treat all children and young people as if they were equal – challenges these ingrained schooling practices. Like Rancière, the artists we researched invited teachers to test equality as a principle of practice (Biesta, 2017).

An epistemology of uncertainty

Artists also bring into school a particular epistemology. Contemporary art and performance practices, for example, almost always assume that the ways in which we 'know', and thus speak and act and live our lives, can and should be questioned. This view is more than understanding knowledge as culturally produced, contingent, specific and partial. When artists query knowledge and its production, they also query knowing per se. 'Why do we want to know?', 'Why do we need to know?', 'Why do we value knowing over making, or being?' they ask. Holding the quest to know up to scrutiny results in seeing not knowing as a positive, rather than a negative and alarming state (Barthelme, 1997), something to be rectified as quickly as possible.

Not knowing is a place where things happen (Fisher and Fortnum, 2014). As Schechner (2013, 111) argues: 'Arts, once the home of strict choreography, precise scores, and fixed mise-en-scènes has for some time been open to chance processes, unpredictable eruptions from the unconscious and improvisation.' The not-knowing processes of thinking and exploring – delaying leaping to a conclusion and staying with the unknown and uncertain positions – are valued and valuable practices for working and being. Artists' commitment to the value of a practice of liminality creates new spaces and times for being, relating, doing and thinking, disrupting the dulled patterns of everyday life in schools. (For an example of artists who challenged a school to un-know their use of time and space, see Box 5.2.)

Box 5.2: Querying what schools know and do

The head teacher, Lesley, described the artists' initial analysis of her school in this way:

> [The artists] came in with an objective eye and began to develop this space analysis document, which was really a set of photographs and questions. So they just came into school and wandered around and took photographs of areas of the school and then they raised questions about why is that like that. What is that doing there? Who works here? So it showed all these different areas: it showed ways in; getting around; what was on the wall; storage. And there were lots and lots of issues around our school.... We've got a lot of spaces ... we've got playgrounds that were surrounded by lots of walls so you can't see anything out of it. You've got the guinea pig space which, again, is a tiny area. You've got all these little add on bits of space.... They did some work as well, not just on those spaces and what they saw there, but also on tracking how people use the space. So they went out and they put pedometers on some of the children and some of the staff and they just watched where people went – followed them around and made notes of what they were doing. And incredible things came out of it, about people walking – one of our teaching assistants walked seven miles in a day and she was going up and down the stairs in a big building. (Hall and Thomson, 2017b: 141)

The artists also looked carefully at the classrooms. In Lesley's words:

> they looked at what they called 'stuff'. So they talked about what we had in that room and do we use it all? How is it stored? Is it too much? Is stuff beautiful? And as a result of that, we began to look at the classrooms and think about what the ideal environment might be for our children. (Hall and Thomson, 2017b: 141)

An unknowing state is in considerable tension with a national curriculum in which learning outcomes are fixed, explicit and presented as targets, levels and grades. Atkinson argues that, in reality, these are pedagogical choices – in England, two opposing pedagogical existences are possible:

> The first is driven by a desire for specific preordained pedagogised subjects that will meet the needs of economic

> competition and which is held in place by controlled curriculums, assessment and inspection programmes. Such existence follows planned routes determining educational success or failure. The second advocates a more uncertain pedagogical adventure characterised by novel modes of subjective engagement that emphasise a subject-yet-to-come and where the notion of the not-known is immanent to such adventures. (Atkinson, 2015: 43)

Atkinson does not underestimate the difficulties of pedagogical choice-making – even arts teachers who understand not knowing are still required to fulfil demands imposed by the systemic desire for the measurable and well-disciplined subject and subjectivity.

Material ethics

Artists are often concerned with materials. Performers accumulate clothing and objects that help them to become something other than their habitual selves. Visual artists respond to the affordances of different materials and push what materials can do to their (collaborative) limits. Musicians and their instruments work together to make music; music comes from their work in concert. Artists understand that materials can have profound influence on human activity.

The artists that we documented routinely proffered a variety of materials as invitations to students. They assumed that students would be drawn by and to particular materials, and through experimenting with them, would produce a narrative, relationship and/or object that had meaning to them. (For a typical example of the ways in which play with materials was structured, see Box 5.3.)

Box 5.3: Materials in action

Each session opened with Stanley reviewing the previous week, going through images on his laptop and encouraging the parents to comment on the children's learning and their progress. This broad invitation tended to result in murmurs of assent and shared moments of recognition rather than sustained discussion. Stanley then invited the parents to go outside and begin to arrange the materials he has brought with him into some sort of order. The materials consist of a huge number cardboard boxes, tubes, grips, plastic sheets, felt tips, rubber bands, ties, tape and other kinds of 'safe' found materials in relatively good condition. He also brought three digital cameras for use by children and adults, as well as his own camera, which he used for documenting the day.

The materials were arranged in the playground according to type. The staff marked off the playground with chairs. When the parents judged the play area to be ready, the staff brought out the selected children – those whose parents have come along that day – and 40 minutes to an hour of intense play ensued.

The purpose of the activity was for the children to make structures and then engage in imaginative play. Stanley encouraged the parents and the children to engage with the tactile, 'felt' qualities of the play: he was interested in the use, experimentation and manipulation of materials and the structures that were built. Most of the play involved single children engaging with their parents. The staff made notes about the children's learning, particularly their language use and the points where tactile and experimental play moved into narrative.

About ten minutes from the end of the session, Stanley encouraged the children and parents to visit each edifice and ask the child to describe what it was and what it meant. When the session had come to its natural end, the constructions were dismantled and the materials were re-sorted for use next time. The adults then sat in a small group and discussed what had happened. Stanley encouraged each parent to reflect on his or her own child's play and the other parents to join in the discussion. The parents were keen to participate, to get validation of their own child's play and also to find a way of supporting other children's achievements. Stanley then put photographs of the session onto the computer in preparation for next time. (Thomson et al, 2012b : 31–2)

The materials that the artists used were often discarded, second-hand or natural – feathers, leaves and twigs, card, plastic, cord, and metals. These 'loose parts' (Nicholson, 1971) could be repurposed and reused multiple times to create new 'things'. They were uncategorised and uncategorisable except as primary material and were thus open to interpretation and remixing in ways that commercially produced objects are not. Materials varied in colour, shape and texture. They invited students to play and construct complex, diverse and emergent meanings. Reassembling drew on imagination and supported the development of a range of concepts and skills.

The reuse of materials was important. It was not that artists thought children unworthy of new materials, but rather that they wanted to instil the idea that artistic practices could use the most ordinary, and often apparently 'waste', materials (compare with the Arte Povera movement). Many of the artists adopted an ecological perspective, which resonates with Bennett's (2010) argument for working with materials to re-imagine politics – to 'articulate a vibrant materiality that runs alongside and inside humans to see how analyses of political events might change if we gave the force of things more due' (Bennett, 2010: viii). Bennett focuses not on 'the macro-level politics of laws, policy, institutional change but the micro-politics of sensibility-formation' in the hope to achieve 'a greater attentiveness to the active power of things – a power that can impede, collaborate with, or compete with our desire to live better, healthier, even happier lives'.[1] This view was expressed by many of the artists we watched and interviewed. They believed that creative work with used materials was a process of learning the value of reuse.

A redistributive ethos

The ontological, epistemological and ethical positions that artists assumed did not exist in isolation from each other. Brought together, they formed a particular emancipatory commitment that was openly directed at supporting people to engage in arts-supported learning. They did not see what they did as a substitute for formal arts education, itself sometimes highly conservative and elitist (Addison and Burgess, 2012). They understood that they were bringing the being-thinking-doing of artists to bear on school pedagogies in order to resist and change them.

The artists we observed often expressed strong desires to disrupt what Rancière called 'partage de sensible' – the distribution of 'a system of a priori forms of determining what presents itself to sense experience' (Rancière, 2004b: 12). This was a double move, working against both the art and the educational worlds. Rancière suggested that a contradiction exists between the aesthetic systems of the arts and the ideal of a democratic society, that contemporary arts are a system that produces hierarchies of knowledge, participation and status. This argument was reflected in the lived experience of many of the artists who chose to work in schools. Often wary of elite institutions and marketised art-world systems through which they might or might not become individually successful (see Thornton, 2008), they had a commitment to working in communities and social institutions such as schools where they could in small ways make arts available to more people, more of the time, to say and do what they chose. Often, they saw working in schools as an art practice in and of itself, a form of social engagement. Analogous to the Arte Util (useful art) movement in the visual arts, this practice puts the self-professed transformative power of the arts to the test.

Artists believed that in working with teachers, they might effect some change, albeit possibly only temporary, in schools. They understood that the arts are not 'the answer' to all of the problems in society – or in schooling (Illeris, 2006) – but they thought that they might be a helpful interruption. Due to the 'aesthetic deficit' in school education as it is practised in neoliberalised policy contexts (McDonnell, 2016), aesthetic and affective experiences can work to disrupt – and draw attention to – the production and reproduction of inequalities. As Rancière (2004b: 8) notes: 'Artistic practices [are] "ways of doing and making" that intervene in the general distribution of ways of doing and making as well as in the relationships they maintain to modes of being and forms of invisibility.'

Artists who worked in schools were often interested in the ways in which schooling distributes its goods and benefits: the use of money, space and time; the ways in which education is measured and monitored; who is able to speak, to have ideas, knowledge, narratives and truths; and how these are represented. They sometimes tackled this directly, but more often through indirect means.

The artists' emancipatory intent was evident in the ways in which they worked to humanise schools in which students are increasingly seen as performing outcomes. Their interactions with students tended to be highly reciprocal: they gave time to students to air their views, they listened intently and they responded positively. They answered questions that might be deemed inappropriate in lessons. They offered information about themselves and invited students to do the same. They promoted and produced a highly 'person-centred' environment (Fielding, 2004). (For an artist's talk during an aesthetic exploration of affect, see Box 5.4.)

Box 5.4: Talking differently

> There was a session focussed on self-expression through the arts.... It happened off site in The Friends' Meeting House, a community space that was unfamiliar to the children. As before, the resources for the session were idiosyncratic and provided by Iona but the main teaching method was the facilitation of independent activity. The focus was on producing

representations of stress, and then of contentment, through the production of collages. The materials for making the collages were stored in what Iona referred to as her 'Tinker's Box'. The Tinker's Box comprised about 30 small crates full of beads, the hooked lids of shower gel containers, cones, feathers, drinking straws and other, mainly plastic, objects derived from domestic or packaging sources. The children assembled – and later dismantled – the collages on large circles or squares of coloured card. They worked individually in a self-chosen space on the hall floor, having selected their own collection of materials from the Tinker's Box. Once they were satisfied with their collage, they were encouraged to write about it, in prose or in poetry.

The patterns of Iona's language use were focused on the children's experiences and creativity; she offered no anecdotes or sustained personal references as she had in the previous session. The emphasis of the session was on exploring, creating images, interpreting symbols, finding language that captured emotions. Instructions were couched gently, as invitations. Most of Iona's time in the session was spent crouching on the floor in private conversation with individual children, listening to their points about their work. This was in contrast to the teacher, who was also circulating and showing obvious appreciation for the artwork, but offering semi-public suggestions and prompting certain interpretations. Photography was used as part of the recognition of each child's efforts ('Can I take a picture of that?' The child nods and smiles and, when it's taken, they both look at the image together). The use of photographs also served to develop the theme – introduced in the first session – of making something from nothing and, in doing so, creating something that persists. (Hall and Thomson, 2017b: 162)

While school systems of meaning remained, they were often, through the use of artist-teacher produced conversations, artefacts, exhibitions, performances and displays, made more 'considerate, convivial and capacious' (Bragg and Manchester, 2017). The distribution of who could offer representations and meanings was broadened.

Conclusion

We have argued that artists can offer teachers and students very particular ways of being, knowing and acting in and with the world. Working with teachers, they can use pedagogies that are, at their best, open-ended, exploratory, deconstructive and reconstructive, collaborative, inclusive, and disruptive. The development of embodied expertise and connoisseurship embedded in the arts requires 'slow' and 'deep' thinking and doing. The pedagogies that develop and sustain these characteristics stand in contrast to the norm of micro-targets, ritualised lesson structures and test-oriented learning that constitute the dull daily diet of so much neoliberalised schooling. Working together, artists and teachers can resist and even change the 50 shades of neoliberal grey.

Note

1 See: https://philosophyinatimeoferror.com/2010/04/22/vibrant-matters-an-interview-with-jane-bennett/

References

Addison, N. and Burgess, L. (2012) *Debates in art and design education*, London: Routledge.

Atkinson, D. (2015) 'The adventure of pedagogy, learning and the not-known', *Subjectivity*, 8(1): 43–56.

Ball, S., Maguire, M. and Braun, A. (2012) *How schools do policy. Policy enactments in secondary schools*, London: Routledge.

Barthelme, D. (1997) *Not-knowing. The essays and interviews*, Berkeley, CA: Counterpoint.

Bennett, J. (2010) *Vibrant matter. A political ecology of things*, Princeton, NJ: Princeton University Press.

Biesta, G. (2017) 'Don't be fooled by ignorant schoolmasters: On the role of the teacher in emancipatory education', *Policy Futures in Education*, 15(1): 52–73.

Bragg, S. and Manchester, H. (2017) 'Considerate, convivial and capacious? Finding a language to capture ethos in "creative"' schools', *Discourse*, 38(6): 864–79.

Fielding, M. (2004) 'Transformative approaches to student voice: Theoretical underpinnings, recalcitrant realities', *British Educational Research Journal*, 30(2): 295–311.

Fisher, E. and Fortnum, R. (2014) *On not knowing. How artists think*, London: Black Dog Publishing.

Galton, M. (2010) 'Going with the flow or back to normal? The impact of creative practitioners in schools and classrooms', *Cambridge Journal of Education*, 25(4): 355–75.

Gillborn, D. and Youdell, D. (2000) *Rationing education. Policy, practice, reform and equity*, Buckingham and Philadelphia, PA: Open University Press.

Hall, C. and Thomson, P. (2017a) 'Creativity in teaching: what can teachers learn from artists?', *Research Papers in Education*, 32(1): 106–20.

Hall, C. and Thomson, P. (2017b) *Inspiring school change. Transforming education through the creative arts*, London: Routledge.

Hall, C., Thomson, P. and Russell, L. (2007) 'Teaching like an artist: The pedagogic identities and practices of artists in schools', *British Journal of Sociology of Education*, 28(5): 605–19.

Illeris, H. (2006) 'Museums and galleries as performative sites for lifelong learning: Constructions, deconstructions and reconstructions of audience positions in museum and gallery education', *Museums and Society*, 4(1): 15–26.

Kulz, C. (2017) *Factories for learning. Making race, class and inequality in the neoliberal academy*, Manchester: Manchester University Press.

McDonnell, J. (2016) 'Is it "all about having an opinion"? Challenging the dominance of rationality and cognition in democratic education via research in a gallery setting', *International Journal of Art & Design Education*, DOI: 10.1111/jade.12107.

Nicholson, S. (1971) 'Now not to cheat children: Theory of loose parts', *Landscape Architecture*, 62: 30–4.

Ranciere, J. (1991) *The ignorant schoolmaster. Five lessons in intellectual emancipation* (trans by K. Ross), Stanford, CA: Stanford University Press.

Ranciere, J. (2004a) *The philosopher and his poor*, Durham, CA: Duke University Press.

Ranciere, J. (2004b) *The politics of aesthetics. The distribution of the sensible* (trans by G. Rockhill), London: Bloomsbury.

Schechner, R. (2013) *Performance studies: An introduction* (3rd edn), New York, NY: Routledge.

Thomson, P. and Hall, C. (2015) '"Everyone can imagine their own Gellert": The democratic artist and "inclusion" in primary and nursery classrooms', *Education 3–13*, 43(4): 1–13.

Thomson, P., Jones, K. and Hall, C. (2009) *Creative whole school change. Final report*, London: Creativity, Culture and Education and Arts Council England.

Thomson, P., Hall, C. and Jones, K. (2010a) 'Maggie's day: A small scale analysis of English education policy', *Journal of Education Policy*, 25(5): 639–56.

Thomson, P., Hall, C. and Jones, K. (2012a) 'Creativity and cross-curriculum strategies in England: Tales of doing, forgetting and not knowing', *International Journal of Educational Research*, 55: 6–15.

Thomson, P., Hall, C., Jones, K. and Green, J.S. (2012b) *Signature pedagogies*, London: Creativity, Culture and Education.

Thornton, S. (2008) *Seven days in the art world*, London: Granta.

Ward, G. and Quennerstedt, M. (2018) 'Curiosity killed by SATs: An investigation of mathematics lessons within an English primary school', *Education 3–13*, 47(3): 261-76. DOI: 10.1080/03004279.2018.1429479

6

Resisting the neoliberal: parent activism in New York State against the corporate reform agenda in schooling

David Hursh, Sarah McGinnis, Zhe Chen and Bob Lingard

Introduction

On 8 February 2018, the New York State Board of Regents Chancellor and Commissioner, and the Board of Regents, who are together responsible for the general supervision of all educational activities in the state,[1] filed a lawsuit against the State University of New York (SUNY) Charter Schools Committee and other SUNY committees for adopting a proposal in which charter schools would not need to hire certified teachers, but could grant certification to their own novice teachers (Clukey, 2018). Such a process, Chancellor Rosa and Commissioner Elia argued, would lower standards and 'allow inexperienced and unqualified individuals to teach those children most in need – students of color, those who are economically disadvantaged, and students with disabilities – in SUNY authorized charter schools' (Prothero, 2017). A lawsuit, in which the Chancellor, Commissioner and the Regents challenged the charter schools, would have been unthinkable until recently, if for no other reason than the fact that the previous Chancellor, Merryl Tisch, was a strong supporter of charter schools; indeed, so strong that she now sits on the SUNY Charter School Committee (State University of New York, no date) that passed the proposal to have charter schools certify their own teachers.

To understand how New York's leading policymakers came to sue several committees, including the SUNY Charter Schools Committee, one needs to understand how parents, teachers and students have reasserted the right of the public to determine or at least have a strong say about education policy against those who wish to adopt neoliberal reforms of privatisation, accountability based on scores on standardised tests and managerial techniques that shift power away from teachers and parents towards philanthropists, such as the Bill and Melinda Gates Foundation, hedge fund managers and investors (Hursh, 2015). The lawsuit reflects the increasing resistance from New York State parents, students, educators and community members to neoliberal reforms, including the privatisation of education, the Common Core State Standards and assessing students, teachers and schools via standardised tests.

Our focus in this chapter is explicitly on the two most influential opt-out groups in New York State, namely, New York State Allies for Public Education (NYSAPE) and Long Island Opt Out (LIOO). More specifically, the focus of this chapter is on understanding how, over the last three years, 20 per cent of the parents, who are typically hesitant to defy educational mandates and authorities, refused to submit their children to the standardised tests. Importantly, we also show that these parent activists have a broader target than standardised tests, namely, the neoliberal or corporate reform agenda in public schooling (see Burch, 2009; Au and Ferrare, 2015).

The evidence for our argument comes from interviews, media reports, websites and relevant policy documents. More specifically, we draw on interviews with parents who have leadership roles in NYSAPE, LIOO, the Alliance for Quality Education (AQE), the Rochester Coalition for Public Education and other grass-roots organisations. We also interviewed the Chancellor of the New York State Board of Regents, members of the Board of Regents, teacher union leaders, district superintendents, principals, teachers and community activists. We show how the parent activists have created an effective grass-roots, social media-based social movement for the 21st century, which has been successful in reducing the length and effects of the tests, as well as in limiting privatisation efforts. These parent activists have rejected policies that construct them as simply consumers in an education market and have reclaimed a stance of active citizens with a right to have a say about the schooling that their children receive.

In what follows, we first document the rise of the neoliberal reform agenda in schooling at both federal and New York State levels. We then consider in some detail NYSAPE and LIOO and their organising strategies, followed by an account of their successes and the current issues they face, including claims that they are in decline. We conclude with a summative and speculative account of the ongoing success of both NYSAPE and LIOO.

The rise of high-stakes testing and the neoliberal agenda at the state and federal levels

In New York, for more than the last two decades, parents, educators, students and community members have increasingly sought to resist and repeal high-stakes testing by speaking out at hearings and meetings with the Chancellor, the Commissioner, members of the Regents and state legislators, all to limited effect. In the 1990s, New York State phased in the requirement that to graduate from secondary schools, students would need to pass five standardised exams in four subject areas, making them high-stakes tests. The scores were manipulated by the State Education Department to yield the desired passing rate, which would make it appear that the students were being held to high standards and yet not significantly lower the graduation rate. Parents, teachers and students protested that the tests were harmful and began a now two-decade effort to roll back high-stakes testing through demonstrations and meetings with legislators and the Regents but, until the rise of the opt-out movement, with few positive results (Winerip, 2011; Hursh, 2013). Next, in 2002, President George W. Bush signed into law the No Child Left Behind Act (NCLB), which required testing all third- through eighth-grade students in language, arts and mathematics each year. These too were criticised by educators, parents and students for their negative impact on what was taught and how, but also remained unchanged.

Most recently, in 2015, NCLB's testing requirements were replaced by President Obama's Every Student Succeeds Act (ESSA), requiring states to link their standardised tests to some recognised national standards, which were most often the Common Core State Standards. Under ESSA, in New York, students in grades three through eight (approximately ages eight through 14) were required to sit for the Common Core exams in literacy and mathematics for two hours per day for three days, which has been reduced to two hours a day for two days, with the test scores used to evaluate students, schools and, initially, teachers.

If the time and effort devoted to standardised tests were not harmful enough, the scores on the Common Core tests were intentionally manipulated to yield a state-wide failure rate of 70 per cent, with cities like Rochester in upstate New York yielding a 95 per cent failure rate. Such low passing rates assisted proponents of charter schools and standardised testing in portraying public schools as failing and calling for more charter schools and even more standardised assessments. Parents, students, educators and community members began lobbying to change how the test scores were to be used, but the Chancellor, Merryl Tisch, and Commissioner, John King, who eventually replaced Arne Duncan as President Obama's Secretary of Education, resisted all appeals and ridiculed these protesting parents. When middle-class, mostly white parents protested that the tests scores were not accurate reflections of their schools, Secretary of Education Duncan dismissed their complaints, suggesting that they could not handle the fact that their children 'were not as brilliant as they thought they were' (Strauss, 2013).

Parents, observing that lobbying and protests were ineffective, began opting their children out of the tests, which had two beneficial consequences. First, because the scores were to be used to evaluate not only students, but also teachers and their schools, it removed their children from an onerous two-week-long testing experience in which students felt enormous pressure to do well. Second, if enough students refused to take the tests, it would undermine the validity and reliability of the tests.

The opt-out movement: NYSAPE and LIOO

The opt-out movement in New York State has been the most successful such movement in the US, with 240,000 children opting out of the Common Core tests in 2015 and 225,000 in 2017, for example. It is noteworthy that the two counties on Long Island – Nassau and Suffolk – which are typically referred to as Long Island, are generally represented by the Republican Party and are politically conservative. Yet, as reported by LIOO, more than 50 per cent of eligible students were opted out by their parents in 2014 and subsequent years.

In this section, we focus on the two central opt-out groups in New York, NYSAPE and LIOO, and their ways of working both vertically by pressuring policy makers, and horizontally through a grass-roots strategy. These two parent activist groups have actively resisted the neoliberal agenda. They have done so because of the negative impact of this agenda on the schooling that their children receive (Duetermann and Rudley, personal interview, 28 March 2018; Deutermann, 2014) Here, we focus on their goals and strategies.

Rather than accepting the deceptive test data and demanding that schools be privatised, our analysis shows that these parents rejected trusting data over their own lived experiences. Many of them knew from experience that their schools and children were better than the test scores portrayed, and were offended that Duncan suggested that their children were not 'as bright as they thought' (Strauss, 2013).

Duncan derided what he called 'soccer moms'. In interviews with the leaders of NYSAPE and LIOO, they proudly and assertively saw their activism as, in a sense, soccer moms speaking back to this derision. Parents also rejected the neoliberal construction of them as simply individual choosers in a schooling market. Instead, they reconstituted themselves as active citizen groups, demanding a say over the quality and type of schooling that their children receive. The evidence suggests that they are opposed to the broad neoliberal reframing of schooling and to the increasing involvement of corporate, for-profit businesses in public schooling, and thus have a political focus beyond testing and its effects.

Furthermore, both organisations have recently critiqued the increasing reliance on educational technology and digital learning that replaces teacher and student decision-making regarding what they are to teach, with lessons based on algorithms created by corporate technicians from big data. They also successfully defeated New York State's adoption of inBloom, 'a $100 million educational technology initiative primarily funded by the Bill and Melinda Gates Foundation that aimed to improve American schools by providing a centralised platform for data sharing, learning apps, and curricula' (Bulger et al, 2017: 3). Their concern here was keeping data about their children private. InBloom, aimed to create a data infrastructure across a number of states, including New York, to make all data about all students interoperable. Parents were also concerned about the possible on-selling of these data to third parties. Lisa Rudley, a leader in NYSAPE, indicated in interviews that she initially got involved in the opt-out movement because of her deep concern about the edu-business management of student data and the privacy issues that this raised. Additionally, as well as being opposed to detrimental high-stakes testing (Koretz, 2018), the New York opt-out movement has pushed for school reform that promotes students' academic, emotional and physical health. LIOO is increasingly organising public forums on transforming schools to focus on the whole child.

From our interviews with Deutterman and Rudley, we gained a real sense of very savvy political operators, both in terms of very up-to-date knowledge of policy developments and their potential effects, and in terms of effective political strategies. The leaders of the opt-out movement have been very smart to deliberately work in two directions: horizontally and vertically. Horizontally, they have created a grass-roots organisation based on thousands of parents who are willing to opt their students out of the Common Core tests that are administered in grades three through eight in late spring of each year, and they work to elect members of local school boards and state legislators who will push back against neoliberal reforms.

At the local level, school boards can promote policies that either support or undermine standardised testing, the Common Core curriculum and different classroom technologies. Furthermore, the opt-out movement has worked to replace state legislators who favour high-stakes testing and privatisation with legislators who are critical of such reforms. It is crucial who a legislator is because it is the legislature that appoints the 15 members of the SUNY Board of Regents and it is the Regents who select one of their own members as Chancellor of Education for New York State. The Regents determine policy for all the educational institutions in the state and also appoint the Commissioner of Education, who is the top executive.

It is by organising voters to oust members of the legislature who supported the Common Core tests and other neoliberal reforms (for example, the introduction of charter schools), that the legislature replaced enough members of the Regents with critics of the Common Core curriculum and tests; subsequently, the Regents selected Dr Betty Rosa as Chancellor to replace Dr Merryl Tisch, who was an advocate of high-stakes standardised testing and privatisation. It is through the advocacy of its tens of thousands of grass-roots members that LIOO and NYSAPE were able to effect the legislative change that led to Chancellor Rosa replacing Tisch, and Rosa and the Regents filing a lawsuit against the SUNY Charter Schools Committee, which includes the previous Chancellor Tisch.

It is because of their success in shaping education policy that we focus on NYSAPE and LIOO. NYSAPE originated at a meeting in New Paltz New York in 2013, and is a coalition of 70 mostly local organisations guided by a steering committee of 14 people, of whom seven are parents of school-age children, six are educators and one is the director of a non-profit education group. As stated on their website, their mission is: to address 'excessive standardised testing'; to ban the storing and sharing with private companies of children's 'private, personal information … without the permission of parents'; and 'uniting groups from across the state … to work for the betterment of education' (New York State Allies for Public Education, no date[a]). Lisa Rudley, our primary source for the history and politics of NYSAPE, was at the first meeting, as was the lead author of this chapter, David Hursh, representing the Rochester Coalition for Common Sense in Education.

In contrast, LIOO is not a state-wide organisation and was begun by an individual, not a group (Deutermann, 2014). Geographically,

Long Island refers to the 120-mile-long island that includes on its western border the two New York City boroughs of Queens and Brooklyn (also called Kings). Nassau and Suffolk counties make up the eastern two thirds of the island and are to what 'Long Island' refers in this case. Both Long Island counties are dominated by conservative Republicans, while New York City is strongly Democratic. Jeanette Deutermann, a parent whose children went to school in Nassau County, began LIOO in 2014 in response to the negative effects the Common Core curriculum and tests were having on her son. LIOO is a member of NYSAPE, so Deutermann is a member of both organisations. Neither Rudley nor Deutermann had previous experience as political organisers. Jeanette Deutermann is the primary source for our understanding of LIOO.

Deutermann and Rudley owe their success to hard work, becoming deeply informed about schooling and policy, and, as we describe later, using social media such as Facebook, websites (nysape.org), Twitter and email to communicate with members and organise events. LIOO has over 23,900 members on its Facebook page. Over 6,400 people 'like' NYSAPE's webpage. This is the horizontal, grass-roots work of the opt-out movement in New York State.

On the NYSAPE website, Deutermann has created and posted guidelines for 'Growing the resistance to corporate education reform – grassroots organizing' (New York State Allies for Public Education, no date[b]) (hereafter, GRCR) in this era of social media. This manifesto of grass-roots organising emphasises bottom-up, local organising and affiliations across such groups. The GRCR manifesto is outlined around nine strategies (New York State Allies for Public Education, no date[b]):

- Parent motivation, need to 'keep it local';
- educate yourself, the need to be very well informed;
- organising – establish structure at grassroots and use social media;
- messaging – positive, simple, non-partisan, only inform, not inflame, no teacher bashing, fact check;
- spreading the word – hold local forums;
- legislation, campaign, elections, use of voter scorecards;
- build coalitions;
- create local leaders from within the movement; and
- use random actions.

We will consider each of these briefly in turn. In terms of motivation, it is suggested that most of the efforts should focus on the effects of the neoliberal reforms, including testing and privatisation, with a particular emphasis on the local schools that their children attend. In addition, parents, students and teachers, GRCR argues, need to become educated regarding relevant local, state and federal laws, legislation and regulations. NYSAPE regularly posts two-page statements on their website composed of pronouncements from steering committee members and others regarding state education policies. Besides educating anyone who comes to the site, journalists often use the postings to identify potential informants regarding a particular issue. Both organisations rely on their members as experts on a variety of issues, including lawyers, educators and parents. Pizmony-Levy and Green Saraisky (2016) found that, nationwide, 45 per cent of opt-out activists were teachers. Our research shows that this is the case with both the New York opt-out groups that we are focusing on here. We would suggest that this expertise has been an important element in the success of the groups.

The opt-out movement seeks to challenge and change the dominant discourses about schooling and schooling policy, and attempts to do so through extensive messaging. The GRCR manifesto advises keeping the message simple and non-partisan, only informing and not inflaming, and importantly prohibiting any 'teacher bashing' in the messaging. Before the election of President Trump, membership of NYSAPE and LIOO was largely Democratic, with some conservative Republican members (mainly on Long Island) involved largely because of their opposition to the Common Core State Standards on states' rights grounds. This uneasy political alliance has collapsed somewhat since the election of President Trump, who expressed opposition to the Common Core and tests during his presidential campaign. However, he has been silent regarding the Common Core since taking office. The leadership of both NYSAPE and LIOO observed that staying politically non-partisan had become more difficult following the election of President Trump and the appointment of billionaire and pro-Charter school and pro-privatisation advocate Betsy DeVos as Secretary of Education. This is indicative of the varying motivations for differently politically aligned groups involved in the opt-out movement: opposition solely to the Common Core State Standards or broader opposition to the neoliberal reform agenda in schooling.

As mentioned earlier, NYSAPE responds to policy developments with press releases created by their network of activists, which provides the media with direct quotes. Spreading the word involves multiple modes of free advertising, for example, in local bookstores and through flyers posted at local sites, libraries, grocery stores and cafes. Their manifesto states that advertising should be done at the lowest possible cost, such as via T-shirts, lawn signs, bumper magnets and car stickers (for example, 'Our children are more than a score', 'More teaching, less testing', 'Choose to refuse'). The opt-out movement has also strategically placed buses with anti-testing messages on them and advertised on strategically located billboards. LIOO has built a grass-roots team of liaisons that represent nearly all of the 124 school districts on Long Island (Hildebrand, 2018). State-wide affiliations with NYSAPE are also important. Deutermann points out that local media often search for stories and that this is where opt-out activists should start. Local forums are also important in building the movement, which is how LIOO began. While the opt-out movement is a parent movement, there also are many teachers involved, who provide expert professional advice about high-stakes testing and its effects.

Advice is also outlined in GRCR for dealing with legislators and elections, suggesting, for example, 'Realize that most likely you know more about the education issues than they do. Be very specific on what you want, what they can do and what you expect from them' (New York State Allies for Public Education, no date[b]). Producing 'voter scorecards' on the policy matters of interest to activists is a useful strategy at election time. Additional effective strategies include: establishing automatic emails to local, state and national politicians; endorsing suitable candidates for school board membership; and rallying for or against local candidates. LIOO has successfully supported 53 candidates in winning election to local school boards.

Central to successful coalition building are the effective usage of social media, building grass-roots leadership and innovative acts that capture the media's attention. An example of the latter was the 'paint the road red' activity, whereby union groups, parents, children and community members all wore red and, in opposition to the corporate reform agenda, lined a road on the south shore of the island that extended from New York City to Montauk Point (the eastern end).

Opt-out successes and the current moment

It is the horizontal and vertical activism of both NYSAPE and LIOO that has resulted in many political successes. Thus, they appear to have had an impact on the neoliberal policy commitments of New York Governor Cuomo's schooling agenda. They have been successfully changing the composition of the Board of Regents, which resulted in the appointment of the new Chancellor. They also seem to have modified the strongly pro-privatisation views of State Commissioner for Education MaryEllen Elia. They have been successful in electing pro-opt-out supporters to local school boards and to the legislature. They have kept the momentum for opting out going, despite some changes to the test and their usages for teacher and school accountability purposes. They have worked collaboratively with the Alliance for Quality Education around equitable funding for government schools. They successfully blocked inBloom. They continue to oppose the EdTech company-driven, computer-based curriculum, pedagogy and assessment.

Despite these palpable political successes, for some, especially critics, the opt-out movement seems to be in decline as the Common Core tests have been shortened by a few questions (an achievement of the opt-out movement) and the resistance to high-stakes testing seems less visible. However, in interviews, Deutermann and Rudley (personal communication, 29 February 2018) suggested that arguing that there has been a decline in the opt-out movement fails to take into account four significant factors. First, the initial push state-wide to increase the percentage of students opting out came in the spring of 2013, when organisations across the US held forums and other events to promote resisting the Common Core tests. In New York State, in the area west of Syracuse, which includes Rochester and Buffalo, the lead author of this chapter counted 55 events in the month before the tests. Often, there were two such events on the same night. The two events that the lead author attended were in a rural suburban community, at which about 600 people attended, with 350 at an event in a wealthier suburb. There have been fewer such events as criticisms of the Common Core standards and tests have become more ubiquitous. The resistance has become less visible, but no less effective.

Second, Deutermann and Rudley (personal communication, 29 February 2018) noted that the percentage of opt-outs has remained almost the same, even though 40,000 new test refusers need to be added each year to replace the eighth-graders who are promoted to the ninth grade and, therefore, no longer take the Common Core tests. Third, even if the percentage of students opting out were to decline by half to 10%, it would still statistically invalidate using the tests to evaluate students, teachers and schools. Fourth, as we have described, Deutermann and Rudley (personal communication, 29 February 2018) observed that the opt-out movement has been about not only the Common Core standards and tests, but also the larger neoliberal effort to privatise education, to hand over student information to private companies and to increase the datafication and digitalisation of education through heavy edu-business involvement. New York State began to implement inBloom, but opt-out opposition led to its demise (Lingard et al, 2017: 67). Interestingly, in the reasons listed on the NYSAPE website for opting out of the tests in 2018, it noted that 'State tests will serve as a vehicle for corporate digital learning platforms, data mining, and privatization', and also that 'All state tests must be computer-based by 2020', which are further indications of the ongoing and broader political targets of the opt-out movement in New York State (New York State Allies for Public Education, no date[c]). Lisa Rudley (personal communication, 29 February 2018) restated just how important the issue of data privacy is and how it is one of the opt-out movement's top priorities: 'one piece that we tend to not talk about is data privacy anymore. That's a big part of some of the emerging technology that's coming outta the ed. reformers and some of those things that are shifting – how we teach our kids.'

Conclusion

Our analysis has documented the successful methods of the opt-out movement in New York State. As we have shown, NYSAPE and LIOO have worked horizontally, creating a grass-roots, social media and Internet-based social movement for the 21st century, which has resisted a neoliberal construction of parents as mere consumers of the schooling that their children receive. The success of the opt-out movement's horizontal work has enabled other more vertical political work, pressuring the Governor, Board of Regents, Chancellor, Commissioner of Education and legislature for change, and with some real success. As we have also illustrated, this parental resistance and activism has had a broader set of political targets than simply the Common Core tests. The progressive participants in the opt-out movement, at least, also target and seek to resist the broader corporate reform agenda in education. Pizmony-Levy and Green Saraisky (2016: 27–8), in their survey of opt-outers, noted that 'a large share of the sample said they take part in the movement because they oppose the growing role of corporations in schools and because they oppose the CCSS [Common Core State Standards]'. Our research reveals this to be the case with NYSAPE and LIOO. Our data and analysis also show that parents, through the opt-out movement, have reconstituted themselves as active citizens who want a say in their child's public education. They have vehemently resisted and rejected the neoliberal construction of them as simply consumers of schooling in an education market. As such, they have succeeded in reducing testing time, and the tests are not currently being used to evaluate teachers. They defeated the introduction of the inBloom data infrastructure and data collections.

They are also expanding their support for a whole-child philosophy and opposition to computer-based instruction.

The NYSAPE website in the Opt-In Toolkit lists seven demands that need to be met before parents will opt into the tests. These basically turn on limiting the scope and effect of the test to serving educative purposes in order to professionally assist teachers in their classrooms, to help policymaking, and to frame more equitable school funding. On the latter, they support the concept of 'opportunity to learn standards' (Darling-Hammond, 2010), that is, communities have the right to demand and expect that policymakers and legislators provide the necessary resources so that schools can achieve the goals set for them. The final demand states:

> Halt immediately the misuse of assessment data: test results are not to be used to evaluate teachers to punish schools. Instead, this information must be used to help provide the needed supports to ensure that every child receives a well-rounded, high quality public education with access to a curriculum rich in the arts, music and sciences.

We agree with the observation proffered to us by Jeanette Deutermann and Lisa Rudley that the opt-out movement is not in decline in New York State, as some have suggested. However, we see that the very much changed political and policy context for schooling federally in the US under Trump and DeVos, and an even greater push for neoliberal privatisation, will challenge their unity and bipartisanship, and pressure for new political strategies, particularly in terms of their vertical political work. It is the case, we would argue, that their successful opposition to the neoliberal corporate reform agendas in schooling in New York State to this point has been because their horizontal grass-roots strategies have worked very successfully off the very localised structure and governance of schooling in the US. Local governance of schooling has been central to the image of the American public school and its relationship with democracy. The opt-out movement in New York has successfully reworked school governance for the 21st century with their social media-based, grass-roots activism and resistance to the neoliberal corporate reform agendas in schooling.

Note

1 See: www.regents.nysed.gov/

References

Au, W. and Ferrare, J. (eds) (2015) *Mapping corporate education reform*, New York, NY: Routledge.

Bulger, M., McCormick, P. and Pitan, M. (2017) 'The Legacy of inBloom', Data and Society Research Institute. Available at: https://datasociety.net/pubs/ecl/InBloom_feb_2017.pdf

Burch, P. (2009) *Hidden markets: The new education privatization*, New York, NY: Routledge.

Clukey, K. (2018) 'Education Department, Regents file complaint over SUNY charter teacher certification', *Politico*, 9 February. Available at: www.politico.com/states/new-york/albany/story/2018/02/09/education-department-regents-file-complaint-over-suny-charter-teacher-certification-245635

Darling-Hammond, L. (2010) *The flat world and education: How America's commitment to equity will determine our future*, New York, NY: Teachers College Press.

Deutermann, J. (2014) 'Long Island opts out: My story of resistance', in J. Hagopian (ed) *More than a score: The new uprising against high-stakes testing*, Chicago, IL: Haymarket Books, pp 195–204.

Hildebrand, J. (2018) 'Test boycotts top 50% on LI as large opt-outs continue', *Newsday*, 13 April. Available at: https://www.newsday.com/long-island/education/state-test-ela-opt-outs-1.18005317

Hursh, D. (2013) 'Raising the stakes: High-stakes testing and the attack on public education in New York', *Journal of Education Policy*, 28(5): 574–88.

Hursh, D. (2015) *The end of public schools: The corporate reform agenda to privatize education*, New York, NY: Routledge.

Koretz, D. (2018) *The testing charade: Pretending to make schools better*, Chicago, IL: The University of Chicago Press.

Lingard, B., Sellar, S., Hogan, A. and Thompson, G. (2017) *Commercialisation in public schooling: Final report summary*. Sydney: New South Wales Teachers Federation.

New York State Allies for Public Education (no date[a]) 'Who we are'. Available at: www.nysape.org/about-us.html

New York State Allies for Public Education (no date[b]) 'Growing the resistance to corporate education reform – grassroots organizing – By Jeanette Deutermann'. Available at: www.nysape.org/grassroots organizing.html

New York State Allies for Public Education (no date[c]) 'Why opt out in 2018?'. Available at: www.nysape.org/2018-opt-out-factsheet.html

Pizmony-Levy, O. and Green Saraisky, N. (2016) *Who opts out and why? Results from a national survey on opting out of standardized tests*, New York, NY: Teachers College, Columbia University.

Prothero, A. (2017) 'Charter schools in New York can now certify their own teachers', *Education Week*, 12 October. Available at: http://blogs.edweek.org/edweek/charterschoice/2017/10/charter_schools_in_new_york_can_now_certify_their_own_teachers.html?override=web&print=1

State University of New York (no date) 'Charter Schools Committee charter'. Available at: www.suny.edu/media/suny/content-assets/documents/boardoftrustees/Charter-Schools-Committee-Charter-REVISED.pdf

Strauss, V. (2013) 'Arne Duncan: "White suburban moms" upset that Common Core shows their kids aren't " 'brilliant" ', *The Washington Post*, 16 November. Available at: www.washingtonpost.com/news/answer-sheet/wp/2013/11/16/arne-duncan-white-surburban-moms-upset-that-common-core-shows-their-kids-arent-brilliant/?utm_term=.0945ab8da214

Winerip, M. (2011) '10 years of assessing students with scientific exactitude', *The New York Times*, 19 December: A24. Available at: www.nytimes.com/2011/12/19/education/newyorkcitystudenttestingoverthepastdecade.html

7

Nourishing resistance and healing in dark times: teaching through a Body-Soul Rooted Pedagogy

Shiv Desai, Shawn Secatero, Mia Sosa-Provencio and Annmarie Sheahan

Introduction

The Trump administration's 2018 policy of separating nearly 2,700 mostly Central American children from their families as they cross the US–Mexico border in search of asylum is yet another iteration of the US's long history of harming diverse people(s) of colour (Menchaca, 2002; Lomawaima and McCarty, 2006; Gomez, 2008; Almendrala, 2018). From slavery, to Indian boarding schools, to Japanese internment camps, children of colour have experienced schooling policies of cruelty, dehumanisation, criminalisation and trauma (Wilkins, 2012; Desai and Abeita, 2017; Emdin, 2016). Dominant schooling has inflicted *soul wounds* (Duran and Duran, 1995) upon the academic, psychological, emotional and spiritual well-being of marginalised communities. Educators who work in these communities must act as *healers* to treat these soul wounds through wholeness of mind, body and spirit, while instilling education as the *practice of freedom* (hooks, 1994). In Rendón's (2009: 2) work lies a similar call for a 'refashioned dream of education based on wholeness, consonance, social justice, and liberation'. Rendón utilises Latino/a place-based ancestral knowledge to challenge the colonising and increasingly market-driven Western paradigm of education, which privileges intellectual/rational knowing, separation, competition, perfection, monoculturalism, goal-oriented outer work and socio-political and interpersonal unconsciousness.

In this chapter, we detail the painful histories of US schooling, outline its modern-day manifestations, connect it to the neoliberal school reform agenda and contextualise it within the institutionalised racism, intellectual invalidation, economic disparity and educational inequity that people(s) of colour have sustained (Stovall, 2013; Au, 2016). We summarise six pedagogical tenets comprising *Body-Soul*[1] *Rooted Pedagogy* and conclude by focusing on tenet six, which illuminates the ways in which educators may counter the traumas of schooling and curricularly harvest health and well-being. We define *Body-Soul Rooted Pedagogy* as a soulful and living pedagogical framework wherein teaching, learning and knowing take root within body/spirit/land epistemologies of resistance, resilience and wholeness. This decolonising pedagogy galvanises the complex lived realities, intersectional identities, contested bodies, intellectual legacies, spiritualities and ancestral healing practices of communities of colour to bring about social and educational equity, which provides a vibrant source for resistance (Sosa-Provencio et al, 2018). We theoretically centre *survivance*, which Vizenor (2008) defines as the spectrum of coping responses that indigenous people(s) have developed amid imperialist genocide and forced assimilation. As a result, communities of colour have galvanised the remarkable ability to meld struggle as a source of strength, survive and even thrive amid attempts at erasure, and recall ancestral spirits despite being forced to practise colonising religions. In the following section, we historicise the role that Western schooling has played in the suppression and control of diverse people(s).

Historicising the trauma of US schooling

> [I]n accomplishing the colonizing goals of the United States … formal education has consistently been at odds with indigenous cultural and educational needs and desires. (Calderón, 2014: 85)

US schooling has been used to erase the knowledge systems of African-American, Indigenous, Mexican-American, Asian/Asian-American, immigrant and Latina/o communities. Herein, mind/body/spirit knowing has been diminished while the bodies of youth of colour have simultaneously been criminalised and regulated (Desai and Abeita, 2017; McCarthy and Benally, 2003; Asher, 2010). We borrow the term *cognitive imperialism* from indigenous scholars Battiste and Henderson (2000) to describe the ways in which this systematic stratification has been used to consolidate power and knowing into the hands of the dominant culture. To this end, schooling has enacted trauma through neglect, segregation, cultural/linguistic erasure, bodily regulation, community removal (including deportation and boarding schools) and labour stratification (Lomawaima and McCarty, 2006; Valencia, 2011). Today, the young inheritors of these heavy histories experience the institutionalised violence of circumscribed invisibility (Taliaferro-Baszile, 2010), hyper-visibility and criminalisation via surveillance (Desai and Abeita, 2017), and reduced access to public schools (Monahan, 2003; Senger et al, 2004). Trauma extends beyond school as well, with the increasing number of school shootings (Metzl and MacLeish, 2015), immigration raids (Lopez et al, 2017) and extrajudicial killings (Lim, 2017). Institutional violence targets even young children, as seen with the Trump administration's separation of refugee babies, toddlers and preschoolers, as well as parents, who were also incarcerated and deported back to the violence from which they fled (Almendrala, 2018; Lind, 2018). Such abuse creates enduring physical, mental and emotional scars for all future generations.

We believe that resisting and reconciling the educational disparities and trauma of settler colonialism begins in recognising the following: youth experience schooling through the pain of its history in their communities (Solórzano and Delgado Bernal, 2001; Martinez, 2010); youth resistance to school is often unexamined alienation met with punishment and neglect (Desai, 2016); and the dominant culture that instituted public schooling still regulates it and experiences disproportionate success therein (Spring, 2010). Furthermore, dominant culture educators have wittingly and unwittingly played central roles in centuries of educational wrongdoing rooted in colonialism, labour stratification and white supremacy (Matias and Zembylas, 2014). Today, educators at all levels are charged with administering and enforcing neoliberal mechanisms of curricular standardisation, test proctoring, school grading and punitive 'reforms', and are silenced and castigated when they oppose these policies.

Within what Stovall (2013) terms the *politics of desperation*, marketing strategies seduce especially economically vulnerable communities of colour with few educational options other than to endorse reforms that they had no hand in shaping. These neoliberal, market-driven measures reify structural racism by exacerbating school segregation, gentrification and educational neglect through school closures (Buras, 2011; Lipman, 2011). They further stigmatise public schools in communities of colour and the children who live there as 'failing', and coerce these communities to lose or deny their linguistic, cultural and historical identities in exchange for 'achievement' (Alim and Paris, 2017). State and federal initiatives then institutionalise this *data-driven accountability* and *achievement gap* discourse with little inquiry into who benefits from these reforms (Ladson-Billings, 2006; Stovall, 2013; Au, 2016), how learner identities and curricula are impacted (Apple, 2006; Ravitch, 2010), or the ways in which knowing and achievement are defined by Eurocentric epistemologies (Kumashiro, 2008; Spring, 2010; Emdin, 2016). In the following section, we outline the resistance/resilience that germinates in the strength-based pedagogies, ancestral wisdom and critical consciousness of indigenous and indigenous-heritage Chicana feminist frameworks that affirm *pedagogy* as living and breathing within the *embodied landscape* (Calderón, 2014), where mind, body and spirit co-mingle.

Essence of Body-Soul Rooted Pedagogy

Black and Chicana feminists have long integrated the body epistemologically as the place where our histories and complex, intersecting identities converge (Lorde, 1978; Moraga, 2011). As body becomes both birthplace of theory (Dillard, 2000; Cantú, 2001) and anti-colonial text (Cruz, 2006; Trinidad Galván, 2016), it offers a *theory in the flesh* (Hurtado, 2003; Cervantes-Soon, 2014) to mend fractures of oppression. According to Sosa-Provencio (2017: 8), the body layered upon by histories of oppression is a fractal of our capacity for resilience and regeneration because the physical body itself 'carries within it the genetic material for creation – of newness and possibility. Within our cells [lies] the power to conceive a future never before imagined.' We name this resilient, embodied, historicised knowing *Body-Soul Rooted Pedagogy* and illuminate a tangible-transcendent pedagogy of connectedness, curiosity, joy, critical consciousness and agency towards transformation.

This work takes place in New Mexico, where land, like the body, has been an object of desire and conquest. For more than 500 years of Spanish and US occupation, this sacred land has witnessed the gross exploitation of resources and the conquest and massacre of indigenous and indigenous-heritage Mexican/Mexican-American/Chicana/o[2] people(s) (Menchaca, 2002; Gomez, 2008; McCarty and Lee, 2014). Due to this history, there is an intimate relationship with land because communities of colour have witnessed first-hand the devastation of settler colonialism. Through an indigenous epistemology, the body is a sacred part of the earth and sky (Cajete, 1994). This relationship is illuminated by the traditional Navajo practice of burying a newborn child's umbilical cord in the ground east of the home, which signifies connection to Mother Earth and further establishes a sense of place (Secatero, 2015). In New Mexico, indigenous and indigenous-heritage Chicana/o and Mexicana/o communities are often (mis)constructed as *minorities*, which discursively masks the fact that they are living in their ancestral homeland and constitute the numerical majority, even as they experience the lowest socio-economic and educational outcomes of any group (New Mexico Fiscal Policy Project, 2011; US Census Bureau, 2017). These groups battle daily to protect their respective knowledge systems, land, resources and rights to water, language, economic stability and citizenship/residency.

Our own vibrant and knowing Navajo, US, urban East Indian diaspora and Mexican-American communities shape in us a chromosomal, spiritual and land-bound knowing that educational endeavours at transformation must be led by the community. We particularly acknowledge the work of communities of colour and educators of colour who shape their own educational efforts at reclamation and revitalisation (Ladson-Billings, 1994; Darder, 1995; Siddle Walker, 1996; Donato, 1997; Sims, 2005; Brayboy and Castagno, 2008; McCarty and Lee, 2014; Secatero, 2015; Desai, 2016). Within our collective consciousness as scholars of colour, we posit *Body-Soul Rooted Pedagogy* to challenge pedagogical frameworks situating outside educators in the role of *sustaining* or *revitalising* (McCarty and Lee, 2014) students' cultures, and nowhere has this been more egregious than in indigenous nations, who have endured Catholic mission schools, the Bureau of Indian Affairs and state education departments fighting to control the education of Native children for the purpose of social control and deculturalisation (Pewewardy, 2005). McCarty and Lee (2014: 102) remind us that although issues facing marginalised communities bear similarities, 'the experiences of Native American peoples have been and are profoundly shaped by a unique relationship with the federal government'. While we utilise indigenous epistemologies as pedagogical guides, we respect the tribal sovereignty, unique history and situated knowledge of indigenous nations, which lie beyond the grasp of the Western academy.

In line with those who urge that culture be understood as a holistically rooted, fluid essence of being and knowing that is intersectional and body-bound (Pewewardy, 1999; Ladson-Billings, 2014; Anzaldúa, 2015; Alim and Paris, 2017), *Body-Soul Rooted Pedagogy* works to expand common notions of *culture*. We define culture as a shared and historicised way of doing, being, seeing, growing, understanding, connecting, communicating and moving through worlds, which is shaped by membership at complex intersections of race, ethnicity, tribal affiliation, class, gender, sexuality, dis/ability, mental and emotional diversity, geography, generation, residency status, language, dialect, familial configurations, and spirituality. To contend with the organic, embodied, geographical and spiritual essence of culture that germinates along familial, community and ancestral lines and grows through life forces of experience, we utilise the living language of *rootedness* and bind this pedagogy to *Body*, touchstone of heavy histories and the living, breathing chromosomal landscape from which resistance, healing and creation spring (Pendleton Jiménez, 2006; Sosa-Provencio, 2017). This work is likewise tethered to *Soul*. While *spirit* is often understood as elevated from the body and material world, *Soul* is a gut-bound entity that electrifies the embodied geography, which likewise gives it breath (Anzaldúa, 1990, 2015). Next, we briefly describe the six tenets of *Body-Soul Rooted Pedagogy*.

Six tenets: an overview

We posit *Body-Soul Rooted Pedagogy*, which: (1) constructs education politically; (2) enacts schooling as decolonisation/empowerment; (3) centres the epistemologies and multiliteracies of marginalised groups; (4) fosters critical frameworks for navigating oppression; (5) engages social action pedagogy; and (6) engenders hope and well-being. By galvanising the histories of oppressed people, the wounds and resilience mechanisms enduring in body/spirit/land, and the corporeal, ethereal life bonds of our common humanity, we may bring about transformation and intergenerational healing to a legacy of US schooling. Tenet one describes how educators work to deepen understandings of power, privilege, equity and inequity, including the policies and practices reifying them. Tenet two discusses how educators engage students in shaping a more just, peaceful world to counter a schooling paradigm of assimilation, body control and silencing. Tenet three takes into account how educators utilise resources reflecting the everyday lives, world views, languages/dialects, histories and intellectual and resistance legacies of marginalised people(s). Tenet four illustrates how educators enact the curriculum to illuminate and demystify the workings of complex social systems. Tenet five involves how educators bring students into social action beyond the classroom towards social equity. In the next section, we detail tenet six, which centres pedagogy as 'continuance rather than … extinction' and moves 'from pessimism to optimism, from despair to hope' (Allen, 1992: 262).

Tenet six: enacting resistance as hope, healing and well-being

Tenet six is particularly informed by the tenacity of those for whom criminalisation, social and economic subordination, land theft, and gentrification run deep in their bearings (Moraga, 2011; Smith,

2012). We utilise *survivance* (Vizenor, 2008) not to generalise trauma or oppression across groups, but to inform an education of radical mind/body/spirit healing for youth of all cultures that has the power to challenge structural oppression and engender hope. In other words, a main premise of *Body-Soul Rooted Pedagogy* is that as much as historical trauma, institutional violence and settler colonialism has been passed down for generations, so have the power and will to resist them. Without the fortitude and the ingenuity of our ancestors to (re)claim and (re)assert our humanity, we would not be here. Tenet six moves educators towards supporting students' self-determination, self-identification, hope and regenerative possibility, especially for youth who carry their own personal traumas and the historical traumas of their cultural groups. Tenet six draws upon the work of Shawn Secatero, Navajo elder and scholar. Through his Medicinal Well-Being model, Secatero (2015) illuminates an indigenous healing process to restore and reconnect with spiritual, mental, physical and social well-being. *Body-Soul Rooted Pedagogy* epistemologically draws from Secatero's (2015) interconnectedness model as a nourishing elixir for ongoing wounds and urges educators across identity to ground themselves within epistemologies reclaiming wholeness and health.

Manifestations of tenet six in the classroom

One example of tenet six is seen in one secondary school, the Native American Community Academy, which serves 90 per cent Native American students and centres an indigenous epistemology. Herein, indigenous teachers designed a final capstone assessment project in which 12th-grade students collaboratively research, design and present their own health and well-being plans. Students delve into their own tribal histories of ancestral food practices and physical/spiritual healing and goodness that have long enabled their resistance/resilience as indigenous people(s). In this way, students and educators repair the disconnectedness and decontextualisation of capitalistic, white-dominant schooling (Nakata et al, 2012).

Tenet six is likewise illuminated by the work of Travis M., a Chicano middle-school educator/activist who teaches a gardening elective that fosters students' creativity, multiple literacies and connectedness to land as spiritual restoration (Anzaldúa, 2015). Travis and his students work towards understanding and institutionalising food justice through interdisciplinary multimodal literacy strategies. These include researching and enacting ancestral indigenous-heritage planting rituals and creating music, dance, spoken word, poetry, mural, hip hop and activist art, and materially and metaphorically bringing dirt, water, plants and food into the curriculum and assessment.

Lastly, research among school districts across the nation has revealed that Ethnic Studies in K-12 educational settings can tremendously improve academic achievement for students, especially among low-income, underserved students of colour (Sleeter, 2011; Cabrera et al, 2014; De los Ríos et al, 2015; Dee and Penner, 2016). Ethnic Studies stresses three important concepts: Access, Relevance and Community (ARC) (Tintiangco-Cubales et al, 2015). *Access* refers to providing students with a high-quality education and enriching academic experiences. *Relevance* refers to how Ethnic Studies serves to infuse formal educational spaces with civic involvement, advocacy, organising and activism. *Community* refers to how Ethnic Studies can be leveraged towards the betterment of communities. In other words, Ethnic Studies promotes a social justice pedagogy that reduces racial and minority ethnic opportunity gaps (Cabrera et al, 2014) by simultaneously empowering students to develop democratic leadership and affirm racial/ethnic identities (Cabrera et al, 2013; Dee and Penner, 2016). Most importantly, successful Ethnic Studies teachers model a decolonising, community-based pedagogy (Tintiangco-Cubales et al, 2015) that fosters the principles of *Body-Soul Rooted Pedagogy* and challenges the poverty of neoliberal educational policies.

Conclusion

We write at a trying time in the US and globally, where the embers of hatred seek to divide and overcome education practised as justice and critical love. We write at a time where the present is repeating the darkest moments of history, which manifest in racist, xenophobic policies that rip families apart, criminalise hope for a brighter future, ban groups of people based on religion, and explicitly label refugees and immigrants as coming from '*shithole countries*'. Now more than ever, educators must implement pedagogies wherein mind and body come together in acts of imagination and resistance (Anzaldúa, 2015) to transform pain, suffering and horror into regeneration, hope and love. *Body-Soul Rooted Pedagogy* taps into a resiliency that we have witnessed in youth in Parkland, Florida, who *marched for their lives*, chanting '*not one more* school shooting' and, in doing so, added their voices and bodies to a collective of thousands of youth who have for decades advocated for gun control and safer schools in urban and working-class communities of colour. This work taps into the deep mind/body/spirit knowing of peoples of colour, who often demonstrate uncanny fortitude, collectivism and optimism in the face of hopelessness. *Body-Soul Rooted Pedagogy* enacts education as a corporeal, soulful practice whose lifeblood is students' untapped knowing, critical consciousness and artistic, performative and civically engaged selves.

Implications

This pedagogy has implications for teacher educators, pre-service students and school-site educators at all levels to establish an agentive pedagogical language of mind/body/spirit to challenge the win/lose accountability and global marketability discourse diminishing educators' professional expertise and positioning educators, districts, students and families at odds (Kumashiro, 2008; Crawford-Garrett et al, 2016). *Body-Soul Rooted Pedagogy* advances a theory and practice of *schooling as medicine, healing, and hope* to embolden youth and educators across cultures in order to mend heavy histories of US schooling and (re)frame education as the human right to connection, empowerment and well-being wherein teaching and learning are regenerative and life-giving.

Acknowledgements

This work was supported by the W.K. Kellogg Foundation's award to the University of New Mexico's College of Education.

Notes

1 Although *soul* conjures European imperialism's conversion, domination, colonisation and attempted extinction of indigenous peoples (Cajete, 1994; Smith 2012), we utilise *soul* as it resonates through Anzaldúa's work – as entity that finds life and meaning within the body itself in relationship to ancestral lands. *Soul* is the symbiosis of body/land/spirit, a sacred chromosomal essence living within and beyond the flesh.

2 We interchange *Mexican/Mexican-American* and *Mexicana/o* to transcend man-made borders in naming a blended cultural identity of indigenous, Spanish and African ancestry formed within Spain's 16th-century conquest of Mexico (Delgado Bernal, 2006). We use 20th-century terms *Chicana/Chicano*, which have been used as self-identifiers among some Mexican-Americans. We frame Chicana/Chicano as a decolonising consciousness that (re)claims indigenous ancestry, (re)connects to ancestral land and practices, and resists colonial nomenclature (Diaz Soto et al, 2009).

References

Alim, H.S. and Paris, D. (2017) 'What is culturally sustaining pedagogy and why does it matter', in H.S. Alim and D. Paris (eds) *Culturally sustaining pedagogies: Teaching and learning for justice in a changing world*, New York, NY: Teachers College Press, pp 1–21.

Allen, P.G. (1992) *The sacred hoop: Recovering the feminine in American Indian traditions* (2nd edn), Boston, MA: Beacon Press.

Almendrala, A. (2018) 'Separating "tender age" children at the border is a specific kind of child abuse'. Available at: www.huffingtonpost.com/entry/still-separated-immigrant-families-government-child-abuse_us_5b2bf345e4b0321a01cf38f2

Anzaldúa, G.E. (1990) *Making face, making soul/Haciendo caras: Creative and critical perspectives by women of color*, San Francisco, CA: Aunt Lute Books.

Anzaldúa, G.E. (2015) *Luz in the dark/Luz en lo oscuro: Rewriting identity, spirituality, reality*, Durham, NC: Duke University Press.

Apple, M. (2006) *Educating the 'right' way* (2nd edn), New York, NY: Routledge.

Asher, N. (2010) 'Decolonizing curriculum', in E. Malewski (ed) *Curriculum studies handbook – The next moment*, New York, NY: Routledge, pp 393–402.

Au, W. (2016) 'Meritocracy 2.0', *Educational Policy*, 30(1): 39–62.

Battiste, M. and Henderson, J.Y. (eds) (2000) 'Decolonizing cognitive imperialism in education', in *Protecting Indigenous knowledge and heritage: A global challenge*, Saskatoon, SK: Purich Pub, pp 86–96.

Brayboy, B.M.J. and Castagno, A.E. (2008) 'Indigenous knowledges and native science as partners: A rejoinder', *Cultural Studies of Science Education*, 3(3): 787–91.

Buras, K.L. (2011) 'Race, charter schools, and conscious capitalism: On the spatial politics of whiteness as property (and the unconscionable assault on black New Orleans)', *Harvard Educational Review*, 81(2): 296–331.

Cabrera, N.L., Meza, E.L., Romero, A.J. and Cintli Rodríguez, R. (2013) 'If there is no struggle, there is no progress: Transformative youth activism and the school of ethnic studies', *Urban Review*, 45(1): 7–22.

Cabrera, N.L., Milem, J.F., Jaquette, O. and Marx, R.W. (2014) 'Missing the (student achievement) forest for all the (political) trees: Empiricism and the Mexican American studies controversy in Tucson', *American Educational Research Journal*, 51(6): 1084–118.

Cajete, G. (1994) *Look to the mountain: An ecology of Indigenous education*, Durango, CO: Kivakí Press.

Calderón, D. (2014) 'Anticolonial methodologies in education: Embodying land and indigeneity in Chicana feminisms', *Journal of Latina/Latin American Studies*, 6(2): 81–96.

Cantú, N. (2001) 'Reading the body', in Latina Feminist Group (ed) *Telling to live: Latina feminist testimonios*, Durham, NC: Duke University Press, pp 264–5.

Cervantes-Soon, C.G. (2014) 'U.S.–Mexico border-crossing Chicana researcher: Theory in the flesh and the politics of identity in critical ethnography', *Journal of Latino/Latin American Studies*, 6(2): 97–112.

Crawford-Garrett, K., Perez, M., Sánchez, R.M., Short, A. and Tyson, K. (2016) 'Activism is good teaching: Reclaiming the profession', *Rethinking Schools*, 30(2): 22–5.

Cruz, C. (2006) 'Toward an epistemology of a brown body', in D. Delgado Bernal, C.A. Elenes, F.E. Godinez and S. Villenas (eds) *Chicana/Latina education in everyday life: Feminista perspectives on pedagogy and epistemology*, Albany, NY: State University of New York Press, pp 59–75.

Darder, A. (1995) 'Buscando América: The contribution of critical Latino educators to the academic development and empowerment of Latino students in the U.S', in C.E. Sleeter and P.L. McLaren (eds) *Multicultural education, critical pedagogy, and the politics of difference*, Albany, NY: State University of New York Press, pp 319–347.

Dee, T.S. and Penner, E.K. (2016) 'The causal effects of cultural relevance: Evidence from an ethnic studies curriculum', *American Educational Research Journal*, 54(1): 127–66.

Delgado Bernal, D. (2006) 'Learning and living pedagogies of the home: The Mestiza consciousness of Chicana students', in D. Delgado Bernal, C.A. Elenes, F.E. Godinez and S. Villenas (eds) *Chicana/Latina education in everyday life: Feminista perspectives on pedagogy and epistemology*, Albany, NY: State University of New York Press, pp 113–32.

De los Ríos, C.V., López, J. and Morrell, E. (2015) 'Toward a critical pedagogy of race: Ethnic studies and literacies of power in high school classrooms', *Race and Social Problems*, 7(1): 84–96.

Desai, S. (2016) 'From a gangsta to a spoken word poet: The multiple identities of spiritual', *The Urban Review*, 48(5): 799–816.

Desai, S. and Abeita, A. (2017) 'Breaking the cycle of incarceration: A young black male's journey from probation to self-advocacy', *Journal of Urban Learning, Teaching, & Research*, 13: 45–52.

Diaz Soto, L., Cervantes-Soon, C., Villarreal, E. and Campos, E.E. (2009) 'A Xicana sacred space: A communal circle of compromise for educational researchers', *Harvard Educational Review*, 79(4): 755–75.

Dillard, C.B. (2000) 'The substance of things hoped for, the evidence of things not seen: Examining an endarkened feminist epistemology in educational research and leadership', *Qualitative Studies in Education*, 13(6): 661–81.

Donato, R. (1997) *The other struggle for equal schools: Mexican Americans during the Civil Rights era*, Albany, NY: State University of New York Press.

Duran, E. and Duran, B. (1995) *Native American postcolonial psychology*, Albany, NY: State University of New York Press.

Emdin, C. (2016) *For white folks who teach in the hood ... and the rest of y'all too: Reality pedagogy and urban education*, Boston, MA: Beacon Press.

Gomez, L.E. (2008) *Manifest destinies: The making of the Mexican American race*, New York, NY: NYU Press.

hooks, b. (1994) *Teaching to transgress: Education as the practice of freedom*, New York, NY: Routledge.

Hurtado, A. (2003) 'Theory in the flesh: Toward an endarkened epistemology', *Qualitative Studies in Education*, 16(2): 215–25.

Kumashiro, K. (2008) *The seduction of common sense: How the Right has framed the debate on America's schools*, New York, NY: Teachers College.

Ladson-Billings, G. (1994) *The dreamkeepers: Successful teachers of African American children*, San Francisco, CA: John Wiley & Sons.

Ladson-Billings, G. (2006) 'From the achievement gap to the education debt: Understanding achievement in U.S. schools', *Educational Researcher*, 35(7): 3–12.

Ladson-Billings, G. (2014) 'Culturally relevant pedagogy 2.0: A.k.a the remix', *Harvard Educational Review*, 84(1): 74–84.

Lim, H. (2017) 'Police bias, use of deadly force, public outcry: Vicious cycle?', *Criminology and Public Policy*, 16(1): 305–8.

Lind, D. (2018) 'The Trump administration's separation of families at the border, explained'. Available at: www.vox.com/2018/6/11/17443198/children-immigrant-families-separated-parents

Lipman, P. (2011) 'Contesting the city: Neoliberal urbanism and the cultural politics of education reform in Chicago', *Discourse: Studies in the Cultural Politics of Education*, 32(2): 217–34.

Lomawaima, K.T. and McCarty, T.L. (2006) *To remain an Indian: Lessons in democracy from a century of Native American education*, New York, NY: Teachers College Press.

Lopez, W.D., Kruger, D.J., Delva, J., Llanes, M., Ledón, C., Waller, A., Harner, M., Martinez, R., Sanders, L., Israel, B. (2017) 'Health implications of an immigration raid: Findings from a Latino community in the Midwestern United States', *Journal of Immigrant and Minority Health*, 19(3): 702–8.

Lorde, A. (1978) *The black unicorn*, New York, NY: W.W. Norton.

Martinez, G. (2010) *Native pride: The politics of curriculum and instruction in an urban public school (Understanding education and policy)*, New York, NY: Hampton Press.

Matias, C.E. and Zembylas, M. (2014) '"When saying you care is not really caring": Emotions of disgust, whiteness ideology, and teacher education', *Critical Studies in Education*, 55(3): 319–37.

McCarthy, J. and Benally, J. (2003) 'Classroom management in a Navajo middle school', *Theory Into Practice*, 42(4): 296–304.

McCarty, T.L. and Lee, T.S. (2014) 'Critical culturally sustaining/revitalizing pedagogy and indigenous education sovereignty', *Harvard Educational Review*, 84(1): 101–36.

Menchaca, M. (2002) *Recovering history, constructing race: The Indian, black and white roots of Mexican Americans*, Austin, TX: University of Texas Press.

Metzl, J.M. and MacLeish, K.T. (2015) 'Mental illness, mass shootings, and the politics of American firearms', *American Journal of Public Health*, 105(2): 240–9.

Monahan, T. (2003) 'The surveillance curriculum: Risk management and social control in the neoliberal school', in A. Darder, M. Baltodano and R.D. Torres (eds) *The critical pedagogy reader*, New York, NY: RoutledgeFalmer, pp 123–34.

Moraga, Ch. (2011) *A Xicana codex of changing consciousness: Writings, 2000–2010*, London: Duke University Press.

Nakata, N.M., Nakata, V., Kech, S. and Bolt, R. (2012) 'Decolonial goals and pedagogies for indigenous studies', *Decolonization: Indigeneity, Education & Society*, 1(1): 120–40.

New Mexico Fiscal Policy Project (2011) 'New Mexico voices for children: Race, ethnicity, and economic outcomes in New Mexico'. Available at: https://www.nmvoices.org/wp-content/uploads/2013/05/State-of-Working-NM-2013.pdf

Pendleton Jiménez, K. (2006) '"Start with the land": Groundwork for Chicana pedagogy', in D. Delgado Bernal, C.A. Elenes, F.E. Godinez and S. Villenas (eds) *Chicana/Latina education in everyday life: Feminista perspectives on pedagogy and epistemology*, Albany, NY: State University of New York Press, pp 219–29.

Pewewardy, C. (1999) *The holistic medicine wheel: An indigenous model of teaching and learning*, Boulder, CO: Winds of Change.

Pewewardy, C. (2005) 'Ideology, power, and the miseducation of indigenous peoples in the United States', in A. Wilson and M. Yellowbird (eds) *For indigenous eyes only*, Santa Fe: School for Advanced Research Press, pp 139–56.

Ravitch, D. (2010) *The death and life of the great American school system: How testing and choice are undermining education*, New York, NY: Basic Books.

Rendón, L.I. (2009) *Sentipensante (sensing/thinking) pedagogy: Educating for wholeness, social justice, and liberation*, Sterling, VA: Stylus Publishing.

Secatero, S. (2015) '"The leadership tree": Our roots of indigenous leadership and well-being in higher education', in A.F. Chavez and R. Minthorn (eds) *Indigenous leadership in higher education*, New York, NY: Routledge Publishing, pp 114–27.

Senger, J.M., Villarruel, F., Arboleda, A. and Walker, N. (2004) *Lost opportunities: The reality of Latinos in the U.S. criminal justice system*, Washington, DC: National Council of La Raza.

Siddle Walker, V. (1996) *Their highest potential: An African American school community in the segregated south*, Chapel Hill, NC: University of North Carolina Press.

Sims, C.P. (2005) 'Tribal languages and the challenges of revitalization', *Anthropology & Education*, 36(1): 104–6.

Sleeter, C.E. (2011) 'The academic and social value of ethnic studies: A research review', National Education Association Research Department, Washington, DC. Available at: http://eric.ed.gov/?id=ED521869

Smith, L.T. (2012) *Decolonizing methodologies: Research and Indigenous peoples* (2nd edn), New York, NY: Zed Books.

Solórzano, D.G. and Delgado Bernal, D. (2001) 'Examining transformational resistance through a critical race and LatCrit theory framework: Chicana and Chicano students in an urban context', *Urban Education Journal*, 36(3): 308–42.

Sosa-Provencio, M.A. (2017) 'Curriculum of the mestiza/o body: Living and learning through a corporal language of resistance and (re) generation', *Diaspora Indigenous and Minority Education*, 12(2): 95–107.

Sosa-Provencio, M., Sheahan, A., Desai, S. and Secatero, S. (2018) 'Tenets of *body-soul rooted pedagogy*: Teaching for critical consciousness, nourished resistance, and healing', *Critical Studies in Education*. Available at: https://doi.org/10.1080/17508487.2018.1445653

Spring, J. (2010) *American education* (14th edn), New York, NY: McGraw-Hill.

Stovall, D. (2013) 'Against the politics of desperation: Educational justice, critical race theory, and Chicago school reform', *Critical Studies in Education*, 54(1): 33–43.

Taliaferro-Baszile, D. (2010) 'In Ellisonian eyes, what is curriculum theory?', in E. Malewski (ed) *Curriculum studies handbook – The next moment*, New York, NY: Routledge, pp 483–95.

Tintiangco-Cubales, A., Kohli, R., Sacramento, J., Henning, N., Agarwal-Rangnath, R. and Sleeter, C. (2015) 'Toward an ethnic studies pedagogy: Implications for K-12 schools from the research', *Urban Review*, 47(1): 104–25.

Trinidad Galván, R. (2016) 'Collective memory of violence of the female brown body: A decolonial feminist public pedagogy of engagement with the feminicides', *Pedagogy, Culture & Society*, 24(3): 343-57.

US Census Bureau (2017) 'State and county quickfacts'. Available at: www.census.gov/quickfacts/fact/table/nm,US/PST045217

Valencia, R.R. (ed) (2011) *Chicano school failure and success: Past, present, and future*, New York, NY: Routledge.

Vizenor, G. (ed) (2008) *Survivance: Narratives of native presence*, Lincoln, NE: University of Nebraska Press.

Wilkins, A. (2012) 'The spectre of neoliberalism: Pedagogy, gender and the construction of learner identities', *Critical Studies in Education*, 53(2): 197–210.

PART III

Higher education

8

Everyday activism: challenging neoliberalism for radical library workers in English higher education

Katherine Quinn and Jo Bates

Introduction

Despite libraries often being termed the 'heart' or the 'laboratory' of the university campus, and featuring heavily in literature, publicity and shared memories of academic life, they are frequently overlooked as institutions of political and pedagogical influence. Not only acting as something of a weathervane of broader social processes such as neoliberalisation, libraries also engender, reproduce and extend these processes in the lives of those who use them. Even with the transformation of libraries by the advent of the Internet and the increasing use of digital technologies (Goodfellow and Lea, 2013), library work is still a central intermediary in the teaching, research and everyday practices of the university. Although unassuming, libraries are neither silent nor neutral, and they have both radical and reactionary potential. As agencies within the institution of education (Hansson, 2006), libraries are affected by their context, and as sites where information is acquired, stored and communicated, the nature of this context has significant influence on the metrics of expertise used and the nature of knowledge made available.

As will be argued, processes of neoliberalisation are damaging to the pedagogic possibility of libraries. However, equally as damaging as denying the permeability of neoliberalisation would be to naively hark back to some imagined golden age of education where access and information was freely given to all, and it is for this reason that we focus on the idea of radical possibility. In resisting neoliberalisation in libraries, we should remember the innately conservative tendencies within librarianship, which have been well researched over several decades within Library and Information Studies (LIS) (Radford, 1992; Budd, 1995; Hjørland, 2005). As Drabinski (2018) argues, libraries have finite, material boundaries, and selection is an inescapably subjective component of what library work is. Despite the rise of automated acquisitions, expertise in libraries is only held in a relatively small number of hands and can only ever represent 'one kind of world, one that can never encompass all the possibilities of how we might organise ourselves' (Drabinski, 2018). As such, our hope is not for libraries to be restored to how they might have been prior to neoliberalisation, but rather for them to be critiqued and extended.

The library as a living, evolving and undirected space is key to our argument. Beyond formal education, they are spaces for everyday life to be performed and difference to be negotiated. Radical education alludes to an unknown (Ellsworth, 2005: 6), risk-laden (hooks, 1994: 4), creative and potentially wonderful (Ahmed, 2014: 178) possibility. It can hereby be associated with an active process of becoming, the possibility of learning experiences that enhance both individual self-consciousness and dignity under capitalism (Freire, 2013), but is also contributing to social engagement and shared communities. This supports hooks's (1994: 4) view of the possibility of education as 'enabling' and as 'enhancing our capacity to be free' – suggesting its outcome – while also seeing the process of learning itself as an opportunity for 'noncompliance and knowledge in the making', as argued by Ellsworth (2005: 17). In the politically straitened circumstances in which we currently live, the task facing library workers is therefore considerable, but not insurmountable.

The purpose of this chapter is twofold: to examine the political position of academic librarianship in the context of recent changes in English higher education; and to explore existing and emergent moments of radical educational possibility through the everyday practices of library workers. In the first section, we develop a case for critical attention being paid to the university library within what is presented as an incomplete but largely hegemonic moment of neoliberalisation. In the second section, we turn to the emergence of the Radical Librarians Collective (RLC), an open, horizontalist organisation of library workers and supporters formed in 2013, as a potential site through which to counter these developments and foster radical alternatives. Empirical data collected through interviews and participant observation with members of the RLC are analysed using thematic and critical discourse analysis. We find the RLC's successes to be primarily within its radical aims to provide solidarity, space for discussion and mutual aid nationally between like-minded library workers, and in its support for everyday workplace practices of resistance. We also offer reflections on the challenges of unstructured forms of organisation and considerations for the RLC's future success.

Methods

The empirical aspect of this article is drawn from a small-scale ethnographic study carried out from late 2013 to June 2014, involving interviews, reflective diary writing and participant observation. It primarily concerned Katherine's involvement in the RLC, a horizontalist network of library workers and supporters based in the UK, and culminated in participant observation at their annual day-long gathering, on 10 May 2014 at the London Action Resource Centre (LARC) in Whitechapel.

In addition to reflective diary writing, six semi-structured interviews were undertaken with members of the RLC, library workers, academics and managers. In line with ethical considerations of the political positions that these library workers were taking, all identifying names were anonymised. We are aware of the limitations of such a small-scale study but hold that such critical reflection is appropriate for our aim to 'illuminate particular moments of neoliberal reproduction and contestation' through individual and everyday experience rather than aiming erroneously for objective truth (Quinn and Bates, 2017: 318).

Neoliberalisation, the library and the enclosure of educational potential

The university library is a key site through which the cultural effects of neoliberalisation are made visible in the lives of not only university students, but also their wider communities. As higher education becomes more financialised around individualised fees and perceived individualised benefits, the university's insertion within a broader conception of public education as a social right becomes more dubious (Hall and Winn, 2017). Practices of education and learning in this context of an increasingly fragmented higher education sector become reified so much as to redefine academic study as asocial and outside of the wider public. Student fees, though still making up only part of the funding of higher education and mainly being paid through a state-organised loan, have come to be imagined as a straightforward transaction between the student and the university. Rather than a feature of public life, the privatisation of university funding has encouraged tertiary education to become a private affair.

University libraries represent a site through which the individualisation of higher education's benefits are made plain. They are the building through which many members of the non-university-going public would previously have engaged with higher education; library architecture is often the most striking on the university campus and, historically, there has been significant overlap and cooperation between public, further education and higher education libraries (McNicol, 2005). In recent years, most have become highly securitised and gated spaces with very low access rights to the non-university-going public. Turnstiles are now ubiquitous in academic libraries, despite evidence that they do little to reduce book theft (Harwell, 2014: 64) but potentially do much to deter non-university students from accessing knowledge that they have a right to. Adding the movement online of much academic output, the enclosure of previously public knowledge is quite profound: even if a member of the public can get limited access to a university library, they are very unlikely to be able to get past the paywalls on previously (physically) open access journal articles, for example.

This shift in the economy of scholarly communication is a further area of library work in which the external pressures associated with neoliberalisation have enclosed educational potential. Harvie et al (2012), Pirie (2009) and Monbiot (2011), among others, all highlight the extent to which the marketisation of scholarly communication has created publishing monopolies that negatively impact libraries in so far as they take up greater and greater proportions of budgets. Publishers have exploited a 'captive audience' by creating the 'big deal' scenario that exclusively suits them. The big deal is defined by Davis as 'an arrangement where a library can purchase unlimited access to a publisher's entire suite of journals', which frequently includes journals that the library had never previously bought or needed, and often includes a non-cancellation clause (Davis, 2003: 552). While boycotts by academics, librarians and researchers of Dutch publishing giant Elsevier has had some impact in some European countries (Matthews, 2017), there has been minimal success of such tactics in the UK, and no structural change worldwide.

This scenario, which sees the proportion of library budgets spent on periodicals come second only to staff costs (Banks, 2014), radically reduces discretionary item purchasing. While this may seem innocuous, it represents a shift in the role of the subject-specialist librarian and means that collection development is brought within the control of markets, rather than people and ideas. Seeing library collections as discrete objects in themselves that evolve, push boundaries and represent a diversity of challenging views is essential to their continuation as something more than 'storehouses' of knowledge (Williams and Deyoe, 2014). If marketability and short-term popularity is to replace deliberative selection by library workers, the space for serendipity, comprehensiveness and knowledge for its own sake is also at risk.

Finally, the vocabulary of business and management in both the discipline and practice of library work is having a corrosive effect on the capacity of those involved to imagine any future beyond neoliberal common sense. In most professional qualifications for LIS, a course in management is compulsory, which heavily reinforces a business-oriented approach to an institution that is not predicated on profit making. New Public Management, in which management is considered the primary activity through which an organisation succeeds, has permeated LIS literature (Quinn and Bates, 2017) and has dwarfed alternative models of running libraries through horizontal management or cooperation. In practice, the rebranding of students as customers, librarians as 'information officers' and success as measurable outputs undermines the radical potential of libraries. As Lossin (2017: 100) has pointed out, such neoliberal language is 'both symptomatic and generative', and removing references to the foundational principles of libraries – books and access to them – promotes a re-imagining of the library as 'a brick and mortar portal into the private sector' (Lossin, 2017: 112).

After having demonstrated the enclosure of education potential via neoliberal developments, the next section explores the ways in which the RLC and radical librarians contribute to a politics of possibility and resistance.

The challenge for radical librarians: the RLC

The RLC was conceived in 2013 on the social media site Twitter via serendipitous exchanges between like-minded library workers. These initial conversations were sparked by expressions of frustration 'about increasing commodification and marketisation in libraries, about creeping neoliberalism and managerialist attitudes within the profession, about the decimation of the public library system, and much more' (Brynolf, no date). Since then, the RLC has developed online as a place for conversation, collaboration and research. It has a Twitter feed, website, online open access journal (the *Journal of Radical Librarianship*) and collaborative documents aimed at information sharing and solidarity. While the readership is not prescribed, and no formal membership exists, the resources include reading lists, guides and strategies primarily useful to fellow library workers. Offline, there have been five annual gatherings for physical meet-ups across the UK in Bradford, London, Huddersfield, Brighton and Glasgow. Sporadic regional groups have also met in between those larger annual meet-ups in London, Oxford, Yorkshire and Dublin.

Someone who was involved in the foundation of the collective suggested that the initial stage of the RLC's foundation was a cathartic moment of "Do you think what I think? I think I think what you think … we should do something about this!". Another RLC supporter described realising they "were not alone" (Quinn and Bates, 2017) through such encounters. These exclamations express both a feeling of release shared among people who did not otherwise know each other, and happiness at being relieved of what felt like isolation in their respective workplaces. They also speak, in part, to the isolation associated with work in capitalism. Since the RLC began and developed on Twitter, the paradox of social media is also relevant, something both Iber (2016) and Back (2016) have recently alluded to. This paradox speaks to the fact that although the job precarity and demand for self-marketing engendered by neoliberalism have arguably created at least some of the perceived need for professions, including librarianship, to use Twitter for a type of self-publicity (Iber, 2016), it also allows users to 'inhabit the attentiveness of another' (Back, 2016: 110) in a very positive way. Interestingly, therefore, connections and moments of empathy and solidarity are facilitated by the very tool that has also been criticised for being symptomatic of the anxiety, isolation and precarity felt to characterise academia.

Political positions from the RLC appeared fluid and not clearly defined, but that fact was acknowledged and justified by members of the RLC in interviews and online. Keeping 'radical' as undefined beyond its etymological definition of 'grasping at the root' of librarianship was a tactic designed to promote inclusivity. Using the definition of 'grasping at the root' is perhaps telling of a belief that librarianship and libraries have a 'root' that has been lost or at least damaged in recent years. While such claims to universality could be problematic, this 'root' appeared a lot to do with democratic values of free information, and a belief that such information could enable politically engaged non-compliant education. One interviewee described her personal political position and occupational identity as a librarian in the same breath, saying:

> 'I always came from a relatively active political position anyway … and became a librarian because I found libraries

> really scary when I was a student and I realised that there had to be a way where it wasn't scary, because information should be empowering and you should be able to help people find information.'

As such, an important aspect of the RLC is seen as being in facilitating conversations and meetings between people who identified themselves in their work, who saw there being a 'radical root' to librarianship, but who saw their paid work detracting from it.

As a collective, the RLC aims to organise this inclusive politics in a manner one supporter described as "prefiguratively". They defined this as "doing things as you want them to be", aligning with a common anarchist notion of prefiguration, which is the 'embodiment, within the ongoing political practice of a movement, of those forms of social relations, decision-making, culture, and human experience that are the ultimate goal' (Boggs, 1977: 100). For the RLC, as for many other radical social change initiatives, this value is carried into its organisation and practice. For example, gatherings are held at cooperatively managed social centres or libraries, such as the Larc, the Cowley Club social centre in Brighton and the Women's Library in Glasgow. These organisations are themselves working as alternatives to profit-seeking corporations and have radical social change aims that align with the politics of the RLC. Several of our interviewees pointed to the importance of getting away from the physical and bureaucratic infrastructure of their workplaces in higher education. One said that not having the "institutional baggage" that came with university conference set-ups, which are "there to generate income" for the university, made different conversations possible.

At the gatherings themselves, prefiguration is shown through their horizontalist approach and lack of 'keynote'-style presentations. Topics are 'pitched' either online in advance or spontaneously on the day. 'Pitches' are suggestions for topics to be discussed in groups at the gatherings, and usually the person pitching gives a brief and informal explanation of the subject and why it is relevant to radical librarianship. Topics at previous RLC gatherings have included: feminism and librarianship; radicalising professional status; the imposter syndrome; metrics; and the role of libraries in challenging oppression. Beyond these specific issues, among the RLC's core interests are the promotion of critical information skills, web privacy, the defence of public libraries through supporting local and national campaigns, and union organisation against declining working conditions across sectors. Such values highlight their political, as opposed to purely professional, identity concerns and a desire to connect librarianship with broader societal concerns. Thus, the RLC operates as an agitator to the official professional body for librarians – the Chartered Institute for Library and Information Professionals (CILIP) – which one of the interviewees called "utterly pointless", and has been criticised for aiming at unattainable political neutrality.

Outside of the collective meet-ups, everyday practices were a particularly interesting element of interviews in connection with radical librarianship. As Chatterton and Pickerall (2010) argue, these molecular-level actions are essential for resistance within imperfect structures, rather than separated from it. They argue that 'it is through its everyday rhythms that meaning is given to postcapitalism' (Chatterton and Pickerall, 2010: 476). One such tactic was so-called 'guerrilla collection development'. Acquiring books and materials for higher education libraries that were challenging to neoliberalism meant leveraging institutional budgets, however small the opportunity was, for resistance. In one case, a subject librarian with responsibility for business and nutrition spent some money on books covering permaculture, agribusiness, cooperative management and Marxism. The practice, identified by several interviewees, involved using what was available to them – in this case, their budget – to "secretly develop a whole alternative collection" of challenging texts for library users to benefit from. The interviewees felt that this was entirely within their remit as subject librarians since the "alternative voices" are valid, but may be overlooked: "it's about combating where the dominance is really, I think … and encouraging people to believe that those are OK sources to be using as well, and critiquing the state of play". Recently, Hudson (2017: 13) has argued insightfully against believing that 'diversity' is sufficient for anti-racist library development, saying 'to be included in a space is not necessarily to have agency within that space'. However, it seems an important, if small-scale, act of resistance.

Further practices of radical librarians were articulated as everyday interactions with students or the public in the workplace. These included talking to students about their assignments in an honest and emotionally invested way, suggesting challenging topics and material, and even discussing the ethics of their institution's technology usage. For example, the bibliographic management software used by many universities, like Endnote, is proprietary, for profit and inaccessible to those without subscriptions. This is the same with Windows, Photoshop and much other software relied upon institutionally. Open-source software – like Linux, Etherpad and Zotero – is, in contrast, transparently built and adaptable by a community of users, and so is more in keeping with the RLC's politics. One interviewee suggested that librarians in general were too concerned about "balance" and overestimated the "danger" of having divergent opinions. There was a tension here between ethics and legality, especially around questions of copyright. As one interviewee queried:

> 'how much "ethically" as a librarian are you allowed to scrabble around trying to find a free, probably illegal copy of a document that you find on the Internet? And how much shouldn't you do that? And … I think … we're not allowed to have those kinds of conversations within the library service.'

Having these conversations with students, even if stopping short of providing the 'illegal' copy, is important for enriching understanding of the political economy of academic publishing but poses a personal risk to librarians employed by university institutions.

Finally, self-reflection and consciously embedding radical aspirations within the working day is crucial for the RLC. All interviewees mentioned their use of reflective journals and diary writing as ways to deal with problems at work and think about the way in which they had handled things. While recognising that this can threaten to be one more thing to do and be an additional burden, interviewees stressed reflective journal writing's merits in relieving the stress associated with neoliberalised work patterns, as well as helping to engage them in reasons for why they wanted to be a librarian in the first place: "it's about … reinforcing your mindset, helping you to … reflect on things, and then how you approach things in your day-to-day life, so, yeah, praxis is what you do all the time, every day, so it's about reinforcing and working with that". Another stressed the importance of making this critical reflection a part of the working day, and forcing it onto the agendas of colleagues and bosses: "what's useful is giving yourself the time, and legitimising in your workplace, the space to work and the space to reflect and evaluate your practice". Going even further, another radical library worker set up a discussion group in their workplace under the banner of continuous professional development (CPD). He said:

> 'There're no outcomes, we don't have to present to any higher group, there isn't any of that. I've managed to sneak it in under the CPD framework, and it was ticking a box. So one of the management group was like "Oooh great,

> you'll do that, that's fine". And so nothing has to come out of it, no work, or anything, so people kind of like it. We've only had a couple, but people seem to like how they can just come along and read an article and just talk about what we do at work and then we try and reflect on it and we try and ask, "What is it we're doing there?".'

What is interesting here is not only the immediate association, and associated revulsion of, activities like presenting to a "higher group" and having "work" and "outcomes" – illustrative of audit fatigue common under neoliberalism – but also how people who are not calling themselves 'radical' are feeling welcomed and supported in what feels like an unusual activity for some – that of talking about the bigger picture.

Although the RLC has many strong points, both in terms of offering mutual aid to self-identifying radical librarians and in terms of intervening in students' everyday lives, we found it to have areas in need of improvement on its own terms. First, although its horizontal and open nature is often alluded to, without deliberate processes or structures, it was hard to know what or who the RLC really was, and this gave rise to informal hierarchies that were difficult to navigate (Quinn and Bates, 2017). Balancing a desire to focus on issues that were pertinent to those attending the gathering with a stated desire to be radical also needs constant re-evaluation. If issues are self-selected, there is a tendency for status quo concerns to be tacitly supported, even within 'radical' groups. As Ahmed (2013) argues, 'open' calls with 'invisible' restrictions (who is speaking, who is attending, what is being discussed), work to reproduce rather than resist 'what we inherit' in terms of class, ethnicity, gender and ability. As she says:

> it would be timely to re-state the arguments that sexism and racism are not incidental but structural, and thus to understand sexism and racism, requires better, closer readings of what is being gathered. Attending to the restrictions in the apparently open spaces of a social world brings us into closer proximity to an actual world. (Ahmed, 2013)

This is a question for all of LIS, not just the RLC, but a focus on such issues seems a very appropriate project for a collective with the aims that it has.

As elaborated in Quinn and Bates (2017), many of these criticisms have been taken on, and there seems to be a positive development in the RLC, with more explicit processes and named organising committees (Radical Librarians Collective, no date). Being critical and reflective practitioners necessitates a willingness to visit and revisit aims, structures and practices, and also to learn from where others have gone before. To this end, a constructive collaborative document entitled 'Barriers to participation' (Radical Librarians Collective, 2017) was created, and resources from other anti-capitalist organising groups were flagged up for possible training. Overall, the RLC has potential to become a space through which radical alternatives to neoliberal hegemony within librarianship can be explored and fostered.

Another way in which the RLC could improve its work is by focusing more on what it wants to build, and in strengthening its local activism in addition to the national gatherings. Following Gibson-Graham's (2006: 125) concept of 'capitalocentric', a framing of reality whereby all 'non-capitalist' alternatives are connected and contingent on a dominant and dominating conception of capitalist society, the RLC could work to re-envision their role positively. The RLC can sometimes be seen to fit within a framework that positions individual librarians as 'activists', or experts with perhaps superior ways of understanding the world, and as though the key to unlocking radical educational possibility rested with them. As such, it places less emphasis on the broader context in which education, libraries and library workers exist, and on the many ways in which a range of people in education and broader society work to struggle with the dehumanising aspects of capitalist education every day, often without self-consciousness.

We will conclude by opening up to the RLC's implications for the broader remaking of our society. Our observations of the practices of the RLC have wider implications for resistance to the neoliberalisation of higher education beyond librarianship. Their principles rely on critical knowledge production and dissemination, and therefore represent fruitful areas for reflection in wider resistance movements in higher education and beyond. Learning from, and engaging with, the RLC's critical use of technologies would allow the further growth of anti-capitalist and open-source technology platforms and practices to flourish. The RLC's radical appropriation of 'management-friendly' activities such as reflective practice and reading groups are also transferable beyond the library. Finally, engaging in critical and honest conversations with students and colleagues represents a small-scale but profound practice through which to work towards remaking our worlds on a daily basis.

References

Ahmed, S. (2013) 'Making feminist points', *Feminist Killjoy*, 11 September. Available at: https://feministkilljoys.com/2013/09/11/making-feminist-points/ (accessed 11 May 2017).

Ahmed, S. (2014) *The cultural politics of emotion* (2nd edn), Edinburgh: Edinburgh University Press.

Back, L. (2016) *Academic diary*, London: Goldsmiths Press.

Banks, P. (2014) 'Resource allocation for libraries in higher education', *SCONUL Focus*, 60. Available at: www.sconul.ac.uk/publication/resource-allocation-for-libraries-in-higher-education (accessed 31 May 2018).

Boggs, C. (1977) 'Marxism, prefigurative communism and the problem of workers' control', *Radical America*, 11(6): 99–122.

Brynolf, B. (no date) 'A history of the radical librarians collective'. Available at: https://rlc.radicallibrarianship.org/about-2/history-of-rlc/ (accessed 9 September 2017).

Budd, J.M. (1995) 'An epistemological foundation for library and information science', *The Library Quarterly*, 65(3): 295–318.

Chatterton, P. and Pickerall, J. (2010) 'Everyday activism and transitions towards post-capitalist worlds', *Transactions of the Institute of British Geographers*, 35(4): 475–90.

Davis, P.M. (2003) 'Tragedy of the commons revisited: Librarians, publishers, faculty, and the demise of a public resource', *Libraries and the Academy*, 3(4): 547–62.

Drabinski, E. (2018) 'Are libraries neutral?'. Available at: www.emilydrabinski.com/are-libraries-neutral/ (accessed 13 February 2018).

Ellsworth, E. (2005) *Places of learning: Media, architecture, pedagogy*, Abingdon: Taylor & Francis.

Freire, P. (2013) *Education for critical consciousness*, London: Bloomsbury.

Gibson-Graham, J. (2006) *A postcapitalist politics*, Minneapolis, MN: University of Minnesota Press.

Goodfellow, R. and Lea, M.R. (eds) (2013) *Literacy in the digital university*, London: Routledge.

Hall, R. and Winn, J. (2017) 'Social co-operatives and the democratisation of higher education', paper presented at the Co-operative Education and Research Conference, 5–6 April, Manchester, UK.

Hansson, J. (2006) 'Just collaboration or really something else? On joint use libraries and normative institutional change with two examples from Sweden', *Library Trends*, 54(4): 549–68.

Harvie, D., Lightfoot, G., Lilley, S. and Weir, K. (2012) 'What are we to do with feral publishers?', *Organization*, 19(6): 905–14.

Harwell, J.H. (2014) 'Library security gates: Effectiveness and current practice', *Journal of Access Services*, 11(2): 53–65. Available at: https://doi.org/10.1080/15367967.2014.884876

Hjørland, B. (2005) 'Library and information science and the philosophy of science', *Journal of Documentation*, 61(1): 5–10.

hooks, b. (1994) *Teaching to transgress: Education as the practice of freedom*, London: Routledge.

Hudson, D.J. (2017) 'On "diversity" as anti-racism in library and information studies: A critique', *Journal of Critical Library and Information Studies*, 1: 1–36.

Iber, P. (2016) 'A defense of academic twitter', *Inside HigherEd*, 19 October. Available at: www.insidehighered.com/advice/2016/10/19/how-academics-can-use-twitter-most-effectively-essay (accessed 9 September 2017).

Lossin, R. (2017) 'Against the universal library', *New Left Review*, 107: 99–117.

Matthews, D. (2017) 'German universities plan for life without Elsevier', *Times Higher Education*. Available at: www.timeshighereducation.com/news/german-universities-plan-life-without-elsevier#survey-answer (accessed 20 February 2018).

McNicol, S. (2005) 'Library co-operation in the inter-war period: Lessons from history', *Library History*, 21(2): 85–9.

Monbiot, G. (2011) 'Academic publishers make Murdoch look like a socialist', *The Guardian*. Available at: www.theguardian.com/commentisfree/2011/aug/29/academic-publishers-murdoch-socialist (accessed 9 September 2017).

Pirie, I. (2009) 'The political economy of academic publishing', *Historical Materialism*, 17(3): 31–60.

Quinn, K. and Bates, J. (2017) 'Resisting neoliberalism: The challenge of activist librarianship in English higher education', *Journal of Documentation*, 73(2): 317–35.

Radford, G.P. (1992) 'Positivism, Foucault, and the fantasia of the library: Conceptions of knowledge and the modern library experience', *Library Quarterly*, 62(4): 408–24.

Radical Librarians Collective (no date) 'Who is RLC?'. Available at: https://rlc.radicallibrarianship.org/who-is-rlc/ (accessed 20 February 2018).

Radical Librarians Collective (2017) 'Follow-up to "barriers to engagement"'. Available at: https://rlc.radicallibrarianship.org/2017/03/08/follow-up-to-barriers-to-engagement/ (accessed 1 May 2018).

Williams, V.K. and Deyoe, N. (2014) 'Diverse population, diverse collection? Youth collections in the United States', *Technical Services Quarterly*, 31(2): 97–121. Available at: https://doi.org/10.1080/07317131.2014.875373

9

Strategies of resistance in the neoliberal university

Mary Hamilton

Introduction

This chapter draws on data from a UK research council-funded project 'The Dynamics of Knowledge Creation: Academics Writing in the Contemporary University Workplace'.[1] The field that has come to be known as 'academic writing' has largely focused on student learning and support. We took a different, workplace approach, exploring the writing that staff in a range of higher education institutions do as part of their work, interviewing and observing people from different disciplinary and career backgrounds. We worked with full-time academics and administrative staff at different career stages, across three disciplines (Maths, History and Marketing) and three institutions chosen to illustrate the range that exists in the UK. In this chapter, I focus on the data from academic staff, but the division of labour between academics and support staff is an important aspect of the working context, especially in relation to digital technologies.

Writing work is at the heart of knowledge production in many cultures, and the university has traditionally been a pivotal and highly valued site for this. We argue that writing practices offer a window through which the changing institutional environment, values and strategies that constitute academic work can be explored (see Tusting et al, 2019). These writing practices are, in part, professional (assembled within wider disciplinary networks) and, in part, institutional (assembled through immediate university affiliations and employment), and while we did not ask directly, we expect our data to be able to tell us something about resistance and complicity.

We interviewed people several times, exploring their practices, their life histories, their institutional and disciplinary contexts, and the tools and resources that they draw on as they write. We documented the activities in which people engage on a day-to-day basis, including teaching, administrative and service-related writing tasks. We took a socio-material approach to our study (see Edwards et al, 2015), looking at both physical and discursive aspects of academics' experience and the networks that sustain these. We looked at material artefacts handled and produced by staff, not only written texts, but also devices like mobile phones, and we observed the buildings and other spaces where academic teaching and writing work was carried out. While the research-based book or journal article is the 'gold standard' for success as an academic, participants mentioned a wide range of writing activities in their interviews with us (see Box 9.1). We counted nearly a hundred kinds of writing tasks involving different texts, procedures and collaborations with others, including academic and administrative colleagues, funding bodies, parents, reviewers, editors, and publishers. Much of this writing is done to satisfy institutional demands related to teaching, administration, external impact, generating publicity and resources, and – of course – collecting and recording data for accountability purposes.

Participants told us that their official role falls into three main areas, which, in some cases, are written into contracts and allocated a nominal percentage of their time using workload models. These are usually teaching, research and administration but there is a fourth area of more 'optional' work that we have called service – much of it outward-facing (see Macfarlane, 2006).

This variety of writing tasks are sometimes still done using pen and paper but many are done using digital tools and platforms of various sorts. There are institutional pressures to use some of these tools, especially for teaching, and many are learned informally on the job. Increasingly, social media such as Twitter, blogging and using academia.edu or similar sites are an expected part of professional writing.

Box 9.1: The complex worlds of academics' writing

- *Teaching-related* writing included course outlines and validation documents, handouts, PowerPoint slides for lectures, and many documents related to marking and giving student feedback.
- *Research-related* writing included the complex paperwork for applying for research grants, such as the proposals themselves and ethical statements; documenting and organising data collection; and many kinds of research outputs, from journal articles and books to popular summaries and press releases.

- *Administrative* writing included writing agendas, inputting to databases and compiling job descriptions, reference letters, expenses claims and explanations of policies and procedures (for example, quality assurance paperwork) for colleagues.
- *Service-related* writing included evaluative reviews of articles and books, external examining reports, responding to surveys and committee policies, and mentoring and pastoral care.

What is 'the neoliberal university' and why might it provoke resistance?

Universities in England have seen considerable change over the last three decades. As a working environment, the academy has been reconfigured through the increasing use of digital resources, new forms of funding, governance and accountability, and internationalisation (Barnett, 2000; Olsen and Peters, 2005; Deem et al 2007; Robertson, 2008). Higher education is now a global industry that is estimated to contribute around £73 billion to UK gross domestic product (GDP) per year (Kelly et al, 2014). Direct public funding has been reduced while income from student fees and private corporate sponsors has increased. Links with industry are encouraged, and research is assessed for its demonstrable benefits beyond the academic community. Institutional status and public funding are allocated through international and national rankings. Corporate management cultures have developed, replacing traditional university values and governance structures (Sum and Jessop, 2013; Radice, 2013).

Such far-reaching changes inevitably result in tensions and pressures within the academy (Kinman and Jones, 2003). These have to be managed by academics, administrative staff and the institutions that employ them (Carrigan, 2015).

Transformations in managerial practices in universities have led to the intensification of the pace of work and job insecurity has increased. There are new forms of accountability and surveillance, especially the Research Excellence Framework (REF), which assesses the quality and impact of scholarly publication. This leads to demands to publish in strategic ways, to respond to new demands around impact and public engagement, and to be accountable to standards that can conflict with disciplinary norms and established practices (Winter and O'Donohue, 2012). The privileging of research articles in highly cited journals, for example, conflicts with the norms of history as a discipline that values monographs above other forms.

Compounding and amplifying these changes are the changing resources and working spaces offered by new digital tools (Goodfellow and Lea, 2013). Academics are required to learn to use new technological platforms for teaching, and to engage with social media in order to maintain a public online persona. As described in the following example, these new practices take time to learn and are often acquired informally "on the job":

> 'I'm still trying to understand [Moodle]. We do course reviews and … I spent an hour this morning trying to work out where the student comments in it – actually, it's not part of Moodle at all; they're sent to you in an email. I thought they'd been on Moodle somewhere and they're not. There are a lot of parts and corners of Moodle that I don't use and understand.' (David Keene, Maths, Uni A)

Changes in the demands and resources of the academic workplace culminate in tensions and pressures, which are vividly described by participants in our study and recall Ball's (2012) observations on 'the terrors of performativity':

> 'I wake up every morning I feel like it's my A levels. I feel panicked all the time that I'm not doing enough. So, I'm involved in lots of projects, probably way too many research projects. I think it's just trying to keep the wolf from the door all the time.' (Charles Cooper, early career, Marketing, Uni A)

> 'So it's this chicken-and-egg situation whereby you can only get the hours if you've proven yourself to be able to get published, but you can only get published if you get the time and hours. So you go around in this circle, sort of like the imponderable cycle of impossibility.' (Mark West, Marketing, Uni B)

People commented on the introduction of surveillance and demands to cede control over their work to administrative procedures. Sometimes, this is a physical constraint placed on routines and the pace of work; sometimes, it is a loss of autonomy in the work of writing itself:

> 'A few years ago, there was this kind of instruction, from on high, that we had to be in our offices at 9:00 on a Monday morning and, with the door open … all to do with student satisfaction and contact hours and stuff.' (Verity Hough, History, Uni C)

> 'For the first time ever, writing [the course handbook] has been out of our control because we've been told what should be in our curriculum. I'm not used to being told what I will write. We've had the size of the modules, the content of the modules and the number of assessments and the type of assessments dictated to us [by] the pro-vice-chancellor. It's the first time we've had that kind of micromanagement.' (Ella Kemp, Marketing, Uni B)

The variety and experience of autonomy, of feeling in control over writing demands, was a really central issue for participants in our project.

Academic spaces are being physically reorganised to respond positively to student needs, but often with little consultation or concern for the working lives of staff:

> 'I cannot believe the way in which academics are being forced into smaller offices, shared offices and into spaces where … you have three bookshelves. If you're a literature and culture person, you need … this is about a third of the books that I have.' (Dolly Blue, History, Uni B)

There are many interruptions to working in the campus-based office, from face-to-face meetings with students and colleagues, to the arrival of emails demanding action. It is a social and service-oriented environment and, consequently, most of our respondents say that they are not able to do 'serious' writing work there:

> 'You think, "I've got two hours. I'm going to get something done", and then it just takes one knock on the door to interrupt that.' (Will Dodd, Maths, Uni C)

> 'It's like every time you sit down to do some writing, an email comes in that takes you away from it.' (Diane Simmons, Marketing, Uni A)

Interestingly, all three of the universities we chose have experienced major building works over the last two decades or more as a result of refurbishment, expansion or the repurposing of campus spaces. Many people told us that they have been moved to smaller, refurbished offices, or spent time in temporary spaces while refurbishment takes place:

> 'I'm sharing at the moment with a colleague who's based in London and he's on research leave, very kindly offered me the use of his office. And so I've parked myself with some of the boxes of books that I was able to salvage before the contents of my room were parcelled up and sent off to a warehouse.' (Collin Whitworth, History, Uni C)

Even though academics are measured by their success in writing, the space for scholarly writing, in particular, is squeezed so hard that our participants tell us that they find it difficult to do it in their allocated office and within normal working hours. Writing needs to be managed and people construct and try to maintain boundaries of various kinds around different kinds of work, in space and time, and around devices for writing (such as laptops, separate email accounts and notebooks) in order to address overwhelming demands.

One strategy for dealing with the tensions and challenges is simply to extend the working day as long as possible and in space as far as possible. The following quote expresses many of the tensions that others also identify (the sheer volume of conflicting demands, dealing with constant interruptions to sustained thought and attempts to allocate writing to particular places or times of the day or week):

> 'I do an awful lot of writing at home. I think I am a cause of some despair, probably, at home because I do work very long hours, and very often, I'm working into the late evening … it might be because I've got inspiration to do something of my own, or it might be because there's a deadline, a student needs a reference, or a document for teaching needs to be updated. And it's easier to do that work at 9:00pm than to feel I will have time in the working day, when I … [will] be interrupted.' (Collin Whitworth, History, Uni C)

Other time boundaries intervene in writing too: the span of insecure contracts; the demands of the REF and other assessment and auditing cycles; deadlines set for proposal writing; or paperwork prepared for exams and validation committees. Yearly cycles of work also have to be managed:

> 'There's not a block where you can say "I'm doing writing". We used to have the summer. But things like overseas partners, it massively intrudes on everything.' (Diane Simmons, Marketing, Uni A)

> 'I will have to do [extended] writing at a time [of year] when I don't have teaching ideally.... It's having a period of a few weeks or something like that, where you don't have to think of another thing. It's really disruptive to your concentration to have to go back and do three hours one day on something [else].' (Ian Fairclough, Maths, Uni A)

Administrative demands placed on people are not felt to take account of the pressure on time and workload that results, and such pressures are felt by people across the spectrum of jobs and seniority, as the following quotes from senior staff show: David Keene, a head of department, comments on the preparation of documentation for the Quality Assurance Agency:

> 'I hate it.... I can see the point of it but ... it takes on its own momentum and people go really crazy about it. I'm not quite sure how much is needed – the university, the people in charge of these things always seem to insist on far too much. Maybe I'm wrong but I think there's no understanding of the amount of time these things take and the fact that it's yet another demand on your time.' (David Keene, Maths, Uni A)

> 'My role as the unit of assessment coordinator for the REF was exhausting and complicated. It involved a lot of drafting of all the documents and also all the dealing with people, about whether they'd be in or out; all the reviewing of the work internally.... Also, it's hard to do; it's not something I'm trained to do. It's very hard to know what's needed.' (Verity Hough, History, Uni C)

What might resistance look like?

We can see from these examples that academics might feel that they have grounds for resisting changes that bring them a loss of autonomy and deteriorating working conditions, as well as intensified, new and sometimes contradictory demands that they have not been trained for. Examples of resistant behaviour range from visible, collective activism involving physical, bodily resistance, to 'everyday tactics' of resistance (Johansson and Vinthagen, 2016). Everyday tactics may be primarily symbolic or language-related and have much in common with the notion of 'strategic compliance' proposed by Shain and Gleeson (1999), whereby practitioners rework existing professional ideologies and commitments to mediate the organisational changes they face. Some situations may be more conducive to overt acts of resistance, while in others, people may have limited room for successful manoeuvre or have conflicted responses due to the multiple role positions they occupy (Scott, 1992). Resistance is not always a commitment to radical action, but may involve holding onto the status quo through refusal to change. As Fleming (2016) points out, such everyday, mundane acts can appear to be insignificant and a 'weak' form of resistance but, as a growing body of international literature shows, it is important to document them in order to understand the genesis and dynamics of collective, organised movements and resistant events.

James Scott's approach seems particularly useful for understanding our data. He not only discusses the observable, micro-interactional manifestations of resistance, but, like Goffman (1959), puts forward the idea of a 'front stage' and a 'backstage' – public 'ritualistic' and 'hidden' transcripts of behaving, relating and speaking about experience that are not available to outside observers unless they work closely with the groups involved, both those in dominant positions and those in subordinate institutional positions. He also speaks about the symptoms of resistance – stress, tensions that build until they burst out as violent interactions, anger or collective mobilisation:

> 'the necessity of "acting a mask" in the presence of power produces, almost by the strain engendered by its inauthenticity, a countervailing pressure that cannot be contained indefinitely.' (Scott, 1992: 9)

Scott argues that riots and strikes are the exception rather than the rule in resistant communities and it could be that our focus on workplace writing practices offers a valuable window onto Scott's metaphorical 'hidden transcripts' and evidence of the build-up of stresses that they express.

Based on these ideas, I interrogated our data for evidence of the following forms of resistance: visible, organised, collective action; everyday workarounds (finding ways of satisfying administrative demands, REF publishing or workload models without conforming to the letter of the law); symbolic resistance (sceptical discourses or challenging gestures that undermine the neoliberal view); refusal to change existing practices; and valuing aspects of work that are unrewarded in neoliberal times (such as collaborations, optional service, positive care to students and alternative strategies of open-access publishing). I elaborate on each of these forms of resistance in turn.

Evidence of resistance from our study

Despite ample and vivid evidence of stress, the acceleration of work and deteriorating working conditions across the three universities in our study, there was little trace in our data of organised, collective resistance. Does this mean that academic staff were passively accepting these changes and the resultant negative feelings, the loss of autonomy and the 'squeezed' spaces and times affecting their work and personal lives?

One answer to this question can be found in the events of March 2018 that occurred soon after our study was completed, when the biggest strike of academic staff in UK higher education history began (as reported in *Times Higher Education*, 2018). It was a serious and enthusiastically supported action, carefully mobilised by the Universities and Colleges Union (UCU) to protect academic pensions. Could we have predicted from our data that such collective action was brewing? I would argue that our research revealed worrying levels of stress and tapped into 'hidden transcripts' that anticipated the outpouring of support for the strike.

When we asked about the strategies that people use to manage the writing demands of academic life, there were many responses that suggested forms of tactical resistance. The motivation for such strategies was often expressed as desperation at needing to fit everything into the available time. People had to make decisions about what to prioritise and how to make sense of the administrative hurdles placed in their day-to-day lives:

> 'We have … an official kind of workload [model] that we sit down with our line manager, and I was going to say gerrymander, that's probably not the right word, they figure out, you know, how many hours you get for being a module

> leader, how many you get for the amount of students you've got, and there is a chunk there which is about research as well.' (Bob Busby, History, Uni B)

> 'Yes, so people talk about it as a game. It is gaming. I had a conversation with a colleague [about submitting a paper to a high-ranking journal], I'd better not mention who it is.... I just thought, "This is a game that I can pretend I'm playing to here, because that's what they want to hear, but I also know that I have no chance". I'm not a positivist, I don't do modelling. I have no way of engaging with that world ... you've got to play the game otherwise you're nobody. You get trampled on.' (Diane Simmons, Marketing, Uni A)

The language of "gerrymandering" and "gaming" signals a strong scepticism about some of the demands placed on their work and is evidence of symbolic resistance, as well as tactical game playing. As Avis (2000) puts it, there is a way in which we manage/police ourselves while recognising the contradictions. There were many examples of 'hedged' discourses and gestures (such as covering transparent door panels to avoid surveillance) that undermined the neoliberal view and articulated an alternative. For example, one of our interviewees, a mathematician (Alan Bradbury, Uni B), started talking about "useless writing", clarifying this as "writing you don't want to do", and how differently he experiences this from the subject-related writing that he enjoys, which is under his own control rather than demanded of him, and on which his academic reputation depends. In our data, refusal to change existing practices mainly focused around digital technologies and the many entanglements of these in the moment-by-moment experience of academic life. One problematic area was that of the electronic marking of scripts, which "tied people to the screen" when they were used to fitting their marking into, for example, travelling time. Another was resistance to the spread of work into personal time because of the ubiquity of digital technologies. Gareth explains:

> 'For years, even when the Internet was around, I refused to learn how to log in to work email from home. I always tried to work a day a week at home and I used to be able to get on with very substantial things, whereas now, 50 per cent of it is constantly ... clearing out emails.' (Gareth Wareing, Maths, Uni A)

The following example refers to resistance to using social media but the underlying issue is about a change to scholarship and the academics' role:

> 'It's become this bit of unspoken pressure, perhaps, or self-imposed pressure, maybe, as well. You see other people doing it and you wonder, "Should I be doing that as well?" … One of the people in another faculty, that's his job, to help people [enterprise officer] … getting academics presented in the media and so on, getting people grants from the government on partnership, or enterprise. I had some interesting discussions with him. He's quite frustrated with academics because they didn't welcome him with open arms. I said to him, "You have to understand the context of what's going on here. This feels like a dumbing down, or like the increased managerial culture in higher education". There's a bit of implied pressure … you're not really doing your job properly unless you use Twitter to publicise it.' (Ian Fairclough, Maths, Uni A)

While some of the workarounds that people described may negatively affect students and other colleagues, there are other, more positive, aspects of resistance where academics organise their work in relation to alternative, strongly held principles, even when these are not rewarded by the neoliberal university. For example, participants talked about extensive service-related activities within and beyond the immediate institution:

> 'Everyone has an admin role, a teaching role and a research role. That's what I do. I have two external roles as well. I'm an external examiner at University X, a Vice Chair at a professional management organisation and I'm on the Advisory Board of Journal X and on various editorial boards as well … it's what we call working for the community. That's what you do for free really.' (Diane Simmons, Marketing, Uni A)

Many attached a high value to collaborative relationships (including with support staff), which are widely and actively sought out:

> 'we set up a small group, which included people from ISS [Information Services Section] and the library and so on,

> to try to support students' learning between the lectures, using things like reflective diaries and online discussion forums and so on … that was interesting and I find the people I was working with really helpful, people from the library and so on.' (Don Robinson, History, Uni A)

> 'I enjoy interaction with colleagues of different generations, especially some of the younger people, who bring in perspectives that might seem unfamiliar, or surprising, or exciting.' (Collin Whitworth, History, Uni C)

Spending time on mentoring and providing positive care to students was felt by some to be an important and rewarding aspect of their role, though this was not widely acknowledged by the institution: "I like the teamwork aspects with PhD students. I like the nurturing aspect of teaching to research and write" (Gareth Wareing, Maths, Uni A); "I would say, yes, teaching is probably the aspect that I love most" (Robyn Alexos, Maths Uni C). The university, of course, benefits greatly from these activities, so as forms of resistance, they are unlikely to change the conditions that undervalue the time and effort put into them.

Conclusions and speculations

Changes taking place in the UK university sector impact strongly on the day-to-day experience, relationships and identities of academic staff. In our data, these changes are tracked through the conversations we had with academics about their writing practices, which are central aspects of creating value for the employing university, as well as being a marker of professional endeavour and satisfaction for individual academics. Our participants told us about positive aspects of these changes in terms of flexible working, the availability of new resources and collaborations. However, the pace of work and volume of demands made on people's time has accelerated. The entanglement of these practices in new management and target-driven cultures, new forms of digital communication, and a diversifying student body sets up pressures and stresses to the system that academics manage more or less successfully, and at considerable cost to themselves.

As a relatively privileged professional sector, academics have not traditionally seen themselves as an exploited workforce. In the English higher education system, many senior academics take on management and administrative roles within the institution and beyond, so that their loyalties may be divided in complex ways. In addition, there are strong disciplinary identities, communities and vocational commitments that academics adhere to beyond their immediate employment.

The academics we spoke to seemed to see the problems and tensions that they faced as ones that should be solved by them as individuals. They feared for their hard-won status and a potential career to which they were highly committed. There seemed to be little sense of shared experience. Indeed, many of the organised consultative forums and shared spaces (such as staffrooms) for academics to air their working problems have been removed from universities. These discussion spaces can act as safety valves in stressful situations but their loss also means that academics are excluded from processes of decision-making and information-sharing about how change is achieved. The arcane governance of universities is opaque to most academics, communicated through the dry technical papers of senate and council meetings, which are rarely read. However, the implications of what look like tiny, inconsequential changes to committees and appointment processes can be crucial in moving neoliberal agendas forward.

All these factors contribute to the fact that visible evidence of collective resistance to the neoliberal university has been sparse and piecemeal compared with the organised struggles that have occurred in other workplaces. Nevertheless, there is plenty of evidence in our data of varied resistance at the micro-interactional level of workarounds, sabotage and subversive uses of language, what Lilja et al (2017) call 'hacking the system'.

Just after our study concluded, an unprecedented collective action took place in UK universities, well supported and strategically organised around proposals to reduce pension benefits. The strike gained support from students and international colleagues. Banners on picket lines, statements on social and other media, and 'teachouts' expressed high levels of discomfort and wider frustration with the directions in which universities are moving. The concept of 'everyday resistance', as proposed and documented in many contexts by Scott and others, helps us to understand these events and to see the dissatisfactions and stresses expressed to us in our data as the creaking of a system that suddenly fractured into visible collective anger.

A great deal of accelerated learning happened during the strike, as is commonplace in social movements everywhere – learning about the universities as employers and organisations, as well as their motives, structures, forms of governance and decision-making. New discourses developed as 'hidden transcripts' became visible and were further articulated in public spaces. Armed with the knowledge gained from this recent industrial action, and a new sense of solidarity and community, it will be interesting to see whether this action changes strategies of resistance within higher education in the longer term or whether, as before, academics will return to accommodate themselves, uneasily, to the neoliberal university.

Note

1 Economic and Social Research Council Grant 2015–2107 Ref: ES/L01159X/1.

References

Avis, J. (2000) 'Policing the subject: Learning outcomes, managerialism and research in PCET', *British Journal of Educational Studies*, 48(1): 38–57.

Ball, S.J. (2012) 'Performativity, commodification and commitment: An I-spy guide to the neoliberal university', *British Journal of Educational Studies*, 60(1): 17–28.

Barnett, R. (2000). 'University knowledge in an age of supercomplexity', Higher Education, 40(4): 409–22.

Carrigan, M. (2015) 'Life in the accelerated academy: Anxiety thrives, demands intensify and metrics hold the tangled web together', LSE Impact of the Social Sciences Blog.

Deem, R., Hillyard, S., Reed, M. and Reed, M. (2007) *Knowledge, higher education, and the new managerialism: The changing management of UK universities*, Oxford: Oxford University Press.

Edwards, R., Fenwick, T. and Sawchuk, P. (2015) *Emerging approaches to educational research: Tracing the socio-material*, London: Routledge.

Fleming, P. (2016) 'Resistance and the "post-recognition" turn in organizations', *Journal of Management Inquiry*, 25(1), 106-110.

Goffman, E. (1959) *The presentation of self in everyday life*, Garden City, NY: Anchor.

Goodfellow R. and Lea M. (eds) (2013), *Literacy in the digital university: Critical perspectives on learning, scholarship, and technology*, London: Routledge, pp 67–78.

Johansson, A. and Vinthagen, S. (2016) 'Dimensions of everyday resistance: An analytical framework', *Critical Sociology*, 42(3): 417–35.

Kelly, U., McNicoll, I. and White, J. (2014) *The impact of universities on the UK economy*, London: Universities UK.

Kinman, G. and Jones, F. (2003) '"Running up the down escalator": Stressors and strains in UK academics', *Quality in Higher Education*, 9(1): 21–38.

Lilja, M., Baaz, M., Schulz, M. and Vinthagen, S. (2017) 'How resistance encourages resistance: Theorizing the nexus between power, "organised resistance" and "everyday resistance"', *Journal of Political Power*, 10(1): 40–54.

Macfarlane, B. (2006) *The academic citizen: The virtue of service in university life*, London: Routledge.

Olssen, M. and Peters, M.A. (2005) 'Neoliberalism, higher education and the knowledge economy: From the free market to knowledge capitalism', *Journal of Education Policy*, 20(3): 313–45.

Radice, H. (2013) 'How we got here: UK higher education under neoliberalism', *ACME: An International Journal for Critical Geographies*, 12(2): 407–18.

Robertson, S.L. (2008) '"Remaking the world": Neoliberalism and the transformation of education and teachers' labor', in Weiner, L., & Compton, M. (eds) *The global assault on teaching, teachers, and their unions: Stories for resistance*, New York: Palgrave Macmillan US, pp 11–27.

Scott, J.C. (1992) *Domination and the arts of resistance: Hidden transcripts*, New aven, CT, and London: Yale University Press.

Shain, F. and Gleeson, D. (1999) 'Under new management: Changing conceptions of teacher professionalism and policy in the further education sector', *Journal of Education Policy*, 14(4): 445–62.

Sum, N. L., and Jessop, B. (2013) 'Competitiveness, the knowledge-based economy and higher education', *Journal of the Knowledge Economy*, 4(1), 24-44.

Times Higher Education (2018) 'The USS strike and the winter of academics' discontent', 12 April.

Tusting, K., McCulloch, S., Bhatt, I., Hamilton, M. and Barton, D. (2019) *Academics writing: The dynamics of knowledge creation*, London: Routledge.

Winter, R.P. and O'Donohue, W. (2012) 'Academic identity tensions in the public university: Which values really matter?', *Journal of Higher Education Policy and Management*, 34(6): 565–73.

10

Moving against and beyond neoliberal higher education in Ireland

Fergal Finnegan

Introduction

Irish higher education (HE) offers an interesting case study of both the transformative power and limits of neoliberalism. In many respects, Ireland is one of the most neoliberal countries in Europe, and as one of the so-called 'PIIGS' (Portugal, Ireland, Italy, Greece and Spain), it was also one of the states that was hardest hit by the 'Great Recession'. Although neoliberalism has also been resisted in significant ways inside and outside the university, most of the literature on the topic in Ireland focuses almost exclusively on the power, reach and hold of neoliberal ideas. With this in mind, the primary aim of this chapter is to offer a less 'one-sided' account and to document how neoliberalism has, and continues to be, resisted by staff and students in HE in multiple ways. Of particular interest here is how 'everyday' practices and values (De Certeau, 1984) that are not explicitly political might be understood in relation to more formal political acts of resistance.

Taking a radical, critical realist perspective (Jessop, 2012; Sayer, 2015), I will use empirical and documentary research on resistance and explore how these hidden or 'marginal' practices might be drawn upon to re-imagine the university as a space in which we can move against and beyond neoliberalism. As Barnett (2013) argues, an analysis of any such alternative requires close attention to the conditions and constraints on action in a given context and period as they operate at various scales and levels. Thus, the chapter begins with a socio-historical analysis of neoliberalism as both a global and national phenomenon, as well as the specific ways in which this has shaped Irish HE, in order to make full sense of the everyday and political resistance of staff and students described and analysed in the second and third sections.

Taking the measure of neoliberalism

Neoliberalism has become, over time, what the geographer Jamie Peck (2013: 133) has called 'an unloved, rascal concept', that is to say, it has become a highly elastic and often analytically overstretched term, used as a catch-all term for everything that is negative and disempowering. There is now an all too familiar mode of analysis of neoliberal politics that offers a melancholy and dystopian vision of a 'totally administered world'. The indiscriminate use of the word 'neoliberalism' in the media and parts of academia has led to a reaction against the term and resulted in highly scholastic debates over the precision and saliency of the concept. However, from a historical perspective, either treating neoliberalism as a measureless dark Leviathan or solely focusing on the conceptual haziness of the term is odd. It is worth recalling that the concept was first popularised by alternative globalisation activists from Latin America, most notably, by the Zapatistas in Mexico, who wanted to highlight significant changes in international socio-political conditions and tackle the idea that 'There is no alternative' to the current social system head on. We certainly need modes of analysis that move beyond sterile scholasticism or immobilising pessimism.

Nevertheless, it would be a mistake to downplay the structural depth and power of neoliberalism, or the difficulties of effectively challenging it. What we now call 'neoliberalism' emerged in an incremental fashion in the early 1970s as an elite response to the disintegration of the Fordist regime of accumulation and growing concerns about social order in the face of the demands of radical social movements. It has since become a truly global phenomenon linked to the political, cultural, economic and spatial reorganisation of capital in the 1980s and 1990s (Brenner et al, 2010; Peck, 2013). As Andrew Sayer (2015: 16–18, emphasis in original) argues, it has three major characteristics. First, '*markets are assumed to be the optimal or default form of economic organisation* and to work best with the minimum of regulation'. This is underpinned by the idea that the role of the state is to provide the economic and regulatory conditions that favour capital and maximise profitability. Second, 'the rise of neoliberalism also involves *a political and cultural shift* compatible with its market fundamentalism'. This can be understood as a bid to define a new 'common sense' in which 'through a host of small changes in everyday life, we are increasingly nudged into thinking and acting in ways that fit with market rationality'. Of particular importance in terms of everyday culture has been the promotion of competitive individualism and the rise of an audit culture obsessed with measuring efficiency and performance. As a political project, it has been defined by sustained attacks on collectivist movements and institutions, especially of the organised working class. Third, 'neoliberalism has ushered in a shift in the economic class structure of the countries most affected. It involves not only the shift of power and wealth towards the rich but also within the rich.' This has primarily been driven by the financialisation of the economy. The impact and importance of this cannot be underestimated, and debt levels have soared not only at a nation-state level, but also for individuals, households and non-financial firms (Lapavitsas, 2013).

Yet, as Brenner et al (2010) note, the application and development of neoliberal ideas through time and across space is highly variegated, contingent and often contested. It is therefore more accurate to speak of uneven processes of *neoliberalisation* rather than the unfolding of a unified programme. Grasping how these multi-scalar and multileveled processes are sometimes disrupted, blocked or altered, creating pockets of resistance and loosely bound spaces in which emergent practices based on other values can flourish, is crucial to understanding resistance in contemporary HE.

The neoliberalisation of Irish society and education

Neoliberal policies have been driving socio-economic development in the Irish Republic since the late 1980s. Following Kirby (2010), I want to acknowledge the distinct historical trajectory of Irish society but contend that the state now operates as a 'market state' oriented to the priorities of corporations and large businesses. In terms of economic policy, this has been reflected in 'light-touch' regulation, low levels of corporate taxation and the marketisation and, to a lesser extent, privatisation of public goods of various sorts, such as water and waste disposal (Allen, 2007). Since the 1980s, there has been significant growth of 'knowledge economy' industries, such as technology, pharmaceuticals and biotechnology. Ireland is currently the second-most economically globalised economy in the world (KOF Index of Globalisation, 2017) and is highly financialised and very dependent on foreign direct investment, especially from the US (McCabe, 2011). As a result, Ireland has become a small but important node in an Atlantic economy, which is peculiarly sensitive to global economic shocks.

Ireland has also become more unequal since the 1980s (Allen 2010; Kirby, 2010). There has been a diminution in the social wage, as measured through wages, pensions and social welfare, and a concomitant increase in the level of private profit. Allen (2010: 26) calculates that the adjusted wage share for employees dropped from

71 per cent of gross domestic product (GDP) in the 1980s to 54 per cent between 2001 and 2007. There has been very little systematic research undertaken on wealth inequality in Ireland, but Credit Suisse data (Brennan, 2017) indicate that, today, as much as 32 per cent of the wealth is held by 1 per cent of the population and the richest 10 per cent control 65.8 per cent of the country's wealth.

Despite decreased control over significant aspects of economic decision-making and rising inequality, throughout this period, Irish policymakers have used corporatist, consensual rhetoric that links the market to notions of meritocracy, modernisation *and* social equality. Moreover, the boom in the 1990s allowed the government to increase public spending in some areas while implementing neoliberal reforms. A high rate of employment, rising levels of income and the promotion of a 'social partnership' in which unions and representatives of civil society were consulted on national policy meant that for most of this period, there was relatively little popular resistance to neoliberalisation.

The crisis and bank bailout in 2010, which cost €64 billion, radically changed the situation in Ireland. The government implemented austerity measures, which were overseen and partially devised by the Troika (the International Monetary Fund [IMF], the European Commission and the European Central Bank). Unemployment grew by 10 per cent and the workforce shrunk by 14 per cent, wages collapsed, and 'fiscal control' and 'budgetary restraint' became the watchwords of the day. As Finn (2017) remarks, by 2015, '475,000 people had left since the crisis began, and 17.5 percent of Irish-born people over the age of fifteen lived outside the state'. Once the initial shock wore off, this led to a wave of protests against neoliberalism and austerity.

As might be expected, the reconfiguration of the Irish state, the influence of European Union (EU) and Organisation for Economic Co-operation and Development (OECD) directives, and international trends in HE led to a clear 'neoliberal turn' in HE over the past two decades (Fleming et al, 2017). While there has been relatively little privatisation and for-profit consortia remain minor players in HE, neoliberal ideas now inform policy, funding models and management culture, and have encouraged the outsourcing of on-campus services (Lynch et al, 2015; Fleming et al, 2017; Mercille and Murphy, 2017). Interviews conducted with senior management and an analysis of key policy documents reveal a clear trend towards less institutional and professional autonomy and the concomitant development of new managerial techniques and practices for assessing performance (O'Malley, 2012; Lynch et al, 2015).

The neoliberalisation of HE has intensified under austerity (Mercille and Murphy, 2017); the state has radically decreased direct funding to HE while student numbers have continued to increase and staff numbers have declined (student to staff ratios went from 16:1 in 2008 to 20:1 in 2015) (see Cassells, 2016: 19). Some of the shortfall has been made up through the reintroduction of fees and there is currently much talk of introducing a student loan scheme. Besides this, there has been an increasing emphasis in policy on making universities more responsive to the needs of business and on tightening links with the private sector (Fleming et al, 2017). The appointment of business people to senior positions in the Higher Education Authority, the state body that oversees the sector, as well as to policy advisory groups, has consolidated this shift (Mercille and Murphy, 2017). Consequently, the key strategy document in Irish HE (DES, 2011), which outlines a plan for the future development of HE up to 2030, is markedly neoliberal in its aims and values.

This macro-level policy shift is reflected, and mediated, on a meso level as well. Individual HE institutions have been extensively 'reformed' by the extension of market logic through cost–benefit analysis and the application of performativity measures in every part of university life (Lynch et al, 2015). There have also been a number of expensive branding exercises as HE institutions seek to position themselves in relation to national and international competitors.

Everyday and political resistance to neoliberal HE

The application of neoliberal ideas in a state-funded system has given rise to new hybrid forms of policy and procedures that have certainly impacted on teaching, learning and research. Yet, it is striking just how much resistance to neoliberalism there has been, especially since the crisis. However, this is rarely noted and hardly ever researched, and there is a tendency to foreground the power of neoliberalism and the extent to which it has captured hearts and minds and lament a 'university in ruins'. I think, though, that it is important to remember that HE is a layered, contradictory social institution and a symbolic and cultural space where ideas, practices and values that are not commensurable with neoliberalism are very firmly rooted. Cultural 'sediments' of the pre-neoliberal university remain influential in a system that has also been qualitatively and quantitatively transformed over the past 30 years through rapid expansion (student numbers have tripled since the late 1980s). HE has become both a crucial site of accumulation for a knowledge-based economy (Jessop, 2012) and widely envisaged as a space of free inquiry, public dialogue and human development. The new social centrality of HE – linked to conflicting and contradictory social forces – in institutions that have evolved over a long time is crucial to understanding HE in a neoliberal era.

However, the possibilities that exist within such a layered and contradictory situation are easy to overlook if we approach it *solely* on a structural and systemic level of analysis. It is important not to overlook the undramatic, but often creative, forms of 'everyday' and political resistance within and at the edges of the university. As De Certeau (1984: 34) points out, people are frequently 'poets in their own affairs', who know how to escape, circumvent and tactically adapt to a dominant logic in culture and institutions. With this in mind, I want to now discuss how staff and students orient themselves and act within HE on a day-to-day basis, drawing on several empirical research projects (Fleming et al, 2010; Finnegan and O'Neill, 2015; Finnegan et al, 2014). These studies on student experience, retention and employability comprise of one mixed-methods (Fleming et al, 2010) and two large-scale qualitative projects (Finnegan and O'Neill, 2015; Finnegan et al, 2014). For these, we conducted 200 in-depth interviews with HE students and graduates, and 40 interviews with staff. However, I also want to draw on documentary research in order to describe the range of ways in which neoliberalism has been politically contested and to explore how everyday and political resistance might be linked.

HE staff: disciplinary passions, critical values and workplace organising

It was noticeable how rarely the staff we met described their work in neoliberal terms. Disciplinary passions remain crucial for many lecturers' sense of identity and purpose. For example, several lecturers, mainly in the social sciences, said that fostering critical reflection on established mores and values was central to their discipline and their teaching. Stephen, a science lecturer, spoke of his passion for his subject and his dedication to encouraging the same passion in others. He was critical of the shift towards funding for scientific research with clear and immediate market applications as he thinks that this is undermining the future development of his field. He devotes a great deal of time and effort to teaching and research conversations that are meaningful for him as a scientist and expressed disinterest in effective networking or winning funding for career purposes despite being in precarious employment conditions. This sort of everyday resistance was also discernible among non-academic staff. For instance, social justice mattered a great deal to staff in access and guidance, who described how they sought to use the dominant language of targets and metrics to support students for this 'deeper' purpose.

These values and commitments often explicitly inform how research and external engagement is approached as well. For example, some interviewees had sometimes done work on inequality and the impact of austerity in collaboration with trade unions, community groups and non-governmental organisations (NGOs). If one looks beyond the interview cohort, it is clear that a small but not insignificant portion of academics have used their specific skills to do 'movement'-relevant research for public campaigns against neoliberalism (for example, on housing policies, the privatisation of water, corporate tax avoidance and the appropriation of natural resources).

There are even degree programmes within the 'entrepreneurial university' where developing academic–activist alliances against neoliberalism is integral to the course. The ones that I am most familiar with are the courses run by the School of Social Justice in University College Dublin and the Masters in Community Education, Equality and Social Activism (CEESA) at Maynooth University. In both cases, staff have had extensive interaction with community groups and political movements, including popular education efforts related to neoliberalism and austerity over the past decade. While this only shaped the experience of hundreds of students and a few dozen academics, such efforts did, and do, create a space for research and social action that is explicitly at odds with neoliberalism.

There is, of course, more visible workplace organising going on as well. The main trade unions in HE have all, in various ways, sought to resist the neoliberalisation of HE. Most of the work has been defensive (that is, specific disputes over contracts and resources), but it also included a one-day strike in 2016 to push the state to acknowledge the extent of the crisis in HE and a broad campaign run between 2013 and 2015 to 'Defend the University' based on a charter that rejected the commercialisation and commodification of education.

Many, for the most part, young and early-career, academics feel that the established trade unions have not done enough to highlight the increasing level of precarity in academic work (Courtois and O'Keefe, 2015). As noted earlier, austerity measures affected the sector very badly, not least in blocking access to meaningful career paths. As a result, in the midst of the crisis, Third Level Workplace Watch was established. They describe themselves as a:

> collective of precarious workers organising to defend our rights to fair wages and working conditions. We wish to make explicit the university workplace as site of struggle.... We feel any discussions on the third-level sector must first and foremost address the casualisation of labour and exploitative workplace practices that allow universities and colleges to function. (Third Level Workplace Watch, no date)

Throughout the crisis up until 2017, the group organised meetings, did independent research on working conditions, lobbied trade unions, published articles in popular and academic forums, networked internationally, and took a series of 'agitprop' actions to generate publicity.

Student lives and student activism

One of the common critiques of the neoliberal university is that it invites students to see themselves as self-interested and instrumentally minded clients and consumers (Lolich and Lynch, 2017). However, while the students we met were certainly seeking upward social mobility, the values and motivations of these people were neither simply individualistic nor straightforwardly instrumental. Among mature students, "becoming more of yourself" (Rachel) was seen as one of the main benefits of attending university. Among younger students, HE was also described as a vital liminal space for learning and for forging relationships, as well as the basis for a career. For many working-class students, going to HE was seen as a valued opportunity to have time for formal learning for its own sake. It was also seen as an opportunity to undo prior misrecognition: "to prove them wrong", as Terry put it (in this case, he was talking about teachers and negative evaluations of him as a working-class man generally). Frequently, students and graduates said that social science courses offered them words and concepts that allowed them to name their world, to understand why certain communities are "overlooked" (Chloe), to try to tackle inequality and to also 'give something back' to their communities. Being in HE was repeatedly linked to profound explorations of worth, identity and meaningfulness. As a result, people were willing to make enormous sacrifices in terms of security and financial stability to get their degree, which simply does not make sense in 'purely' economic terms. A survey of 4,265 students (Lolich and Lynch, 2017) indicates that this multidimensional way of valuing the university and the everyday practice that flows from this is very widespread.

The high value given to education also led a small number of the interviewees to take part in the explosion of political activity by student groups and students unions against the reintroduction of fees from 2008 onwards. As part of this, the student group Free Education for Everyone, which included activists from eight HE institutions, engaged in a campaign of civil disobedience (sit-ins, blockades, pickets and demonstrations). Student unions went on to develop a national campaign against fees and for publicly funded HE, which resulted in large demonstrations of tens of thousands for several years. This is by far the largest and most visible wave of resistance against neoliberal HE, and was a vital part of the learning story given by these interviewees. In the midst of the crisis, this also resulted in an attempt to link students, graduates, the unemployed and young, especially precarious, workers in a campaign called 'We are not leaving'.

Troubling the boundaries: re-imagining the university

There has also been a series of small initiatives to re-imagine the university and find new terms for thinking about the purpose of HE in relation to the activity of wider social movements. The first is 'Occupy University', an offshoot of the Occupy movement. As is well known, the protests in Wall Street during 2011–12 sparked similar events in 950 cities. In Dublin, a camp was set up on Dame Street at the Central Bank Plaza that lasted from October 2011 until March 2012. Szolucha (2013: 23), an ethnographer who was based in Occupy Dame Street, notes that:

> The camps were structured and operated in ways that could prefigure communities in which people would like to live in the future. The direct democratic ways of making decisions may provide some clues as to how to facilitate more democratic ways of self-governance.

Significantly, this included an 'Occupy University' made up of academics, students and activists. The collective organised over 78 talks in the first two months, mainly from a radical perspective. In a contemporaneous report (Burtenshaw, 2012), an academic who was heavily involved, Helena Sheehan, explained:

> The kind of discussions we really needed weren't happening in our universities and that was a big encouragement to us.... What we did, I feel, stands up intellectually. It was of a more rough and ready, certainly less standardised, variety than university lectures.... But we tackled big ideas in difficult circumstances.

This continued for over a year. Interestingly, after the camp lost direction and energy, the group sought to connect with other movements, including a community television station, and hosted and broadcast lectures on radical history.

A project that similarly sought to re-imagine the university was the 'Provisional University' project. This collective of mainly young academic-activists, alongside students, worked between 2010 and 2016. Influenced by international debates on the changing nature of the university, a flavour of their aims and approach can be gleaned from the following statement (Provisional University, no date)

> In the university and the city processes of exclusion and exploitation multiply. These processes are the effect of the governing neoliberal logic: university competes with university, city competes with city, and so are we forced into a competition that generates fewer and fewer winners, more and more losers. As well as excluding those who are unable to play the game, the logic of competition erodes and dismantles the public goods and services that we rely on.... This does not just come in the form of privatizing and marketizing public resources and institutions, but also through the individualization and precaritization of many aspects of our lives: the ways we are forced to see and act as entrepreneurs, against one another.

The project took the form of meetings, pieces of movement-relevant research and publications, and put a very strong emphasis on finding more democratic ways of producing knowledge. As is often the case, these initiatives rely on small groups of individuals and specific contexts, and the project slowly wound down when members were drawn into other campaigns and the demands of paid work.

Building alliances and emergent possibilities

Neoliberalism has been described as a highly variegated phenomenon that has reshaped Irish society in very significant ways, and these ideas have become dominant ones in HE at a policy and management level. Yet, this has provoked widespread, albeit mainly diffuse, resistance within and at the boundaries of HE. Sometimes, this has flared into view but much was 'under the radar'. However, it is significant that in a highly neoliberal country crippled by crisis and austerity, where HE is underfunded and increasingly envisaged in marketised terms, a great deal of teaching, learning, research, access work and career guidance, and workplace organising in HE has sought to confront or tactically circumvent the dominant logic. The range and vitality of this activity should not be discounted. We know, though, that neoliberalism is a deeply rooted, transnational phenomenon, and that the level and type of everyday and political resistance discussed here has not been sufficient to alter the general direction that HE is taking, let alone that of society as a whole.

To reflect on this, I want to turn to Raymond Williams (1977), who argued that it was useful to distinguish dominant from residual or emergent meanings, values and practices in critical historical analysis. He describes residual culture as 'effectively formed in the past, but it is still active in the cultural process' (Williams, 1977: 122), and emergent culture as that which carries 'new meanings and values, new practices, new relationships' (Williams, 1977: 123). Using this framework, I can say that although the dominant culture in HE is clearly neoliberal, this interacts with, and is being resisted through, a variety of emergent and residual cultures. I think that the idea of disinterested scientific inquiry, critical social science and the humanist idea of education for personal development discussed earlier are examples of such residual ideals. As we have seen, these feed into 'tactical' everyday forms of action and also sustain political resistance of various sorts. The idea of education as a public good and a belief in the non-commodifiable nature of organised learning and inquiry appear to be especially important.

However, within and at the edges of the university, there are also emergent forms of critical culture that perhaps offer coordinates for higher education *beyond* neoliberalism. Initiatives such as the Provisional University and Occupy sought a new type of democratic relationship between students and lecturers, were self-consciously internationalist, and explicitly linked education to wider social movements. Here, the university is viewed as a potential space for the elaboration of new forms of democratic knowledge production beyond the terms that have predominated in the past or prevail in the present. The desire is to free knowledge from old hierarchies and recent commodification in order to develop a knowledge 'commons'. In this way, such groups, however fitfully, are beginning to puzzle out how we can best respond to the changing, and changed, political circumstances in which we live.

In Ireland and internationally – in Chile, South Africa, Québec and the UK – the debate over the purpose and funding of HE is now a central and potentially explosive social question. Defensive actions by institutionally embedded groups, which draw sustenance from a conception of HE elaborated within social democracy, can – at best I think – only offset the worst effects of neoliberalism. The social forces and political compromises that made this possible have simply disappeared. However, future-oriented versions of the university that have little or no institutional purchase and do not have the backing of large-scale social movements are destined to fade away as well, leaving only faint traces of activity. As neoliberalism unravels, we need to be able to learn from previous waves of resistance in HE. To move beyond the diverse but limited, relatively fragmented resistance discussed earlier, I think that we will need to build alliances and dialogue between individuals and groups who draw from these residual and emergent cultures. The task, then, I think, is to elaborate a new vision of the university that draws critically on the widely shared belief in the non-commodifiable nature of education and builds on the idea of a knowledge commons in order to imagine new forms of HE altogether (Alcántara et al, 2013).

Acknowledgements

I wish to thank Mariya Ivacheva for her help and advice, and Niamh McCrea, Bernie Grummell and Kathleen Lynch for rich conversations.

References

Alcántara, A., Llomovatte, S. and Romão, J. (2013) 'Resisting neoliberal common sense in higher education: Experiences from Latin America', *International Studies in Sociology of Education*, 23(2): 127–51.

Allen, K. (2007) *The corporate takeover of Ireland*, Dublin: Irish Academic Press.

Allen, K. (2010) 'The trade unions: From partnership to crisis', *Irish Journal of Sociology*, 18(2): 22–37.

Barnett, R. (2013) *Imagining the university*, Abingdon and Oxon: Routledge.

Brennan, J. (2017) 'Swiss bank reveals Ireland has 125,000 dollar millionaires', *Irish Times*, 20 November.

Brenner, N., Peck, J. and Theodore, N. (2010) 'Variegated neoliberalization: Geographies, modalities, pathways', *Global Networks*, 10(2): 1–41.

Burtenshaw, R. (2012) 'Occupy University and rebel political education', *University Times*. Available at: www.universitytimes.ie/2012/02/reclaiming-the-tools-of-resistance-occupy-university-and-rebel-political-education/ (accessed 24 November 2017).

Cassells, P. (2016) *Investing in ambition: A strategy for funding HE*, Dublin: HEA.

Courtois, A. and O'Keefe, T. (2015) 'Precarity in the ivory cage: Neoliberalism and casualisation of work in the Irish higher education sector', *Journal for Critical Education Policy Studies*, 13(1): 43–66.

De Certeau, M. (1984) *The practice of everyday life*, Berkeley, CA: University of California Press.

DES (Department of Education and Skills) (2011) *National strategy for higher education to 2030*, Dublin: DES.

Finn, D. (2017) 'Irish politics after the crash', *Catalyst*, 1(2). Available at: https://catalyst-journal.com/vol1/no2/irish-politics-finn (accessed 19 February 2018).

Finnegan, F. and O'Neill, J. (2015) 'A critical approach to employability', paper presented at the ESREA conference 'Continuity and discontinuity in learning careers', 25–27 November, University of Seville, Spain.

Finnegan, F., Merrill, B. and Thunborg, C. (eds) (2014) *Student voices on inequalities in European higher education*, London: Routledge.

Fleming, T., Loxley, A., Kenny, A. and Finnegan, F. (2010) *Where next? A study of work and life experiences of mature students in three higher education institutions*, Dublin: Combat Poverty Agency.

Fleming, T., Finnegan, F. and Loxley, A. (2017) *Access and participation in Irish higher education*, London: Palgrave Macmillan.

Jessop, B. (2012) 'A cultural political economy of competitiveness and its implications for higher education', in D.W. Livingstone and D. Guile (eds) *The knowledge economy and lifelong learning: A critical reader*, Rotterdam: SENSE, pp 57–83.

Kirby, P. (2010) *The Celtic tiger in collapse: Explaining the weaknesses of the Irish model* (2nd edn), Basingstoke: Palgrave Macmillan.

KOF Index of Globalisation (2017) 'Globalization rankings'. Available at: http://globalization.kof.ethz.ch/media/filer_public/2017/04/19/rankings_2017.pdf (accessed 14 January 2018).

Lapavitsas, C. (2013) *Profiting without producing: How finance exploits us all*, London and New York, NY: Verso.

Lolich, L. and Lynch, K. (2017) 'Aligning the market and affective self: Care and student resistance to entrepreneurial subjectivities', *Gender and Education*, 29(1): 115–31.

Lynch, K., Grummell, B. and Devine, D. (2015) *New managerialism in education: Commercialisation, carelessness and gender* (2nd edn), London: Palgrave Macmillan.

McCabe, C. (2011) *Sins of the fathers: Tracing the decisions that shaped the Irish economy*, Dublin: History Press.

Mercille, J. and Murphy, E. (2017) 'The neoliberalization of Irish higher education under austerity', *Critical Sociology*, 43(3): 371–87.

O'Malley, M. (2012) 'The university and the state in Ireland', unpublished EdD thesis, Maynooth University.

Peck, J. (2013) 'Explaining (with) neoliberalism', *Territory, Politics, Governance*, 1(2): 132–57.

Provisional University (no date) 'About us'. Available at: https://provisionaluniversity.wordpress.com/about-2/ (accessed 20 November 2017).

Sayer, A. (2015) *Why we can't afford the rich*, Bristol: The Policy Press.

Szolucha, A. (2013) 'No stable ground', *Interface: A Journal for and About Social Movements*, 5(2): 18–38.

Third Level Workplace Watch (no date) 'About us'. Available at: https://3lww.wordpress.com/about/ (accessed 22 December 2017).

Williams, R. (1977) *Marxism and literature*, Oxford: Oxford University Press.

PART IV

National perspectives

11

The appropriation of cultural, economic and normative frames of reference for adult education: an Italian perspective

Marcella Milana and Francesca Rapanà

Introduction

This chapter seeks to shed light on the complex dynamic that produces cultural, economic and normative frames of reference for popular adult education, a type of adult education that stimulates learners to critically appraise their lives, and to act to change social conditions (Arnold and Burke, 1983). The authors take the example of the *Università della Terza Età e del Tempo Disponibile* (University of the Third Age and Free Time) (UTETD), a public provider of popular education in the Autonomous Province of Trento (Italy), as an illustrative case of resistance to the dominant neoliberal discourse. Neoliberalism values adult education in the same way as any other goods that provide utility in a global market, resulting in decontextualised forms of provision that do not favour emancipatory learning.

Early European studies centred attention on the working of the European Union's (EU's) institutions, its outputs (that is, European policies) and their domestic implementation. Accordingly, research dealing with European education and lifelong learning policy was primarily concerned with the 'fabrication' of a European educational space (Nóvoa and Lawn, 2002), in an attempt to explain educational convergence (that is, the consequence of integration within Europe) or policy harmonisation (that is, the adjustment of differences in support of European integration).

However, since the late 1990s, domestic adaptation (rather than implementation) has come to serve as a broader concept in Europeanisation research, which comprises the study of administrative adaptation by (national) executive governments, other interest groups and civil society to new institutional opportunities and structures, and their normative consequences (Graziano and Vink, 2008). Accordingly, the study of domestic implementation has been slowly replaced by the study of domestic adaptation, which sought to uncover the direct and indirect effects exerting pressure on single countries towards European regional integration.

Among the direct effects are the adaptation of European legislation and other regulatory frameworks at the domestic level, like the Youth Guarantee agreed between the EU and its member states to ensure that young people under the age of 25 receive a quality offer of continued education, an apprenticeship or traineeship (when not employment), or the Upskilling pathways targeting adults with a low level of skills so that they can progress towards an upper-secondary qualification or equivalent through skills assessment, validation and recognition and/or participation in new learning opportunities. Among the indirect effects is increased cooperation. For instance, the introduction of the Open Method of Coordination in the field of education (Cort, 2008) and the setting up of working groups under the Education and Training 2020 strategic framework for cooperation combine to improve the exchange of information and mutual learning among, and well beyond, (national) executive governments so as to include political institutions, research institutions, adult education and learning institutions, civil society organisations, and other policy actors (Dale and Robertson, 2009).

All these factors have directed attention and resources to the promotion of adult education and learning within Europe, and to recognition that European discourses on, and the international steering of, adult education impact on the ways in which it is perceived, financed and regulated at the national level. This thus frames what opportunities may exist for adults to engage in intentional learning opportunities in their immediate surroundings.

It is equally important to recognise that the immediate surroundings of adults, even within a country, vary substantially, for instance, when they live in cities or villages, metropolitan or rural areas, or even mountain districts. Also, the cultural, economic and normative frames of reference for intentional learning opportunities to be made available to adult citizens vary across and within countries. This is especially evident in a country like Italy, which is historically characterised by large and persistent disparities in economic development between regions, and that has strengthened the financial autonomy of regional and local governments under the principle of subsidiarity inspired by the law of the EU (Groppi and Scattone, 2006).

Against this background, the authors focus on a public provider of popular adult education in the Autonomous Province of Trento (Italy) that resists the dominant neoliberal discourse. Physical, material or symbolic action that in some way challenges or subverts this discourse is what they call 'resistance' (Hollander and Einwohner, 2004). As an illustrative case, the public provider identified allows the authors to: (1) critically examine how cultural, economic and normative frames of reference that result from international–national–local interactions can be locally appropriated and (re)interpreted; and (2) understand what conditions may create spaces for physical, material or symbolic action that resists the dominant neoliberal discourse in popular adult education.

This chapter is structured in three sections. First, the authors outline how they conceptualise cultural, economic and normative frames of reference. They then present and examine UTETD as an illustrative case of resistance to the dominant neoliberal discourse. Finally, building on this analysis, the authors pinpoint a few actions that may open interstices for resistance by popular adult education providers, as well as policymakers, professionals and volunteers that support or are involved in popular adult education.

Frames of reference and the interstices of resistance

The concepts of 'frame', first introduced in psychiatry (Bateson, 1972), and that of 'frame analysis', developed in sociology (Goffman, 1974), have been widely used in the social sciences, and such multidisciplinary applications confirm the explicative strength of the 'frame' conception. At the same time, it makes the theoretical boundaries of this concept permeable, as shown by an exhaustive review of the concept by Porismita Borah (2011). For this reason, the authors take as their point of departure Erving Goffman's (1974) early conceptualisation to explain how a frame of reference is construed in this chapter.

Goffman (1974) argues that people cannot grasp reality as a whole; they can only experience reality through the sharing of basic 'frames' or 'schemata' of understanding. Thus, the primary function of a frame is to reduce the complexity of reality by constructing a system of meaning that makes mutual understanding between people involved in a communication possible. Accordingly, a frame is both a cognitive and an organisational apparatus. From this perspective, social activities are organised according to a series of rules, codes and conventions that represent the organisational premises of social realities (frames), which provide the context of meanings enabling participants to express a shared definition of the situation (Barisone, 2009).

Accordingly, the frame concept has been used especially in communication and media studies to analyse variations and changes in public opinion (Scheufele, 1999). Scholars interested in New Social Movements (NSMs) have also used this concept to study the ability of NSMs to mobilise people (Benford and Snow, 2000). Finally, frame analysis has also been used to understand policymaking processes and their dynamics. For instance, Martin Rein and Donald Schön (1996) argue that frame analysis is critical to the study of policy controversies as it helps to overcome the limits of widespread approaches building on policy rationality. Anna Triandafyllidou and Anastasio Fotiou (1998) further note that policy rationality cannot explain the adoption of the contradictory policy decisions that occur in real life. It is such occurrences, however, that 'remind us that the relevance of rationality in the process of policy-making is not only bounded, but also – when it does occur – highly dynamic and symbolically constructed' (Triandafyllidou and Fotiou, 1998: para 2.8).

In line with the views presented thus far, in this chapter, a frame of reference is construed as a cognitive and organisational apparatus that reduces the complexity of social reality, hence allowing shared understandings of a given situation. Rather than examining the ways in which certain frames of reference are produced or considering their prognostic effects, the authors acknowledge the existence of, and interplay between, different frames of reference that allow those involved to make sense of and communicate about popular adult education within the Italian context. Furthermore, a distinction is made between three types of frames: the cultural, the normative and the economic (see Figure 11.1).

The cultural frame gives meaning, and assigns values, to popular adult education as a context-, place- and time-specific experience. This frame alone, however, is not sufficient. It also needs a normative frame that legitimises popular adult education provision through a system of laws and regulations that, at different levels (European, national and local), allows the institution of popular adult education to function. Yet, without an economic frame that supports such an institution, popular adult education cannot exist as a form of educational provision. All three types of frame (cultural, normative and economic) are thus necessary for a public provider of popular adult education to be established and to remain in operation. It is the authors' argument that examining the interplay between cultural, normative and economic frames of reference can bring to light interstices where resistance is not 'surrender' (Žižek, 2007) to a neoliberal discourse.

Figure 11.1: Interplay between frames of reference

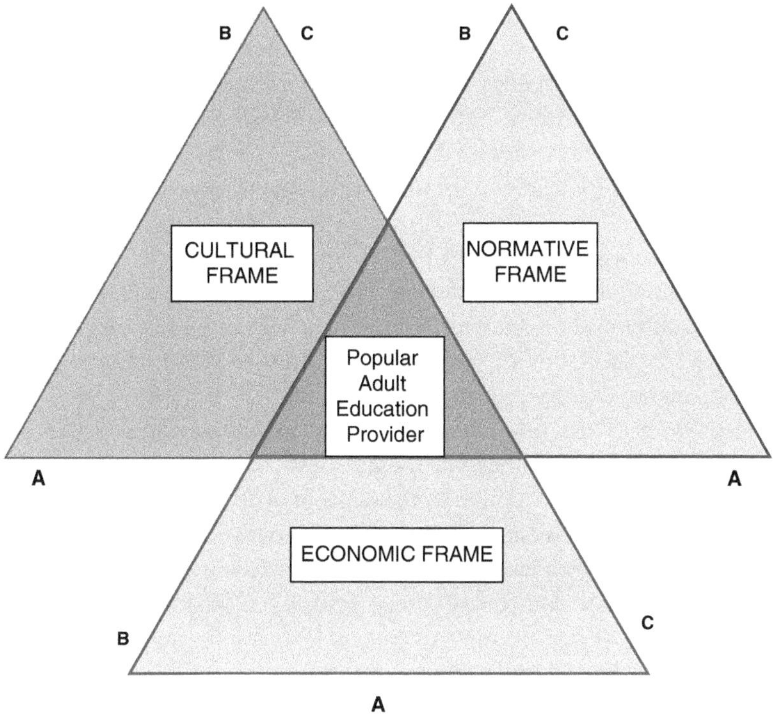

Legend:
A = Local dimension
B = National dimension
C = European dimension

An illustrative case of resistance

In a time when learning, and adult learning in particular, is almost exclusively characterised as a tool that enables people to be more competitive in the world of work, there are some experiences that escape this dominant discourse through an educational provision linked to personal development and a concept of well-being that is not reduced to its economic dimension, but nourished by concepts such as inclusion, participation and culture. To understand which conditions can favour the existence and development of such experiences, the authors focus on an educational provider of popular adult education, UTETD, still active today as part of the Franco Demarchi Foundation. Before looking at UTETD, however, it is necessary to offer a review of popular universities and their specific contribution to popular adult education more broadly conceived.

Popular universities and third-age universities

Popular adult education covers a multiplicity of educational experiences, with varied characteristics as regards to their objectives, programmes, participants and funding. Yet, popular universities, as a type of provider of popular education, present distinctive features that are common across countries. In particular, popular universities: operate in close cooperation with local authorities and are locally rooted; primarily address adults but can reach out to people of all ages; provide access to educational opportunities that are not restricted by people's formal qualifications; build mainly on the voluntary work of teachers and educators; and are financed by local bodies, associations and people's participation fees, which are usually low (Stromquist and Lozano, 2018). However, 'With the greying of the population in advanced industrialised countries, older persons have also become a significant concern.... Some popular universities in fact are inspired by the concept of "third age," which centre on the provision of educational experiences with a high entertainment content for older students' (Stromquist and Lozano, 2018: 787–8).

So-called third-age universities, such as UTETD, fall into the broader category of popular universities, and when compared with other providers of popular adult education, at least in Italy, they tend to be more structured and often represented by national associations (Tramma, 1996). Furthermore, this type of provider recognises that the elderly population, for different reasons than younger age groups, may find themselves in a situation of social exclusion and marginalisation due to factors such as the loss of autonomy, physical debilitation or poor schooling. Accordingly, their provision promotes health education, inspires intellectual as much as physical activity and artistic expression, and supports an active attitude to the local environment in which older adults live (Marcinkiewicz-Wilk, 2011).

The cultural, normative and economic frames of reference

UTETD is the second third-age university to have been established in Italy, and its inception in 1979 was characterised by the desire to be part of larger networks at both national and international levels. From its earliest stage, it became a member of the *Association Internationale des Universités du Troisième Age* (AIUTA), and promoted the establishment, in 1982, of the first national association of third-age universities (*Federazione Italiana tra le Università della Terza Età* [FEDERUNI]).

Some specifics of the Italian experience include the fact that UTETD is a private entity rather than a public one (as is usually the case in other

European countries), and aims at helping, through training, cultural and social promotion, and social participation, the establishment of stronger links with the local community and environment among all adults aged 35+ (although the learners' average age is around 65). The achievement of such aims is made possible by a cultural perspective that frames old age as not only a time for consolidating the existing, delaying decline and recovering what has been lost, but also for expanding, enriching, adding to and repositioning the self. In other words, the elderly condition is perceived as having a risk dimension, but also an often underestimated potential for change due to the disappearance or attenuation of family and professional ties. Thus, since its establishment, UTETD conceptualised older adults as 'people who, apart from production in the economic sense, become essential for production in a cultural sense, especially as a way of being, and therefore valuable personnel for the units of services, voluntary movements, and the community itself' (IRSRS, no date: 190, own translation).

However, the provincial territory of Trento[1] presents some distinctiveness from a national perspective: the capital city, Trento, is one of the two autonomous provinces of Italy and therefore enjoys a certain degree of legislative and financial independence. The provincial territory is mainly mountainous, with small towns spread chiefly in the valleys, from which it is not always easy to reach the capital city. Moreover, there are minority ethnic groups recognised and protected by the autonomous province and through dedicated public funding to preserve their cultures and languages.

For all of the aforementioned reasons, an additional element that characterises UTETD (when compared to other third-age universities) is its strong commitment to strengthening its links with the local environment, communities and authorities in order to avoid potentially interested adults being excluded from its provision due to the difficulty of accessing the capital city of Trento. This was done since its early days, when UTETD's ties with the local territory were created through the establishment of peripheral offices 'with the aim of reactivating the territorial conscience, threatened by the massification of culture' (IRSRS, no date: 190, own translation).

Today, UTETD has an office in Trento that, in addition to running its provision, acts as the headquarters for the entire structure, made up of 82 local branches, through which UTETD's cultural project is enacted through specific educational projects. UTETD's educational project foresees three kinds of actions (education, experimentation and socialisation), so that participants can grow as active protagonists of their lives while also being agents of community change. Accordingly, knowledge is not valued per se by UTETD, but is valued as a tool at the service of people, which supports people's capacity for reflection and critical thinking. It is such capacity that brings to maturity free and autonomous people who can choose and be engaged in crafting their own lives. These are the core cultural principles on which all UTETD's activities build.

However, the cultural frame of reference outlined thus far would not be enough to guarantee the existence and development of UTETD, which, in contrast to other popular universities operating in Italy, and universities of the third age particularly, has not experienced a reduction in the number of learner enrolments.[2] Therefore, the normative frame that gives legitimacy to UTETD's activity and the economic frame that guarantees its sustainability shall also be taken into due consideration.

As a regional state, similar to other federal systems, Italy's legislative power belongs to both the central state and the regions, whereas administrative functions are dispersed among national, regional and local governments. Hence, all levels of government collect taxes.

Since 1972, the Province of Trento has been regulated by a Statute of Autonomy and can, in fact, be equated to a small region. In addition to the usual regional taxes, its financing counts on the attribution of significant quotas (90 per cent or more) of all state taxes that remain in the provincial territory, and are used to finance, among other things, greater provincial powers for the protection and valorisation of culture and language, as well as in education. So, for instance, teachers are employed by the Autonomous Province of Trento, whereas they are employed by the Ministry of Education in the rest of the country.

Although it was created in 1979, since 2013, UTETD has turned into one of the three areas of institutional activity of the Franco Demarchi Foundation, originally the Regional Institute of Social Studies and Research (IRSRS). This institute was established in Trento in 1947 with the aim of educating social workers in the post-Second World War era, and was transformed into a public foundation by provincial law in 2012. Such a transformation was possible thanks to a provincial law that, since 2006, allows the Autonomous Province of Trento to promote and conclude financial agreements in support of public foundations that do research in social development, education, culture, vocational training and continuing education.

The 2013 statutes of the Franco Demarchi Foundation state that it 'pursues interests of a general nature and of public utility' by promoting and implementing (directly or indirectly) research and training in social, cultural and educational fields 'for the benefit of local communities and their development' and in support of public workers' and citizens' competences (Art 1, para 2, own translation). In line with this way of thinking about public utility, education and research are seen as integrated activities 'so that educational activity is constantly enriched by research results and, in turn, research can be stimulated and enriched by relations with the local environment and the communities of practices activated through education' (Art 1, para 2, own translation).

The meanings allocated to these activities are further specified in the preamble to the statutes, which stresses the strategic value of research and education to reinforcing a cohesive 'social fabric' that becomes aware of its human and economic resources, and is responsible for, as well as committed to enhancing all such resources for the good of all. Special emphasis is paid to the appeal that both research and education should have for older adults and younger generations, who, as citizens, should be aware of the need for capable people to develop 'non-superficial thinking and responsible participation' (Preamble, para 3, own translation). Moreover, the Foundation (and, by extension, UTETD's main office and territorial branches) identifies itself as 'a place for meeting, confrontation, reflection, innovation and assessment, open to all the subjects involved in the social, educational and cultural network: institutions, private individuals, volunteers, citizens, families' (Art 1, para 3, own translation).

In short, the Foundation, and UTETD as one of the three areas of its institutional activity, is framed by provincial norms that incorporate national and European ones, with their emphasis on lifelong learning. Yet, contrary to national and European norms, provincial ones reinterpret lifelong learning as an instrument for emancipation, outside of a strictly market-oriented logic. This broader interpretation is evidenced in additional provincial policies that support further interventions based on collaborations between public and private institutions in their respective areas of competence and for the purpose of social inclusion and the elimination of inequalities. Among these is Provincial Law No. 10 of 1 July 2013 in support of lifelong learning through the certification of competences, since it is an opportunity for people 'to improve their own competencies from the perspective of inclusive growth at personal, work, and social levels, and for professional mobility' (Art 1, para 2, own translation). In order to perform its activities, the Foundation signs programme agreements with public bodies other than the Autonomous Province of Trento, namely, the Federation of Cooperatives and the Municipality of Trento, which define the objectives to be pursued, the interventions and the objectives to be achieved, the economic resources, and the methods for assessing the results. Thanks to the programme agreements and registration fees charged to the learners, UTETD specifically has an active budget that allows it to pay those who work there and obtain a profit that is reinvested in training activities. Additional funding is obtained through public tenders at local, national and European levels.

Both these normative and economic frames help shape the specific character of UTETD when compared with other universities of the third age, in Italy and abroad, which are usually run by not-for-profit organisations and rely mostly on voluntarism (or quasi-voluntarism) on the part of teachers and trainers.

All of the foregoing impact on UTETD's provision in different ways. First, UTETD is spread over the provincial territory through its numerous local branches. Accordingly, its provision is available and easy for all to reach, well beyond the urban context of the capital city of Trento. Second, UTETD's teachers and trainers are qualified, paid staff and reimbursed for the expenses they face to reach the different local branches. Third, UTETD's overall provision covers a great variety of content knowledge, spanning the human and social to physical and natural sciences, which is delivered in different forms (courses, conferences, laboratories and so on). Additionally, over time, UTETD has developed a 'cultural programme' that, departing from the person as a unity, proposes different multidisciplinary pathways through their course catalogue for potential learners. Each pathway is organised around a thematic area. For example, in 2017/18 these were: self-care; languages, images and signs; thought, history, culture, memory and beliefs; the citizenship vocabulary; and the world seen through the eyes of science. This model allows for flexible modes of participation, among which the learners can choose the most suitable for his/her entry level of knowledge, interest and time availability.

Interstices for resistance for popular adult education

Drawing on the examination of the ways in which cultural, normative and economic frames are locally appropriated and (re)interpreted by a popular adult education provider, it is possible to bring to light a few interstices where resistance (for example, physical, material or symbolic action that challenges or subverts a certain discourse) is not 'surrender' to a neoliberal discourse. As stated earlier, neoliberal discourse values adult education in the same way as any other goods that provide utility in a global market. Consequently, it favours a physical detachment between teachers and learners through the promotion of teaching–learning transactions that occur at distance, for instance, through

Massive Open Online Course (MOOCs) and other information and communication technologies, which are detached from the sites and immediate surroundings in which adults live and interact with others, both within and outside educational locations. Critical voices, however, have stressed how the initial emphasis on the potential for widening adults' access to learning opportunities through MOOCs, for instance, has turned into an arguably less emancipatory opportunity (Speight, 2018). They have also stressed that technological integration for adult and older learners should follow a learner-centric rather than a technology-centric direction, which implies that teachers and educators should choose the most appropriate technology in response to the learners' needs. These needs should also guide decisions about whether teachers should promote 'knowledge as acquisition', 'learning as participation' or 'learning as knowledge' (Tan, 2018).

Action that does not 'surrender' to the physical detachments embedded in the neoliberal discourse privileges the identification and opening of multiple educational locations within the local environment under the foresight of an educational provider. Such action would guarantee physical access to all locations hosting educational activities, their physical proximity to potential learners and physical encounters between all those involved in the teaching–learning transactions.

Second, the neoliberal discourse brings with it the idea of the adult learner as consumer, hence supporting a decrease in public spending and a simultaneous increase in private funding for adult education. This constructs the adult learner as a citizen-customer, and adult education as a demand commodity. Once again, critical voices point to the condition of the adult learners as inherently social actors, with interests and aspirations that are fundamentally shared and collective (Martin, 2000). Research on public and popular adult education shows how the neoliberal discourse on individualisation also permeates this type of provision in ways that reinforce the shaping of individualised subjectivities among adult learners (Fejes at al, 2018).

Action that does not 'surrender' to considering material conditions as complimentary aspects for adult education secures the conditions for keeping multiple educational locations in operation. Such action would guarantee that the designing, planning and delivering of educational activities are the result of qualified and paid work. However, it would also guarantee that learners can participate in education activities at a reasonable individual investment in terms of both money and commuting time.

Last but not least, the neoliberal discourse brings to the fore 'vocationalisation' in contemporary policies and the provision of adult education at the expense of other epistemic and social meanings and functions that adult education embeds and accomplishes (Bagnall and Hodge, 2018). Action that does not 'surrender' to an instrumental vocationalisation of adult education also values adult education for its contribution to promoting culture, fostering the inclusion of adults (and older people particularly) in the social and cultural life of their local communities, and providing appropriate responses to the educational and learning needs of real, not idealised, citizens.

Conclusion

In this chapter, the authors acknowledge the existence of, and interplay between, different kinds of frames of reference (that is, cultural, normative and economic) that, operating at different levels (that is, local, national and international), allow those involved in popular adult education to make sense of, and communicate about, the special features of this kind of provision. Accordingly, they show that in order to understand what allowed a particular provider of popular adult education to be established and remain in operation for 40 years, one should take into account its context-, place- and time-specific cultural frame, as well as its interactions with the normative and economic frames that legitimised its establishment and made its activity sustainable over time. From this analysis, it was possible to identify some interstices for resistance to the dominant neoliberal discourse that, although drawing on one case study, could be an inspiration for policymakers, providers, professionals and volunteers that support or are involved in popular adult education more broadly conceived, both in Italy and elsewhere.

Notes

1 On 1 January 2017, there were 538,604 residents of the Autonomous Province of Trento, of which one fifth (117,703) lived in the capital city of Trento.

2 Over the years, UTETD has increased the number of seats and registered learners, which after growth during the 1990s, stabilised during the 2000s at an average of 6,500 registered learners per year. Despite the minimum age of access being 35 years, the majority of registered learners are 66–75, while the number of learners in the age group 35–55 is small (160 participants out of 6,349 in 2016/17). Gender differences are also significant, with a predominance of females (in the 2016/17 academic year, there were 5,301 women and 1,048 men).

References

Arnold, R. and Burke, B. (1983) *A popular education handbook*, Toronto and Ottawa: Ontario Institute for Studies in Education and CUSO Development Education.

Bagnall, R.G. and Hodge, S. (2018) 'Contemporary adult and lifelong education and learning: An epistemological analysis', in M. Milana, S. Webb, J. Holford, R. Waller and P. Jarvis (eds) *The Palgrave international handbook on adult and lifelong education and learning*, Basingstoke and New York, NY: HPH and Palgrave Macmillan, pp 13–34.

Barisone, M. (2009) *Comunicazione e società. Teorie, processi, pratiche del framing*, Bologna: Il Mulino.

Bateson, G. (1972) *Steps to an ecology of mind: Collected essays in anthropology, psychology, evolution and epistemology*, San Francisco, CA: Chandler Publishing Company.

Benford, R.D. and Snow, D.A. (2000) 'Framing processes and social movements: An overview and assessment', *Annual Review of Sociology*, 26: 611–39.

Borah, P. (2011) 'Conceptual issues in framing theory: A systematic examination of a decade's literature', *Journal of Communication*, 61: 246–63.

Cort, P. (2008) 'The Open Method of Coordination – a triangle of EU governance', in R. Desjardins and K. Rubenson (eds) *Research of vs. research for education policy: In an era of transnational policy-making*, Saarbrücken: VDM Verlag Dr. Müller.

Dale, R. and Robertson, S.L. (eds) (2009) *Globalisation and Europeanisation in education*, Oxford: Symposium Books.

Fejes, A., Olson, M., Rahm, L., Dahlsted, M. and Sandber, F. (2018) 'Individualisation in Swedish adult education and the shaping of neo-liberal subjectivities', *Scandinavian Journal of Educational Research*, 62(3): 461–73.

Goffman, E. (1974) *Frame analysis: An essay on the organization of experience*, Boston, MA: Northeastern University Press.

Graziano, P. and Vink, M.P. (eds) (2008) *Europeanization: New research agendas*, Houndmills, Basingstoke, Hampshire: Palgrave Macmillan.

Groppi, T. and Scattone, N. (2006) 'Italy: The subsidiarity principle', *International Journal of Constitutional Law*, 4(1): 131–7.

Hollander, J.A. and Einwohner, R.L. (2004) 'Conceptualizing resistance', *Sociological Forum*, 19(4): 533–54.

IRSRS (Regional Institute of Social Studies and Research) (no date) *Rapporto sull'Attività 1976–1979*, Trento: IRSRS.

Marcinkiewicz-Wilk, A. (2011) 'The University of Third Age as an institution counteracting marginalization of older people', *Journal of Education Culture and Society*, 2: 38–44.

Martin, I. (2000) 'Reconstituting the agora: Towards an alternative politics of lifelong learning', paper presented at the Adult Education Research Conference. Available at: http://newprairiepress.org/aerc/2000/papers/51 (accessed 28 March 2018).

Nóvoa, A. and Lawn, M. (eds) (2002) *Fabricating Europe: The formation of an education space*, Dordrecht: Kluwer.

Rein, M. and Schön, D. (1996) 'Frame-critical policy analysis and frame-reflective policy practice', *Knowledge and Policy*, 9(1): pp 85–104.

Scheufele, D.A. (1999) 'Framing as a theory of media effects', *Journal of Communication*, 49(4): 103–22.

Speight, S. (2018) 'The mainstreaming of massive open online courses (MOOCs)', in M. Milana, S. Webb, J. Holford, R. Waller and P. Jarvis (eds) *The Palgrave international handbook on adult and lifelong education and learning*, Basingstoke and New York, NY: HPH and Palgrave Macmillan, pp 939–56.

Stromquist, N.P. and Lozano, G. (2018) 'Popular universities: Their hidden functions and contributions', in M. Milana, S. Webb, J. Holford, R. Waller and P. Jarvis (eds) *International handbook on adult and lifelong education and learning*. Basingstoke and New York, NY: HPH and Palgrave Macmillan, pp 779–96.

Tan, S.G. (2018) 'Technologies for adult and lifelong education', in M. Milana, S. Webb, J. Holford, R. Waller and P. Jarvis (eds) *International handbook on adult and lifelong education and learning*. Basingstoke and New York, NY: HPH and Palgrave Macmillan, pp 917–38.

Tramma, S. (1996) 'Le università della terza età', in Gallina V. and Lichner M. (eds) *L'educazione in età adulta: primo rapporto nazionale*. Milano: Franco Angeli, pp 153-91.

Triandafyllidou, A. and Fotiou, A. (1998) 'Sustainability and modernity in the European Union: A frame theory approach to policymaking', *Sociological Research Online*, 3(1). Available at: www.socresonline.org.uk/3/1/2.html (accessed 12 March 2018).

Žižek, S. (2007) 'Resistance is surrender', *London Review of Books*, 29(22): 7. Available at: www.lrb.co.uk/v29/n22/slavoj-zizek/resistance-is-surrender (accessed 12 March 2018).

12

The marginalisation of popular education: 50 years of Danish adult education policy

Anne Larson and Pia Cort

Introduction

In August 2016, the Danish government set up an expert group on how to improve the Danish adult education system. In the terms of reference,[1] the focus was on how to make adult education more responsive to the needs, first, of public and private organisations and, second, of individuals, with the aim of supporting the development of a productive and highly qualified Danish workforce. The role of adult education was reduced to that of increasing the stock of human capital in order to improve the competitiveness of Danish society (that is, its economy). However, such a narrow, instrumental view of adult education has not always been dominant.

From a historical perspective, adult education has played a much broader role in Denmark as a path to emancipation and a way of creating a sense of community and national identity. Its roots are linked to social movements and the idea of enlightenment, solidified in the form of so-called folk high schools bringing education to the Danish people. The government took popular education under its wings from an early stage. Already in 1851, folk high schools received public subsidies (Ehlers et al, 2011), and from 1896, evening schools were included in the national budget. Central to the Danish tradition is active and voluntary participation in common activities that aim at 'making important subjects topics of conversation among ordinary human beings' (Jensen, 1991: 7). Learning is 'for life' and for democratic citizenship, and, more importantly, the form and content of adult education are to be developed by participants and educators, not the state or the market. This tradition stands in stark contrast to current adult education policy, with its focus on individuals' *qualification* for the labour market.

Three functions of adult education: qualification, socialisation and subjectification

The concepts developed by Biesta (2010) to debate the function of education systems provide us with a framework for understanding the direction that adult education has taken within public policy. Biesta distinguishes between three functions of education: qualification, socialisation and subjectification. By *qualification*, he refers to the relationship between the division of labour in a society and the education system's role of training people to enter the labour market with relevant skills. In the case of adult education, this involves upskilling and reskilling individuals throughout their working lives.[2] *Socialisation* concerns education's role in how a society's norms and values are reproduced. This refers to both the construction of a social identity embedded in a nation state and the ideals of a specific social order, such as democracy. Finally, *subjectification* describes the development of autonomous individuals with the capacity to realise their innate potential and critically reflect on themselves and their positions within a given society (Biesta, 2010).

While popular adult education has played a significant role in socialising Denmark as a democratic nation state comprised of subjectified citizens and human beings whose innate potential is realised as qualifications and life skills, a human capital understanding now dominates the political discourse on adult education. In the early 1960s, economists including Schultz (1961) and Becker (1962) introduced human capital theory, stressing the need for investment in human capital in line with investments in physical capital like land and technology. The influence of human capital theory on education policy has since grown markedly, leading to the marginalisation of popular education.

Although a human capital understanding of adult education has become hegemonic in contemporary political discourse, this chapter demonstrates that this has not always been the case. Popular education was previously considered a central part of adult education policy, contributing to democracy as a Danish life form. This chapter traces the historical development of adult education policy in Denmark. While adult education policy is today couched in a language of economic necessity and technocratic inevitability, adult education reflects the values deemed important in a society. Therefore, in accordance with Biesta (2009), the chapter aims to provoke a discussion about what adult education *should* be good for. The historical reading serves as an act of resistance.

Methodology

The chapter builds on an analysis of historical and contemporary documents concerning Danish adult education policy from the 1960s to the 2010s. Through the study of changes in adult education policy, the authors show how the current understanding of adult education as qualification for the labour market should not be taken for granted (Bacchi, 2009). Adult education is not just a matter of upskilling or reskilling to meet the needs of an insatiable labour market (see Cort et al, 2017); rather, it must consider wider societal demands and needs. The analysis shows that adult education 'can be "thought" differently' (Bacchi, 2009: 9) and that policies are contingent. The analysis adopts a discourse-oriented strategy (Boréus and Bergström, 2017). The selected documents are central strategies representative of the period of time in which they were written. The texts include: Acts and Bills; reports from governmental bodies or committees; and political strategies. In relation to Acts and Bills, annexes attached to the Bill when presented to Parliament are included. Secondary literature is used to support the analysis.

The analysis identifies three phases of development in Danish adult education policy: an initial phase where adult education policy balances the functions of socialisation, subjectification and qualification as equally important in creating a 'good life' for Danish citizens; a transitional phase where the human capital approach, foregrounding the function of qualification, gains ground; and the current phase, where *qualification* for the labour market has become the hegemonic rationality in adult education and the functions of *socialisation* and *subjectification* have become subordinate to qualification.

Balancing the three functions of adult education policy

In the 1960s, the three strands of Danish adult education – work-related adult education, general adult education and popular adult education – were given equal status despite their different aims (Ehlers et al, 2011). Qualification for the labour market was in focus with the 1960 law on training for low-skilled workers, leading to the establishment of schools for semi-skilled workers (*specialarbejderskoler*) (Ehlers, 2010). An upper-secondary programme aimed specifically at adults also saw the light during this period, providing a second chance to qualify for higher education (the higher preparatory examination programme) (Ehlers et al, 2011).

However, in line with international trends at the time (for example, Faure et al, 1972; ILO, 1974a), during the 1960s and the following decades, policies were not only focused on *qualification*. Education for life was part of public policy and encompassed both *socialisation* and *subjectification* as important aspects of adult education. Hence, public policy also focused on encouraging adults to take part in democratic processes, develop critical awareness of societal framing and achieve their potential (self-actualisation). Public subsidies to popular education, both folk high schools and part-time education, increased in the 1960s, and in 1968, the Parliament passed a law on leisure-time education (Ehlers, 2010). According to Korsgaard (2012), the underlying objective was to give adults the best opportunities for personal development in their spare time.

In the wake of the International Labour Organization's (ILO's) Paid Educational Leave Convention (ILO, 1974a), in 1978, the Danish Confederation of Trade Unions presented a proposal for an adult education policy (Thorgrimson, 1978) that included a section on paid educational leave. Among their demands was the right to paid educational leave for vocationally oriented education, general adult education or education for union representatives (Thorgrimson, 1978: 202).

The 'popular education' mark of the Social Liberal Party

In 1984, after a decade of discussions about paid educational leave, members of the Social Liberal Party, a party in opposition, put forward a proposal for a parliamentary resolution on a ten-point programme for adult teaching and popular adult education (Jensen et al, 1984). The proposal was adopted as part of a deal with the four-party government at the time (Conservatives, Liberals, Centre Democrats and Christian People's Party) (Ehlers, 2009). This proposal was to have a major impact on adult and popular education over the next decade as a guiding framework for policy initiatives within the field, not least as one of the leading initiators, Ole Vig Jensen,[3] was later to become, first, Minister of Culture and then Minister of Education.

The proposal stressed the need for long-term planning within the field of adult and popular education and for supporting grass-roots initiatives. One of the first principles in the proposal was to decentralise adult and popular education in order to give 'participants, teachers and initiators an extensive freedom to decide on contents and form' (Jensen et al, 1984: 3853). The proposal underlined that adult and popular education was to be a public good where the individual citizen should be able to decide 'what he/she wants to participate in'.[4] The proposal, thus, stressed not only the need to qualify citizens for a labour market marked by change, but also broader social and individual objectives, not least the individual's right to decide which training or education programmes to participate in.[5] Furthermore, adult and popular education was to be seen not only as a public investment, but also as 'a good in itself'. Although the function of providing people with labour market qualifications was not absent from the proposal, it was given a less prominent role than the functions of socialisation into Danish democratic society and subjectification as a critical and educated (in the German sense of *Bildung*) citizen.

The Social Liberal Party continued to play an important role in defining adult education in the 1980s. In 1988, it put forward a new proposal for a parliamentary resolution on the establishment of an adult education fund (Jensen et al, 1988). The aim was to put pressure on the government to create a fund that would reduce cost-related barriers to participation. In the proposal, access to all forms of education was prioritised. Although the proposal stressed the need for qualifications related to a changing labour market, with a focus on 'adults' opportunities to qualify for a demanding and technically complicated work life' (Jensen et al, 1988: own translation), formal qualifications were not considered the sole purpose of education. Like the 1984 proposal, the emphasis was on education as a good in itself. Furthermore, priority was given to those with a low level of education, especially those at risk of losing their jobs and/or in a 'difficult life situation'.

The proposal was not adopted as the government called a general election in the spring of 1988. After the election, the composition of the government changed and the Social Liberal Party became part of a coalition government. Ole Vig Jensen became Minister of Culture with a portfolio including adult education policy. In January 1989, he put forward a Bill relating to the adult education grant (Danish Ministry of Culture, 1989). Both the intention and content of the Bill were in line with the ten-point programme and the 1988 proposal; however, whereas the original proposal was aimed at giving employees the right to choose the education that best suited their needs, the actual legislation deviated from the ILO convention by not making education a right, but leaving it to the social partners to integrate it within collective agreements, hence emphasising the *qualification* function of adult education (Uddannelsesudvalget, 1989).

Summarising Danish adult education policy from the 1960s to the late 1980s, it is clear that the three functions *qualification*, *socialisation* and *subjectification* are considered equally important, with a slight tendency to focus on the latter two. A human capital understanding can be found in references to the need for upskilling but is overshadowed by a focus on democracy and personal development. Adult education was expected to play an important role in creating democratic citizens who were actively involved in a continuous process of defining and redefining what Danish democracy is and should be. Focus was on adult education as a community practice where the state provides the framework while the participants and educators define the form and content. The concept of 'human capital' is largely absent from policy documents – something that changed markedly in the 1990s.

The transitional phase: increased focus on qualification for the labour market

While the inspiration for Danish adult education policy in the 1970s and 1980s came from the Danish tradition for popular education, as well as the ILO convention on paid educational leave, the inspiration in the 1990s would come from the Organisation for Economic Co-operation and Development (OECD) and the European Union (EU), and particularly the EU's 'White Paper on education and training' (Commission of the European Communities, 1995) and the OECD's (1996) strategy 'Lifelong learning for all'. These transnational policies, which stressed the role of education as giving countries a competitive advantage in a post-industrial society, were to influence national education policies around the globe (Rizvi and Lingard, 2010).

The 1990s, meanwhile, can be characterised as a transitional period where an interest in the functions of *socialisation* and *subjectification* could still be found within adult education policy but gradually became subordinate to a dominant interest in *qualification* and a focus on human capital. In this process, the meaning of the terms *socialisation* and *subjectification* were changed completely. Adults are no longer to be socialised into a democratic Danish society, but into the labour market, while subjectification is no longer about self-actualisation or being empowered as a critical citizen, but about being an adaptable lifelong learner (see Jackson, 2013).

Adult education in between popular education and human capital

Although Ole Vig Jensen was the Minister of Education for much of the 1990s, his background in popular education could not resist the tide of neoliberal education ideology. Already in his 1994 joint statement to Parliament with the Minister of Labour, a drift in the functions of adult education can be detected, with an emphasis on qualification for the labour market (hardly surprising with the Minister of Labour as co-author).

A certain ambivalence crept into the new ten-point plan published in 1995. On the one hand, the significance of the individual's inclination for education is still emphasised: 'In education, it is the desire that is the decisive driving force' (Jensen, 1995: 4). On the other hand, however, the concept of popular education is abandoned in favour of 'recurrent education', a concept used by the OECD in their plan for lifelong learning from 1973 (OECD, 1973).

This development can also be traced in a discussion paper published in 1996, where the Minister of Education encouraged a debate on how the adult education system could/should be organised (Jensen, 1996). Jensen proposed an adult education system parallel to the formal education system, thereby making it possible for adults to complete formal qualifications at all levels of the education system, from basic schooling to master's degrees. The discussion paper was highly influenced by the ideas of lifelong education and made reference to the Delors report from the same year (Delors et al, 1996). However, the paper reflected a predominantly human capital understanding, describing skills as 'goods demanded in the labour market' and an 'investment to be enhanced'. The role of adult education in relation to socialisation as a democratic citizen is only mentioned once.

In 1999, the transition to an economistic view of education was consolidated when a working group led by the Ministry of Finance presented an analysis of the Danish adult education system and suggestions for its development (Finansministeriet, 1999).[6] *Qualification*, in the sense of meeting labour market needs, was now indisputably the primary function of adult education. The proposed strategy was intended to create a more efficient adult education system with reduced public funding. The strategy further mentioned a need for educational programmes of high quality and 'relevance for the society as well as the individual' (Finansministeriet, 1999: 21). Courses within adult education that do not result in formal competences were repeatedly referred to as a problem. For the individual, the aims of education were described in utilitarian terms as getting a new job, having better career options, obtaining higher salaries, lowering the risk of unemployment, maintaining a current job and so on. After listing objectives relevant to the labour market, personal qualifications, development and a better quality of life were mentioned. Gone was any mention of knowledge and learning as a good in itself, and education's ability to offer a better quality of life was only given a minor role compared to qualifications. It was further recommended that people should be encouraged to take part in education in their free time. From being a right, adult education (or rather lifelong learning) started to become an obligation for the individual, an activity in which they were expected to invest time and/or money.

Reviewing policy papers from the 1990s shows the subtle drift in the functions of adult education, from serving the multiple purposes of developing democratic citizens, empowering people and providing them with both vocational and life skills, to a reductive emphasis on qualification for the labour market influenced by international agendas. It also shows that the system is marked by inertia, meaning that policy changes do not occur overnight. At the same time, although the ministers in charge play a role in shaping policies, they cannot resist changing ideological tides. Thus, the 1990s served as a transitional period where adult education policy gradually shifted course.

Qualification, qualification, qualification: adult training for the labour market

By the turn of the millennium, human capital had become the main driver of adult education policy in Denmark. The ideas had been gradually introduced by a Social Democrat-led government in the 1990s but the new Liberal–Conservative government accelerated the transition from a welfare state to a competition state and consolidated the idea of education as a central parameter in the economic defence against globalisation.

The new government started out by changing the Law on Popular Education in 2002. The political debate in relation to the proposal concerned the societal utility of popular education: the state should only subsidise courses offering qualifications of immediate relevance to the labour market, it was argued (Nielsen, 2002: 109). The legislative changes included different subsidy levels for programmes that provide labour market qualifications and those that do not, as well as an increase in the fees paid by participants, which led to a decrease in participation levels among less well-off groups in Danish society.[7] The new law changed the institutional landscape of popular education: many non-residential folk high schools were closed down and the evening schools had to compete under market conditions, leading to a higher degree of commercialisation in the sector (Kandrup, 2013: 46).

In 2006, a new strategy for adult education in Denmark was presented by the government (Finansministeriet, 2006), and the Ministry of Finance was once again the driving force. This time, the social partners were also actively involved through a tripartite agreement on adult education (*Markant styrkelse af voksen- og efteruddannelse*, 2007). The social partners were expected to take greater responsibility for adult education through the establishment of competence funds. The strategy maintained the focus on qualifications and the inspiration from human capital theory found in the 1999 publication.

The title of the report itself indicated the exclusive focus on education for the labour market: 'Lifelong skills upgrading and education for all *in the labour market*' (emphasis added). The aim of adult education was described as improving qualifications, especially among low-skilled and skilled workers and people at risk of labour market exclusion. The aim was to secure continuing competence development, thereby reducing the risk of a future skills mismatch in the labour market. Further aims were to secure mobility in the labour market, continued welfare provisions and relatively even income distribution. It was stressed that 'all parts of the educational system must contribute to securing the needed competences in the light of future challenges' (Finansministeriet, 2006: 5), leaving no room for educational activities not related to qualification. Personal development was mentioned a few times but only as a by-product of adult education. Besides a major role in relation to qualifying people to meet labour market demands, adult education was also to play a role in relation to other policy areas, such as social policy, integration and industrial policy, providing especially the function of socialising marginalised groups into the labour market and Danish society. Adult education was a solution to a number of societal problems, and was no longer described as an end in its own right.

The following ten years were relatively quiet in relation to adult education in Denmark. A national strategy for lifelong learning was published in 2007 (Undervisningsministeriet, 2007) at the behest of the EU, mainly referring to what Denmark had already done and without presenting any fundamentally new developments regarding the adult education system.

It was not until 2017, when the 'expert group'[8] (mentioned in the introduction) presented their suggestions for the future Danish adult education system (Ekspertgruppen, 2017), that adult education returned to the public agenda. The group's task was the 'development of an adult and further education system with a flexibility and adjustability which meets the demands of companies and employees' (Arbejdsgruppen til Trepartsforhandlinger, 2016: 172). Hence, their proposal focused on ensuring the qualifications of the workforce through an adult education system responsive to the needs of the labour market. The recommendations of the group informed a tripartite agreement between the government and the social partners (Trepartsaftale, 2017). In the agreement, a new shift in the perspective on adult education can be detected, from the needs of the individual to the needs of enterprises: 'Adult, continuous and further education thus has to ensure *that public and private enterprises have access to qualified labour*, and that the competences of the labour force are on par with the changes taking place in the labour market' (Trepartsaftale, 2017: 2, own translation and emphasis added). The market has taken precedence over the individual and adult education has become a 'good' for the labour market.

Resisting the neoliberal discourse of adult education

Today, human capital and a neoliberal understanding of adult education have gained a hegemonic role in adult education policy. Adult education has become part of employment and labour market policies, serving the overall neoliberal agenda of global competitiveness. The function of adult education is, first and foremost, to provide a 'productive and well qualified labour force', and the 'highest rate of return' should be ensured in both public and private investments in adult education (Arbejdsgruppen til Trepartsforhandlinger, 2016: 171). The functions of *subjectification* and *socialisation* have been colonised by the function of *qualification*: individuals are expected to invest in their own human capital through lifelong learning in order to be productive citizens contributing to the survival of the competition state. The 2017 policy could not be further away from the ten-point programme of 1984: adult education has been reduced to a question of qualification while ideals of citizenship, community, empowerment and individual learning for learning's sake have been gradually discarded during the five decades at the centre of this study.

The historical account presented in this chapter shows how an economistic idea of education has 'won' over broader ideas of education as important for ensuring a healthy democratic society and the well-being of its citizens. The discussion of what adult education is 'good for' has been abandoned, as have the visions for 'the good society'. It is an important task for research to document the drift in adult education policy as political solutions tend to be naturalised as 'obvious' answers to exogenous societal problems, silencing other discourses on adult education. The Danish tradition of popular education, with its emphasis on dialogue and empowerment through participation, holds the potential to counterbalance the hegemonic discourse of 'qualification for the labour market' and contribute to a debate about common values and the 'good life' of Danish citizens. In line with Biesta (2010: 25), the analysis underlines the need to 'reconnect with the question of purpose in education', especially in times where the concept of 'popular' takes on quite different and threatening dimensions. This debate is necessary if we are to resist the inevitability of the neoliberal discourse about adult education. This is our resistant act.

Notes

1 See Arbejdsgruppen til Trepartsforhandlinger (2016).

2 Biesta (2010: 7) states that qualification is 'particularly, but not exclusively, connected to economic arguments; that is, to the role education plays in the preparation of the workforce and through this, in the contribution education makes to economic development and growth'.

3 Ole Vig Jensen had a past in popular education as the head of *Frit Oplysningsforbund* (The Association of Liberal Popular Education) from 1971 to 1979. His background is evident in the ten-point programme, with its emphasis on popular education.

4 Although Denmark had not ratified the ILO convention on paid educational leave, the ten-point programme was largely in line with the convention and the associated recommendations (ILO, 1974a, 1974b).

5 It is also interesting that, in the proposal, barriers to participation are, first and foremost, structural in the form of economic and working-life barriers. The explanations for non-participation will change over the coming decades from a problem of societal structures to a problem of individual motivation (Ahl, 2016; Mariager-Anderson et al, 2016).

6 In 1998, a new Minister of Education was appointed. Although from the same party as Ole Vig Jensen, the new minister, Margrethe Vestager, did not have a background in popular education.

7 In the period from 2002 to 2012, municipal budgets for evening schools were cut by 45 per cent, leading to a 50 per cent decrease in participation.

8 Another indication of the dominance of an economistic understanding of adult education is the fact that of the six members of the group, four had a background within economics.

References

Ahl, H. (2016) 'Motivation in adult education: a problem solver or a euphemism for direction and control?', *International Journal of Lifelong Education*, 25(4): 385–405.

Arbejdsgruppen til Trepartsforhandlinger (2016) *Kommissorium for ekspertgruppe om voksen-, efter- og videreuddannelse*, Copenhagen: Danish Government, Arbejdsgruppen til Trepartsforhandlinger.

Bacchi, C. (2009) *Analysing policy: What is the problem represented to be?*, Malaysia: Pearson.

Becker, G.S. (1962) 'Investment in human capital: A theoretical analysis', *The Journal of Political Economy*, 70(5): 9–41.

Biesta, G. (2009) *Good education: What it is and why we need it*, Stirling: The Stirling Institute of Education.

Biesta, G.J.J. (2010) *Good education in an age of measurement. Ethics, politics, democracy*, London: Paradigm Publishers.

Boréus, K. and Bergström, G. (2017) *Analyzing text and discourse*, London: Sage.

Commission of the European Communities (1995) 'White Paper on education and training: Teaching and learning – Towards the learning society' COM(95) 590 final. Available at: http://europa.eu/documents/comm/white_papers/pdf/com95_590_en.pdf (accessed April 2019).

Cort, P., Mariager-Anderson, K. and Thomsen, R. (2017) 'Busting the myth of low-skilled workers – Destabilizing EU LLL policies through the life stories of Danes in low-skilled jobs', *International Journal of Lifelong Education, 1–17*, 37(2): 199–215. doi:10.1080/02601370.2017.1404501

Danish Ministry of Culture (1989) 'Lovforslag nr. L 178. Fremsat 12. Januar 1989. Forslag til lov om voksenuddannelsesstøtte (med bemærkninger)'.

Delors, J. et al (1996) 'Learning: The treasure within; Report to UNESCO of the International Commission on Education for the twenty-first century', UNESCO.

Ehlers, S. (2009) 'Livslang læring som politisk strategi i 1900-tallets Danmark: samspillet mellem civilsamfund, stat og marked', *Uddannelseshistorie*, 51: 28–54.

Ehlers, S. (2010) 'Nordic arguments for lifelong learning: Policy making 1960–2000', working paper, Nationalt Center for Kompetenceudvikling, Copenhagen.

Ehlers, S., Wärvik, G.-B., Larson, A. and Thång, P.-O. (2011) *Effektive strategier for livslang læring i de Nordiske lande* (ed T. Geiger), Copenhagen: Nordisk Ministerård.

Ekspertgruppen (2017) *Nye kompetencer hele livet. Fremtidens voksen- og efteruddannelse*, København: Ekspertgruppen for voksen-, efter- og videreuddannelse.

Faure, E., Herrera, F., Kaddoura, A.-R., Lopes, H., Petrovsky, A.V., Rahnema, M. and Ward, F.C. (1972) *Learning to be. The world of education today and tomorrow*, Paris: UNESCO.

Finansministeriet (1999) *Mål og midler i offentligt finansieret voksen- og efteruddannelse*, København: Finansministeriet.

Finansministeriet (2006) *Livslang opkvalificering og uddannelse for alle på arbejdsmarkedet – rapport fra Trepartsudvalget. Sammenfatning*, Copenhagen: Danish Ministry of Finance.

ILO (International Labour Organization) (1974a) *Paid Educational Leave Convention. Convention no. C140*, Geneva: International Labour Organization.

ILO (1974b) *Paid educational leave recommendation – R148*, Geneva: International Labour Organisation.

Jackson, S.E. (2013) *Challenges and inequalities in lifelong learning and social justice*, London: Routledge.

Jensen, J.K. (1991) 'Folkeoplysning', Copenhagen: The Danish Cultural Institute.

Jensen, O.V. (1995) *10-punktsplan om tilbagevendende uddannelse*, København: Undervisningsministeriet.

Jensen, O.V. (1996) *Debatoplæg om et nyt parallelt kompetencesystem for voksne*, Copenhagen: Danish Ministry of Education.

Jensen, O.V., Bilgrav-Nielsen, J., Estrup, J. and Petersen, N.H. (1984) 'Forslag til folketingsbeslutning om et 10 punkts program for voksenundervisning og folkeoplysning. Beslutningsforslag nr. B 114, fremsat den 4. april 1984 af Ole Vig Jensen (RV), Bilgrav-Nielsen (RV), Estrup (RV) og Niels Helveg Petersen (RV)'.

Jensen, O.V., Bilgrav-Nielsen, J., Jelved, M., Lee, K. and Petersen, N.H. (1988) 'Forslag til folketingsbeslutning om etablering af en voksenuddannelsesfond'.

Kandrup, P.E.e. (2013) *Uden tvivl, med stort besvær*, Helsingør: Dansk Oplysnings Forbund.

Korsgaard, O. (2012) *Kampen om folket: Et dannelsesperspektiv på dansk historie gennem 500 år*, Copenhagen: Gyldendal.

Mariager-Anderson, K., Cort, P. and Thomsen, R. (2016) ' "In reality, I motivate myself!". "Low-skilled" workers' motivation: Between individual and societal narratives', *British Journal of Guidance & Counselling*, 44(2): 171–84.

Markant styrkelse af voksen- og efteruddannelse (2007) København Regeringen Landsorganisationen i Danmark, FTF, Akademikernes Centralorganisation, Dansk Arbejdsgiverforening, Sammenslutning af Landbrugets Arbejdsgiverforeninger, Finanssektorens Arbejdsgiverforening, Lederne, KL & Danske Regioner. Available from: https://www.rm.dk/siteassets/vaekstforum/dagsordensbilag/december-2007/punkt_2_bilag_2.pdf (accessed April 2019).

Nielsen, H.e. (2002) *Folkeoplysning – i går, i dag, i morgen*, Odense: Syddansk Universitetsforlag.

OECD (Organisation for Economic Co-operation and Development) (1973) *Recurrent education: A strategy for lifelong learning*. Paris: Organisation for Economic Co-operation and Development, Centre for Educational Research and Innovation.

OECD (1996) *Lifelong learning for all*, Paris: OECD.

Rizvi, F. and Lingard, B. (2010) *Globalizing education policy*, London: Routledge.

Schultz, T.W. (1961) 'Investment in human capital', *The American Economic Review*, 51(1): 1–17.

Thorgrimson, F. (1978) *LO dokumentation om voksenuddannelse*, Copenhagen: Landsorganisationen i Danmark (LO).

Uddannelsesudvalget (1989) 'Betænkning over Forslag til lov om voksenuddannelsesstøtte' Available at: https://www.retsinformation.dk/eli/ft/198814K00178 (accessed April 2019).

Undervisningsministeriet (2007) *Denmark's strategy for lifelong learning. Education and lifelong skills upgrading for all*, Copenhagen: Danish Ministry of Education.

13

Adult basic education in Australia: in need of a new song sheet?

Keiko Yasukawa and Pamela Osmond

Introduction

At the end of 2007, after 11 years of a conservative national government whose adult education policy could best be summed up as rampant privatisation, a new Labor government took office in Australia, bringing with it a mantra of 'The Australian economy needs an education revolution.' This was music to the ears of many adult educators working with equity groups for whom the range of public provision had been diminishing; however, now, more than ten years after the Labor victory and with the conservatives winning back the government, the adult education policy setting is starker than ever before. Historical reflection on the field of adult basic education (ABE) in Australia reveals how radically it has been transformed over a few decades, from one where practitioners worked in, and identified with, a vibrant social justice-motivated community of practice, to a field where practitioner voice in policy deliberations has become restricted.

We examine the emergence of the hegemonic discourse (Mayo, 1999) impacting upon the current Australian ABE field and identify possibilities of resistance to it. We analyse the changes to ABE practices using Engeström's (2001) formulation of Cultural Historical Activity Theory (CHAT). CHAT affords a structured historical analysis of the field that can inform possibilities for the future.

We first explain our claim of a policy vacuum, and why a vacuum of the kind we write about creates a problem rather than affords agency for practitioners in the field. Although the concerns and history that we write about are not unique to the state of New South Wales (NSW), much of our evidence is drawn from our experiences in NSW and the research project on the history of ABE in NSW undertaken by Pamela Osmond (2018). We then outline key concepts from CHAT that we use to examine selected key policy moments in the history of ABE in Australia. The last section looks to the future and what may help activists to reclaim the agenda.

Trapped in a vacuum

Neoliberalism has legitimated an ideological shift from the state assuming responsibility for the provision of lifelong education to individuals initiating ongoing learning by whatever means they have. As the role of government diminishes, the role of the private sphere increases. While governments retain a key role in shaping the landscape of adult education, their direct hand becomes elusive. At the same time, providers and practitioners may find themselves increasingly accountable to new intermediaries, using reporting instruments that are produced by still more intermediaries, which, as a result, can be alien to the practices of the field. Thus, multiple new actors start to occupy the field while the government's role in enabling educational provision recedes into the background, and while the mechanisms by which the government outsources their traditional functions to the private sphere are never totally transparent.

Seeing the future through a critical analysis of our past

To explain the significance of the numerous new actors in the field, we employ a CHAT analysis. CHAT provides us with an analytical resource to understand ABE practice from the perspective of any of its actors or *subjects* as an *object* or goal-oriented, collective activity that is mediated by symbolic and material *tools and instruments*, and is characterised by the *'rules' and traditions* of the field, the composition of the *community* in which it is positioned, and the way in which *roles and power* are distributed within the community (Engeström, 2001). In particular, it enables us to see the critical role of internal contradictions that can emerge or be rendered more visible through changes that disturb the way in which the field operates. In some instances, the resolution of these contradictions can destabilise the activity system to such a degree that the activity system is radically transformed, resulting in what Engeström (2001) calls *expansive learning*.

Central to the study of ABE's trajectory is the gradual change in its community of practice. Although many individuals within this community have come and gone over the 40-year history of this field, the sense of 'community' has never vanished completely. The Australian

Council of Adult Literacy (ACAL) (together with its sister state-based councils) has maintained a presence as the national professional association and continues to bring practitioners together for an annual conference. Within the steering committees of the national and state organisations, there has always been a mix of members, for example, experienced practitioners from public providers, academics in the field of adult education and, in some cases, state bureaucrats. For many years, these committees played a leadership role in policy advocacy, and governments expected to have input from these committees. One of the major changes has been the marginalisation of the voices from these groups in policy debates as other more powerful players reconstituted what policymakers might identify as the ABE community (or, more likely in their language, stakeholders). The new players, including industry groups, employer organisations and multinational consulting firms, have changed the 'division of labour' within the traditional ABE community, removing many of the sources of power that shaped the field in the past, as will be explained later.

The change in the division of labour is one example of how the shift from the public to the neoliberal governance of ABE in Australia has meant a new kind of multi-voicedness becoming a feature of the field. Whereas government policy in the past set out the framework for the practitioner community to develop a range of *tools and instruments* to mediate their work – curricula, courses, teaching and learning resources, assessment frameworks, professional development, and recommended qualifications for teachers – much of this function of policy, not to mention the actual provision, is now outsourced to different organisations and consultants, whose interests may be quite different to those of the practitioners in the field. In other words, these new actors who form part of the larger ABE community may be motivated by *objects* that may or may not be sympathetic to the social justice goals that have motivated ABE practitioners. In CHAT terms, the neoliberal shift has disturbed who is part of the *community* that interacts with ABE practitioners, the relationship between this *community* and the *rules and tools* that mediate the activity of this community, and how *power and labour* is distributed within the activity system.

Each of the new actors constitutes their own activity systems, motivated by their own goals. We argue that the new voices that have entered the field have meant the occupation of the field by multiple activity systems, introducing disturbances to the practitioner community.

Engeström (2006: 1785) uses the term 'runaway objects' as a metaphor for a situation where multiple objects emerge without any coordination or oversight:

> They are objects that are only weakly under anybody's control and have far-reaching, unexpected side effects. Actor-network theorists … point out that such objects are often monsters: they seem to have a life of their own that threatens our security and safety in many ways. They are contested objects that generate opposition and controversy. They can also be powerfully emancipatory objects that open up radically new possibilities of development and well-being.

As Fenwick, Edwards and Sawchuk (2015: 73) explain: '[a]ctivity analysis inevitably becomes ever more complex when we turn our attention toward … contradictions between the wider array of activities that constitute society more broadly'. In the next section, we analyse four policy moments (acknowledging that the 'moments' may cover a period of several years and overlap with another policy 'moment') in which the practitioner field of Australian ABE experienced a major disturbance, and how each of these policy moments became part of the field's journey into an alien land.

From a community of practice to fragmentation in an alien land

The genesis of the field of ABE in Australia was a grass-roots, practitioner-led social movement in the early 1970s, which occurred within the larger socio-political milieu of vibrant emancipatory movements in the Western world. Notwithstanding its origin in this progressive socio-political climate, its first policy moment connected it to the vocational education and training (VET) sector, and, in particular, with technical and further education (TAFE).

Legitimation as a progressive educational sector

This first crucial policy moment that gave the field legitimation within the mainstream of educational policy occurred with the release of *TAFE in Australia: Report on needs in technical and further education* (Kangan, 1974), a report commissioned by a newly elected Labor government. One recommendation of the report was that the brief of the state vocational training systems be widened to encompass those adults who had traditionally been excluded from technical training. This was a highly influential watershed report that foregrounded access and equity concerns and lifelong liberal education alongside the traditional technical focus, and recommended specifically that 'state TAFE authorities … regard literacy programs as a high priority in their use of Australian Government funds' (Richardson, 1975: 96).

Although the Australian economy was already facing challenges by 1972, the new Labor government nevertheless remained driven by Keynesian economic policies, including 'big government', and accepted the Kangan report's recommendation of a considerable injection of funds into the TAFE sector, which was to be ABE's new home in many states. In NSW TAFE, for example, a large number of permanent staff were appointed to new ABE positions and a new TAFE curriculum division was established. Thus, the report helped to articulate the *object* of the emerging field, which, in turn, led to the emergence of *tools and instruments* and the *rules* that came to define the field. For a number of years, adult literacy practitioners had considerable freedom to conduct programmes 'outside the institutional framework' by managing, for example, community-based volunteer tutor programmes. A body of new professional practice knowledge was created that, given its socio-political context, was grounded in a discourse of human rights and progressive liberalism.

The United Nations Educational, Scientific and Cultural Organization (UNESCO) was one of the important actors framing the discourse in these foundation years. Its 1972 publication *Learning to be: The world of education today and tomorrow* (Faure, 1972) was a highly influential publication and was an important informing document for Australia's Kangan report (Kangan, 1974). For a number of years until the early 1980s, this discourse of education as a human right and one that would lead to greater equality and social reform coexisted with the Organisation for Economic Co-operation and Development's (OECD's) human capital view of literacy.

Filling the policy vacuum

The next important policy moment came in 1987 with the implementation of the first national policy for adult literacy, the *National policy on languages* (Lo Bianco 1987), heralding a three-year initiative known as the Adult Literacy Action Campaign. In many ways, this was to become emblematic of Australia's adult literacy golden decade, and enjoyed a significant international reputation (Brock, 2001). The policy secured a specific financial commitment from the commonwealth government for adult literacy and proposed a concerted campaign to attempt to improve levels of adult literacy. It recommended that 'the expert advice and guidance of adult literacy groups' (Lo Bianco, 1987: 20) be sought to guide the implementation of the campaign and the selection and management of a number of 'projects of national strategic significance'.

The recommendation to seek the advice of experienced practitioners was significant, and was perhaps the last occasion at which the views of practitioners and academics in the field were directly sought in the framing of policy. Thus, for a brief period, the *community* in which the practitioners belonged was in dialogue with the policymakers. However, there was to be a bifurcation of the practitioner and the policymaker communities into separate activity systems motivated by increasingly divergent goals. In the late 1980s and early 1990s, the field of adult literacy in Australia had a number of academics and practitioners with a background in adult literacy or allied fields advocating for the field from within the bureaucracy as 'insider policy activists' (Brock, 2001: 48). However, by 1991, when the government released its next policy on adult literacy, their influence was beginning to be sidelined by the discursive shift to the human capital argument. The funding made available under the new Australian Language and Literacy Policy (ALLP) confirmed the government's economic priority, and placed jobseeker and workplace literacy at the centrepiece. These programmes grew and continued to attract even greater funding in future decades.

While welcoming the policy recognition and substantial increase in funding that the ALLP brought, practitioners were nevertheless concerned that the instrumental view of literacy that underpinned the employment-related programmes would ultimately lead to the sidelining of other social justice programmes. Unfortunately, by this time, they had little voice in the policy discussion.

By 1988, the role and identity of bureaucrats who had previously been responsible for welfare programmes within the public service had changed, and the goals of portfolio advocacy that earlier bureaucrats brought to their roles were replaced by goals of economic efficiency, rendering them more impervious to lobbying by special interest groups (Yeatman, 1993). In her article 'Political amnesia: How we forgot to govern', Tingle (2015) refers to the rapid turnover of public servants, who have become generalists and accountants rather than portfolio advocates and who now have little institutional memory. She argues that in Australia, most government departments now have little capacity to develop policy. This poses a particular challenge to those in our field who call for a new national policy on adult literacy: there are no longer any 'insider policy activists' or avenues for practitioner voices to be heard.

'Knotworking' and the emergence of new communities

The economic conditions and discourses that facilitated the establishment of the early adult literacy programmes had changed almost before the recommendations of the Kangan Committee could be enacted. The effects of the global recession from the mid-1970s led to the threat of collapse of Australia's manufacturing industry, growing unemployment and a decline of Australia's status in international markets. By the mid-1980s, there were warnings that unless Australia urgently reformed its industrial base, there were severe risks to the health of the economy. There followed a range of changes to the basic policy settings affecting the field that were to have repercussions for decades to come.

Thus, our next crucial policy moment came as a result of the policy initiatives of a Labor government that came into power in 1983. The initiatives came under the title of the National Training Reform Agenda, and reflected a shift across OECD countries from the UNESCO-influenced human rights discourse to the OECD's almost solely human capital discourse (Marginson, 1997; Limage, 2009).

Reform was achieved through tripartite agreements between government, unions and industry. An industry-driven national qualifications framework was developed, with a competency-based training (CBT) system. However, there was a growing awareness that many in the workforce did not have the literacy and numeracy skills to embark on this retraining. Unions also shared this concern and were particularly keen to safeguard the interests of those on the bottom of the ladder and to optimise their training opportunities.

The power of seduction to become part of this national reform was made clear in the following bold statement made by the Secretary of the Australian Council of Trade Unions at a meeting with members of the ACAL: 'Your time has come. The door of history has opened for you. Award restructure can't happen without you' (Gribble, 1990: 41). Having been co-opted into the cause of economic competitiveness and VET, literacy and numeracy provision shifted from the margins of the VET system into mainstream industrial training. There was to be a cost in joining the mainstream, however. ABE practitioners had to surrender their approach to learner-centred curriculum development, and adopt the much more instrumentally focused CBT framework.

This period was marked by the increasing influence of industry and businesses in VET policy (Marginson, 1997; Ryan, 2011). One consequence was the marketisation of VET, allowing private providers to tender for public funding alongside the newly commercialised TAFE institutes. Prior to this, a large proportion of ABE practitioners had been public servants. Now, an increasing proportion is employed by non-unionised private providers as hourly paid teachers, bringing a change to the dynamic of the community of practice. Over time, many of the *tools and instruments*, such as assessment tools and reporting regimes, were also outsourced to agents from the private sphere. In this way, governance of the field became the responsibility of industry bodies and semi-government organisations, with governments thus exerting influence in indirect ways.

The influence of the OECD was also felt through its series of international research reports during the 1990s that demonstrated apparent inadequate literacy skills for many OECD nations. Foremost among these were the International Adult Literacy Surveys (IALS). With the release of each report, selective media reporting resulted in the creation of a popular discourse of a country facing a 'literacy crisis'.

By the time the 2006 IALS results were released, there were multiple activity systems operating in the ABE field, loosely organised and tenuously linked to the practitioner field of ABE, a phenomenon that befits Engeström's (2008: 21) metaphor of the '*mycorrhizae*, the invisible undergrowth of fungi'. However, in many ways, this undergrowth has filled the policy vacuum through 'knotworking': forming collaborations 'without rigid, predermined [sic] rules or a fixed central authority' (Engeström, 2008: 20).

A new national policy?

In 2012, 20 years since the previous major policy initiative, the profession awaited the launch of the *National foundation skills strategy* (NFSS) (SCOTESE, 2012) in the expectation that the erosion of policy might be redressed. Critically, however, this was not a policy, but a strategy with no funding attached to it.

Recognition was given in the document of the need to assist individuals to develop their foundation skills for both social and economic purposes in the interests of the individual, of civil society and of the national economy. However, a critical reading of the NFSS clarifies the predominant discourse surrounding it. The opening sentence of the ministerial foreword signals the intent, with the familiar claim that 'More than 7.5 million Australian adults do not have the literacy and numeracy skills needed to participate fully in today's workforce' (SCOTESE, 2012: i) and no mention of any objectives other than human capital production. The NFSS renamed our field as *foundation skills*; any reference to education was long gone.

The Australian results for the second IALS had played a powerful role in fomenting another literacy crisis, and mobilising the members of the 'undergrowth' of the field to steer the development of the NFSS (Yasukawa and Black, 2016). The power of the 'knotworking' effect of those whose interest was economistic was formidable in steering the development of the NFSS. The impact of the peak employer organisation, the unions, industry skills agencies and skills advisory agencies working in solidarity was heralded by the then head of the skills policy advisory agency as the result of them all 'singing from the same hymn sheet' (Literacy and Numeracy Are Holding Australia Back, 2010). Rather than filling the education policy vacuum, however, the NFSS was an aspirational document only, open to market forces to determine the areas in and the extent to which it was implemented. Given the government's faith in market forces to indicate funding allocations, the influence of industry bodies continued to ensure that funding was allocated almost exclusively to employment-related programmes to the exclusion of other priorities suggested in the document.

In search of a new tune?

There is a lesson to be learnt from the way in which the *mycorrhizae* reconfiguring the field succeeded. By forming solidarity and ensuring that they sang from 'the same hymn sheet', the voice of business and industry was heard loud and clear by politicians and government bureaucrats. ABE practitioners may also build strengths through solidarity with those who share the core social justice goals of ABE.

For example, researchers specialising in housing policy and its impact on marginalised tenants lent their expertise to an adult education researcher to document the adult literacy needs of a group of homeless people in Sydney (Morris et al, 2017), again, adding a new voice and angle that could be used in policy advocacy.

Another source of strength and solidarity is the international adult basic education community. It is not only in Australia where neoliberalism has impacted on the field (Tusting, 2009; Bowl and Tobias, 2012; Ramdeholl and Wells, 2013); in other countries too, there is a community of practitioners who are motivated by social justice principles and see their accountability to be first and foremost with their learners. In 2016, ACAL and its UK sister organisation Research and Practice in Adult Literacies (RaPAL) collaborated in a project to produce *Resilience*, an anthology of adult learners' writing (Furlong and Yasukawa, 2016). International publications of this kind help to show that the need for a different kind of policy discourse is not just an imagination of Australian adult literacy practitioners; rather, it speaks to the experiences of adult literacy learners internationally.

What the stories in *Resilience* also tell us is that despite the 'official' changes in the ABE field, there are still practitioners and classes that are open to educating the whole person, not just the future skilled worker. One experienced practitioner commented: 'I think one of the really important things that underpin my teaching is the fact that I'm teaching students and I'm not teaching the syllabus' (Yasukawa et al, 2008: 501). Another example of this kind of principled stance was expressed by a participant in Pamela Osmond's research: "Give me a box and I will tick it for you. I won't let it impinge on the way I teach. I won't do it". These teachers exhibit what Johansson and Vinthagen (2016) call 'everyday resistance', routine practices within their relationships with the learners that enable the learner-centred provision to be sustained. Moreover, this widespread practitioner resistance to the rigid audit regime that is part of the neoliberal governance system indicates that, in the eyes of practitioners, that system and all that it represents has lost its legitimacy.

Another source of challenge to the legitimacy of the current regime has emerged from an unexpected direction. The recent OECD Programme for the International Assessment of Adult Competencies (PIAAC) survey produced a great deal of data that are still to be examined but that cast light on the links between social outcomes and adult literacy. Although PIAAC results have so far been used primarily to highlight the human capital argument, these data could be used by ABE activists to support a different kind of argument, one focused on social outcomes such as health, civic participation and social capital (St Clair, 2012). An example of an initiative that reflects such thinking is the Aboriginal literacy programme in Western NSW, where activists and researchers together argued that adult literacy is one of the social determinants of health (Bartlett, 2015; Literacy for Life Foundation, 2017. It is perhaps through the 'knotworking' of those ABE practitioners exercising forms of 'everyday resistance', their learners and social activist groups, including international adult literacy groups, that a new protest song can emerge, leading to the genesis of a new era of ABE that is once again firmly grounded in human rights and social justice goals.

Conclusion

As we have argued, over the last four decades, ABE in Australia has experienced a trajectory of initially sitting outside the gaze of mainstream policy deliberations and gradually being embraced by the mainstream, but, in doing so, losing control over its own *object*, *tools and instruments*, and *rules* of practice as more powerful actors entered the community with their own *objects*. Its spokespersons are now actor outsiders to ABE practice, to the exclusion of practitioners. From the perspective of long-term insiders, the control of the *object* of ABE has been lost to economistic agendas set by industry, businesses and government.

A lesson from our history is that a comprehensive, funded national policy on ABE that is driven by a pursuit of social justice and that strives to develop the individual in order that they can contribute to civil society, as well as to the national economy, is not likely to emerge from a government of either end of the political spectrum. This is not the primary driver of the other activity systems that have come to occupy the field of ABE; moreover, the other activity systems are afforded a louder voice in any policy discussions because of their tight 'knotworking' around a common productivity agenda. In order to survive in this landscape, ABE practitioners have had to adopt the *tools and instruments* and many of the *rules* produced by the *mycorrhizae*. This, in turn, has significantly transformed the 'official' practice of ABE, from a progressive humanist educational practice, to a narrowly defined practice of skills training. In this way, what Engeström would characterise as *expansive learning* has occurred, though with an outcome that sits uncomfortably with many ABE practitioners. In order for the practitioner community to regain something of the earlier moral purpose, a different kind of *expansive learning* is needed. However, there are signs of 'spores' – those local and international practitioners exercising 'everyday resistance', organisations in the wider social arena whose interests are congruent with ABE practitioners' interests, and academic researchers who can critically reinterpret aspects of the dominant discourse – that may grow into a new strand of *mycorrhizae* and weaken the foundations of the neoliberal hold on adult education and civil society.

References

Bartlett, B. (2015) 'Aboriginal adult mass literacy campaign (Yo, Si Puedo) – A circuit breaker for Aboriginal health?', *In Touch*, 32(1): 22–4.

Bowl, M. and Tobias, R. (2012) 'Learning from the past, organizing for the future: Adult and community education in Aotearoa New Zealand', *Adult Education Quarterly*, 62(3): 272–86.

Brock, P. (2001) 'Australia's language', in J. Lo Bianco and R. Wickert (eds) *Australian policy activism in language and literacy*, Melbourne: Language Australia, pp 49–76.

Engeström, Y. (2001) 'Expansive learning at work: Toward an activity theoretical reconceptualization', *Journal of Education and Work*, 14(1): 133–46.

Engeström, Y. (2006) 'From well-bounded ethnographies to intervening in mycorrhizae activities', *Organization Studies*, 27(12): 1783–93.

Engeström, Y. (2008) *From teams to knots: Activity-theoretical studies of collaboration and learning at work*, Cambridge: Cambridge University Press.

Faure, E. (1972) *Learning to be: The world of education today and tomorrow*, Paris: UNESCO.

Fenwick, T., Edwards, R. and Sawchuk, P. (2015) *Emerging approaches to education research: Tracing the sociomaterial*, London: Routledge.

Furlong, T. and Yasukawa, K. (eds) (2016) *Resilience: Stories of adult learning*, Rolleston on Dove, UK: Creative Commons.

Gribble, H. (1990) 'Resisting hijack and seduction', *Literacy Exchange, Journal of NSWALC*, 2: 41–55.

Johansson, A. and Vinthagen, S. (2016) 'Dimensions of everyday resistance: An analytical framework', *Critical Sociology*, 42(3): 417–35.

Kangan, M.C. (1974) *TAFE in Australia: Report on needs in technical and further education*, Canberra: AGPS.

Limage, L. (2009) 'Multilateral cooperation for literacy promotion under stress: Governance and management issues', *Literacy and Numeracy Studies*, 17(2): 5–33.

'Literacy and numeracy are holding Australia back' (2010) *Industry Connections*, June. Available at: http://cit.edu.au/partnerships/industry_connection/2010_june/literacy_and_numeracy_holding_australia_back (accessed 1 January 2016).

Literacy for Life Foundation (2017) 'Measuring long term impact'. Available at: www.lflf.org.au/2017/05/measuring-long-term-impact/ (accessed 20 February 2018).

Lo Bianco, J. (1987) *National policy on languages*, Canberra, ACT: Commonwealth Department of Education.

Marginson, S. (1997) *Educating Australia – Government, economy and citizen since 1960*, Cambridge: Cambridge University Press.

Mayo, P. (1999) *Gramsci, Freire and adult education: Possibilities for transformative action*, London: Zed Books Ltd.

Morris, A., Hanckel, B., Yasukawa, K. and Gamage, S. (2017) 'The perceptions that homeless people and those at risk of homelessness have of literacy classes'. Available at: www.uts.edu.au/sites/default/files/2017-09/Homelessness%20and%20Literacy%20Report.pdf (accessed 20 February 2018).

Osmond, P. (2018) *Adult basic education in NSW 1970–2018: Official stories and stories from practice*, master's dissertation, University of Technology Sydney.

Ramdeholl, D. and Wells, R. (2013) 'Against the grain: Oral histories from adult literacy workers in New York City', National Conference of the Canadian Association for the Study of Adult Education, University of Victoria, British Columbia. Available at: www.casae-aceea.ca/~casae/sites/casae/files/2013_CASAE_Proceedings_0.pdf#page=512 (accessed 30 April 2018).

Richardson, E.C. (1975) *TAFE in Australia: Second report on needs in technical and further education*, Canberra: AGPS.

Ryan, R. (2011) *How VET responds: A historical policy perspective*, Adelaide: NCVER.

SCOTESE (Standing Council on Tertiary Education, Skills and Employment) (2012) *National foundation skills strategy for adults*, Brisbane, Australia: SCOTESE.

St Clair, R. (2012) 'The limits of levels: Understanding the International Adult Literacy Surveys (IALS)', *International Review of Education*, 58(6): 759–76.Tingle, L. (2015) 'Political amnesia: How we forgot to govern', *Quarterly Essay*, 60: 6–75.

Tusting, K. (2009) '"I am not a 'good' teacher; I don't do all their paperwork": Teacher resistance to accountability demands in the English *Skills for Life* strategy', *Literacy and Numeracy Studies*, 17(3): 6–26.

Yasukawa, K. and Black, S. (2016) 'Policy making at a distance: A critical perspective on Australia's National Foundation Skills Strategy for Adults', in K. Yasukawa and S. Black (eds) *Beyond economic interests: Critical perspectives on adult literacy and numeracy in a globalised world*, Rotterdam: Sense, pp 19–39.

Yasukawa, K., Widin, J. and Chodkiewicz, A. (2008) 'The benefits of adults learning numeracy', in J.F. Matos, P. Valero and K. Yasukawa (eds) *Proceedings of the Fifth International Mathematics Education and Society Conference*, Lisbon: Centro de Investigação em Educação, Universidade de Lisboa – Department of Education, Learning and Philosophy, Aalborg University, pp 495–504.

Yeatman, A. (1993) 'Corporate managerialism and the shift from the welfare to the competition state', *Discourse: Studies in the Cultural Politics of Education*, 13(2): 3–9.

PART V

Transnational perspectives

14

Education policy and the European Semester: challenging soft power in hard times

Howard Stevenson, Alison Milner, Emily Winchip and Lesley Hagger-Vaughan

Introduction

In the years following the global economic crisis of 2008, with its particular impact on the Eurozone and many Southern European economies, the European Commission (EC) has been seeking to 'restabilise', while also aiming to continue to develop the European project. One of the key mechanisms at the centre of this process has been the establishment in 2011 of the European Semester as a system of economic governance and social policy coordination (Delors et al., 2011). The Semester's principal purpose is to monitor the economic performance of member states, and specifically their adherence to European Union (EU) rules for managing public finances (Gros and Alcidi, 2015), although the Semester has a wider role in promoting the EU's longer-term strategic goals, including in relation to social and educational issues (Peña-Casas et al, 2015). However, despite the critical importance of the European Semester within EU governance structures, it remains little understood outside of Brussels policy circles.

In this chapter, we seek to 'open up' the European Semester as a 'policy space' (Lawn and Grek, 2012), and at a technical level, to demonstrate both how it works and how it influences and shapes education policy in member states. In so doing, we argue that those committed to shaping democratic public education in communities must engage in this policy space and 'open up' the Semester politically so that it becomes responsive to the voices of citizens, service providers and users at national and local levels. While any attempt to 'democratise' technical European policy processes is difficult, and carries the risk of incorporation into bureaucratic procedures that may make little difference, we argue that there are new opportunities for labour and social movements, as well as civil society organisations, to intervene in the Semester process in order to shape its outcomes, and that seeking to exploit these opportunities is worthwhile.

The chapter draws on research undertaken in 2016 and 2017 on behalf of the European Trade Union Committee for Education (ETUCE),[1] the European regional organisation of the global union federation Education International. The research involved detailed analysis of the European Semester process combined with interviews with key policy actors, including EC officials in relevant directorates, social partners (employer and trade union confederations) and civil society organisations. The study included five country cases based on Denmark, Italy, Lithuania, Malta and Slovenia, including interviews with Ministry officials and education unions in each (Stevenson et al, 2017).

Understanding the European Semester

The European Semester is little understood as a European policy process, in particular, outside of elite policy circles, but it is central to understanding how the EC works and how relations between the EU and member states are framed. It was established in the years following the economic crisis as the EU sought to address the issues generated by an economic meltdown in many member states, with concomitant social consequences (Grahl, 2012). The EU set out its priorities for recovery in a ten-year plan – 'Europe 2020' (European Commission, 2010). Key objectives focused on increasing employment and investment, both of which had been devastated by the economic crisis, but also included a wider set of social and environmental objectives, including those focused on education. The European Semester was established shortly after and can be considered as providing the ongoing monitoring and surveillance of the 2020 plan, most obviously by ensuring member state compliance with EU financial rules. This highlights the key focus of the Semester, and its function principally as a form of 'economic governance'. The need for tighter surveillance was identified in response to a perceived lack of such monitoring prior to the crisis (European Commission, 2015) and a failure by some countries to live within the parameters set out by the Stability and Growth Pact (S&GP) (restricting budget deficits to 3 per cent of gross domestic product [GDP] and public debt to 60 per cent of national income). However, a key element of the process is the provision of a set of European Council-endorsed 'country-specific recommendations' (CSRs) for each member state, and the Semester can therefore be considered as both backward- and forward-looking – monitoring the past performance of member states, but also setting an agenda for future action.

The Semester process is an annual cycle that commences formally in September of each year. Following a detailed analysis of each country's performance against EC targets, a country report is published for every member state in February of the following year. Member states respond formally to these country reports by setting out their own policy plans, and after reviewing these plans, the EC issues a draft set of CSRs that identify priorities for action in each country. Member states are able to respond to the draft CSRs that they have been given and, in due course, the Council of the EU formally adopts the CSRs, by which time the cycle is ready to recommence.

The process just described sets out in descriptive form the Semester as a mechanism. It is important to point out that, in reality, the process is more complex and also evolving (Bekker, 2016), and rather than a tidy series of steps and procedures that unfold in chronological order, there are often multiple processes occurring simultaneously (ETUCE, 2017). It is also important to recognise that the Semester is principally a system of economic governance, intended to ensure that member states live within the rules of the S&GP, with all the problems associated with the S&GP and its role in driving austerity policies across Europe. It is within the Semester system that penalties can be triggered for those countries that have transgressed S&GP rules. Although formal sanctions are applied in only limited cases, the wider impact of the Semester process in ensuring 'fiscal responsibility' is clear. CSRs, the key outcome of the Semester process, always start with a focus on economic policy and there are often several CSRs related to economic policy. We refer to these CSRs as 'first-order' CSRs as they are the principal focus of the Semester and they relate to aspects of national policy that can attract EU sanctions. The role of the Semester in ensuring 'fiscal responsibility' was illustrated by the 2017 CSRs, when 11 countries had the same wording in their CSRs, namely, that countries should pursue their 'fiscal policy in line with the requirements of the preventive arm of the Stability and Growth Pact, which translates into a substantial fiscal effort for 2018' (Stevenson et al, 2017a). A further seven countries had CSRs with wording that was a variant of this. This focus of the Semester on economic policy, and its role as the enforcer of the requirements of the S&GP, has led many to associate the European Semester with post-crisis austerity policies (ETUC, 2016). It is the requirements of the S&GP that drove down public spending in member states in the years after the crisis and that continue to impact public service provision while also depressing demand and preventing growth. It is essential therefore to recognise that without any direct influence on education policy, the European Semester always has significant indirect influence by setting the parameters within which public expenditure decisions are made in member states.

However, despite the dominance of economic policy in the process, the Semester has a broader concern with all of the Europe 2020 objectives, including those relating to social, educational and environmental objectives. It would be mistaken therefore to present the Semester as simply about 'economic governance' as it is important to also recognise its role in 'social policy coordination', reflected most obviously through CSRs relating to health, education and social security reform. These CSRs can be considered as 'second-order' CSRs insofar as they are not linked to elements of the Semester process that have a legislative basis, but rather exemplify the EU's use of 'soft power' (Lawn, 2006), whereby 'policy coordination' is incentivised through a range of measures (benchmarking, sharing 'good practice', developing cross-EU collaborations) that encourage or discourage particular policy responses (Ball, 2017). In the sections that follow, we provide an overview of how the European Semester has influenced education policy across member states and how those representing education workers and civil society organisations are intervening in order to open up and democratise this European education 'policy space'.

The European Semester and education policy

Education policy issues feature prominently in the European Semester, most obviously in the form of CSRs that can be described as 'education-related' and that have a clear, direct or indirect, link to the education policies of member states. Identifying CSRs as 'education-related', or allocating them to particular education sectors, includes an element of arbitrariness as CSRs are not formally allocated to any specific area of policy or EU directorate. However, with that caveat in mind, it is still possible to argue that in each year of the Semester, only a small minority of countries have had CSRs that have had no education content. Indeed, in 2014, every member state participating in the Semester process had at least one CSR that was clearly focused on education (Stevenson et al, 2017).

The specific content of education-related CSRs appears to be a combination of EC priorities and the education policy priorities of member states. 'Second-order' CSRs, such as education, relate to national competences where the EC has very limited formal powers and so CSRs are generated through shared discussions between the EC and national governments within the Semester cycle. These are the processes through which 'soft power' is exercised and social policy is 'coordinated'. By far the most common education recommendations are those that aim to develop human capital and improve labour market responsiveness and flexibility, highlighting the link between education policy and economic policy, and the pivotal role of the European Semester in reinforcing this connection. European education policy has always been intimately linked to the development of the single market and the drive for competitiveness, and within the European Semester, this link is reinforced by the way 'second-order' education-related CSRs serve to support 'first-order' CSRs focused on economic considerations and securing the future of the single market. The following CSR for Portugal in 2014 illustrates the issues and can be considered typical[2]:

> Improve the quality and labour-market relevance of the education system in order to reduce early school leaving and address low educational performance rates. Ensure efficient public expenditure in education and reduce skills mismatches, including by increasing the quality and attractiveness of vocational education and training and fostering co-operation [sic] with the business sector. Enhance cooperation between public research and business and foster knowledge transfer.

The intimate interdependence of economic and social policy priorities within the European Semester highlights both the threats and opportunities inherent within the process. The obvious danger is that education within member states becomes increasingly subjugated to the needs of capital and the demands of the labour market. Education policy is narrowed and becomes increasingly utilitarian. These developments are well understood in general terms but have been identified as a particular issue in relation to the EU's approach to education policy (Borg and Mayo, 2005; Holford and Mohorčič Špolar, 2012). However, there are also clearly progressive possibilities as the Semester has emerged as a mechanism for putting pressure on individual member states to expand educational provision. One illustration of this tension is reflected in the many recommendations related to early childhood education and care (ECEC), which are frequently framed in terms of increasing women's participation in the labour market but that nevertheless point to the need for much improved access to quality ECEC provision. Again, a typical recommendation in relation to ECEC exemplifies the issues: 'Strengthen measures to increase the labour market participation of older workers and women, including by improving the provision of childcare' (Austria CSR, 2015).

Another area of policy where there is progressive potential is in relation to education provision for migrants and the need to ensure enhancements in both the quantity and quality of current services in many countries. CSRs relating to migrant education now feature prominently in the Semester recommendations and can be identified as the second-most common after those focused on improving labour market 'relevance' and the development of human capital.

The role of education policy within the European Semester presented here highlights the intimate relationship between 'economic governance' and 'social policy coordination' and the way in which 'second-order' CSRs are linked to, and can be used to reinforce, 'first-order' CSRs driven by the economy. Such a relationship highlights the coexistence of both threat and opportunity to the development of policy that promotes public provision of equitable and socially just education systems. It also demonstrates how the Semester acts as a policy conduit between the EC and member states in relation to education issues (albeit a rather closed one, with limited input from outside elite policy circles), but one that is intentionally flexible and capable of absorbing a 'push and pull' relationship between the EC and national governments and their relative responsibilities. Education-related CSRs are not externally generated by the EC and then crudely imposed on reluctant member states; rather, they are the product of ongoing dialogue (both formal and informal) from which CSRs emerge through a process of 'co-construction' (in the words of one senior EC official). Often, CSRs were clearly expressions of existing intent from national governments, with the EC urging countries to implement reform programmes that were already priorities (see the country case studies in Stevenson et al, 2017). Such an approach also contains inbuilt flexibility, whereby the EC can 'push' particular agendas when necessary but 'pull' back if member states assert their authority in relation to education as a national competence. This 'push and pull' was described by one EU official in the following terms:

> 'It [the European Semester] has really enabled the Commission to touch upon many policies that are, according to the principle of subsidiarity, are still national competences. I think the Commission is trying, is using this power and trying to move the barriers and bringing

> in different policies, but, you know, we never know when the member states will say "Listen, don't touch. Go away".' (EC official)

Such flexibility is important to the EU at a time when the EU's authority relative to national sovereignty is being challenged in several member states and when the fallout from the Brexit process (Jessop, 2017) is creating instability and uncertainty. However, such an analysis also points to the European Semester as a policy space open to contestation, and one in which trade union and civil society organisations might intervene. In the final section, we discuss what forms such interventions take, but also the obstacles to genuinely opening up the Semester process to the democratic involvement of EU citizens.

Europe, education policy and the European Semester: identifying progressive possibilities

The EU's founding treaties commit the EU to social dialogue between social partners as a basis for policy development at the European level and in Europe's relations with member states (Articles 152, 154 and 155). Social partners are defined as employers and trade unions (bipartite social dialogue) and the EC (tripartite social dialogue). Social dialogue is deemed to include negotiations (including collective bargaining), consultation, information sharing and joint activities between social partners. Such a commitment clearly provides an opportunity for education trade unions, representing education workers across Europe, to make a significant input into shaping the European Semester, and especially with regard to those CSRs focused on education. However, studies of the Semester process have highlighted that the process has been largely technical and bureaucratic, focused on generating the 'correct solutions' (Darvas and Vihriälä, 2013) and with limited input from labour movement and civil society organisations. The European Parliament also has a limited role in the Semester process, and therefore we can argue that the European Semester represents one part of the democratic deficit in EU governance. Part of the explanation for this democratic deficit in relation to the Semester can be attributed to the impact of the economic crisis and the way in which state forces (at both European and national levels) and capital pushed back against organised labour in the period after the crash. It also reflects the way in which the EU's social aspirations suffered in the years after the crisis (Costamagna, 2013) as 'fiscal responsibility' was privileged over social reconstruction. At a European level, the EU quickly took action intended to stabilise the euro and secure the future of the single market. This included the direct intervention of the troika in relation to several member states considered 'high risk', as well as the establishment of the Semester as a key element of new apparatus to ensure enforcement of the S&GP rules. At the same time, research conducted by ETUCE across its membership highlighted attacks on education workers' rights in many European countries following the crisis, and, in particular, the fragile nature of social dialogue and collective bargaining (ETUCE, 2016a, 2016b).

More recently, there has been evidence of a reaction to these approaches and recognition that the EU must reassert its social dimension if it is to maintain legitimacy and support. Evidence of a 'social turn' in EU goals has been evident for some time (Zeitlin and Vanhercke, 2018), and has become particularly associated with the Juncker presidency. In our research project, this was acknowledged by several senior EC officials, who recognised that the legacy of crisis and austerity, combined with increasing migration, was contributing to a toxic populism based on nationalism and racism, hence the EU's commitment to a 'Triple A on social issues' (in President Juncker's address to the European Parliament in 2014) as well as economic ones. One obvious manifestation of this has been the 'European pillar of social rights' (European Commission, 2017), which is now a centrepiece of EU policy (and that will be promoted and monitored through the European Semester), but it is also evident within the Semester itself, which is increasingly focused on social issues. Indeed, the 2018 European Semester was described by Commissioner Thyssen as a 'landmark' given its social orientation and prioritising of social issues (European Commission, 2018). Meanwhile, the EC has committed to a 'new start for social dialogue' (European Commission, 2016), which includes an explicit commitment to strengthening the role of social dialogue in the European Semester process.

Education workers, through their national unions and their European-level organisation (ETUCE), have been seeking to open up the Semester process so that they can more effectively intervene within it. Such efforts start from a low base in which the involvement of education unions was extremely limited. More widely, Sabato and colleagues (2017) have demonstrated that when unions have been involved in the Semester process, it has often been on a very limited basis, where unions have felt 'listened to, but not heard'. This was partly due to the initial *modus operandi* of the EC described earlier, which did not seek to involve social partners meaningfully in the

Semester process. However, this problem was exacerbated in relation to education as early iterations of the Semester did not conceive of the Semester as a process about education and therefore requiring input from education social partners. This has begun to change over time, and changed significantly in the 2017/18 Semester cycle when, following lobbying by ETUCE, education unions were formally invited by the EC to participate in in-country discussions with EC officials as country reports were drafted. However, the process remains technical and remote, with many senior union officials unable to see the relevance or purpose of engaging with what can appear an arcane and detached EU policy process. Inevitably, these issues appear even more remote to rank-and-file members of education unions, if, indeed, they have any awareness at all of the European Semester.

The approach of the ETUCE has been to prioritise the European Semester in its work, with a particular focus on supporting its member organisations in the EU to be able to more effectively engage in the Semester process. Much of this work has been devoted to raising awareness of the Semester with member organisations so that they understand it – both how it has the potential to impact education, and how it works so that national-level unions can make more strategic and effective interventions in the process. For obvious and understandable reasons, not least because education policy is a national competence, individual education unions have not always given a high priority to EU work, but have rather devoted limited resources to national policy priorities. One conspicuous exception to this has been the work of the Danish education unions, who pool resources to support an effective and targeted intervention into the Semester process at the European level. Danish education unions have also sought to pressure their own government to engage with social partners within the Semester cycle, but this has often been resisted by the Danish government. Although this prioritising of the Semester within union activity remains the exception rather than the rule, there is now growing evidence that ETUCE's campaign of awareness raising is paying dividends and that individual member unions are taking an increasingly proactive response in relation to intervening in the Semester cycle (see ETUCE, 2018).

All of this work is reinforced through a linked strategy of alliance building, with ETUCE developing its campaigning through the European Trades Union Confederation as well as with European civil society organisations. Much of this work is focused on identifying the key points in the Semester process where coordinated interventions can be most effective, and, to this end, a number of resources have been developed to help individual member organisations identify strategies accordingly.

What remains an ongoing challenge is for education unions to be able to align this work at a European level with their aspirations and campaigns at a national and local level. The danger is that even where unions are involved in social dialogue in the Semester process, this takes the form of high-level discussions with a small number of senior union officials taking place in meetings far removed from the wider union membership. As unions are able to insert themselves more effectively into the Semester process, the obvious next step is to connect this activity with wider union goals and in ways that make the discussions meaningful and transparent to grass-roots members. There is a particular need to make much more accessible both the processes and the language that underpin the Semester. Processes remain complex and the language used is dense. Both militate against promoting popular participation and can serve to exclude and silence rather than engage and debate.

The European Semester has considerable potential to impact education policy in member states and, by definition, the experience of education workers. It is vital that these processes are made more democratic, but that can only really happen when there is the meaningful participation of grass-roots union members in EU processes.

Conclusion: opening up the European Semester

In this chapter, we have described the role of the European Semester and how it is able to shape education policy in member states. We have also set out how education workers across Europe, through their unions, are seeking to 'open up' and democratise this technical and oftentimes remote process of governance and policy coordination. What remains unclear is whether this 'opening up' of the Semester process represents something significant and meaningful in which genuine social dialogue is able to develop, or whether the changes are more rhetorical than real, where the participation of labour movement and civil society organisations is little more than a token. There is little doubt that there is a genuine danger that the EU's stated commitment to social dialogue represents no more than a complex and bureaucratic form of corporatism in which unions are sucked into elaborate processes of consultation that promise much but deliver little. The real fear is that unions become associated with, and even forced to defend, policies that they have nominally been privy to developing, but over which they have had little real influence. The danger is therefore that the

EU's new-found commitment to social dialogue is little more than an elaborate incorporationism.

Labour movement and civil society organisations are right to be cautious about the democratic possibilities presented by the European Semester; however, our view is that they would be mistaken to not engage with the process, and to seek to open it up much more than is currently the position. In this chapter, we have sought to demonstrate that the European Semester does have significant implications for education policy in member states. Although not an EU competence, education policy features prominently in the Semester, and through its use of soft power influence, there is the ability to shape education policy in individual countries. Seeking to influence these policy debates, and to shape them in ways that promote a progressive commitment to social justice issues and public service provision, seems to us to be essential. A failure to engage effectively vacates this key policy space and leaves it open to those advocating much more damaging policy options, including marketisation and an expanded role for private providers of education services (all of which are visible in some form within the Semester's CSRs).

The challenge for education unions, and the European trade union movement more widely, is to take up these opportunities while simultaneously criticising their limited nature. European-level union organisations such as ETUCE have long been pushing to open up the Semester process, but this work needs further developing through the efforts of labour movement organisations at the member state level. At this moment, the potential to 'democratise' the European Semester looks uncertain; however, new spaces for influence are opening up, and the EU's own commitment to renewing social dialogue creates an opportunity that can and must be exploited by education unions. The challenge for labour movement and civil society organisations is to seek to force open this space and ensure that obscure European-level policy debates are made accessible to the service users and providers who 'experience' policy but rarely feel that they have any role in shaping it.

Notes

1. *Investing in education: Strengthening the involvement of teacher trade unions in the European Semester on education and training* (European Commission reference – VS/2015/0329).
2. CSRs are published annually for all countries participating in the European Semester. They are available online at: https://ec.europa.eu/info/business-economy-euro/economic-and-fiscal-policy-coordination/eu-economic-governance-monitoring-prevention-correction/european-semester/european-semester-timeline/eu-country-specific-recommendations_en

References

Ball, S.J. (2017) *The education debate*, Bristol: The Policy Press.

Bekker, S. (2016) 'Is there flexibility in the European Semester process? Exploring interactions between the EU and member states within post-crisis socio-economic governance', 1 January, SIEPS Swedish Institute for European Policy Studies, Tilburg Law School Research Paper No. 10/2016. Available at: https://ssrn.com/abstract=2743238 or http://dx.doi.org/10.2139/ssrn.2743238

Borg, C. and Mayo, P. (2005); The EU memorandum on lifelong learning. Old wine in new bottles?', *Globalisation, Societies and Education,* 3: 203–25.

Costamagna, F. (2013) 'The European Semester in action: Strengthening economic policy coordination while weakening the social dimension?', LPF-WEL Working Paper No. 5. Available at: https://ssrn.com/abstract=2367768 or http://dx.doi.org/10.2139/ssrn.2367768

Darvas, Z. and Vihriälä, E. (2013) 'Does the European Semester deliver the right policy advice?', Bruegel Policy Contribution. Available at: http://bruegel.org/2013/09/does-the-european-semester-deliver-the-right-policy-advice/

Delors, J., Fernandes, S. and Mermet, E. (2011) 'The European Semester: Only a first step', Notre Europe Policy Brief, 22. Available at: https://institutdelors.eu/wp-content/uploads/2018/01/bref22-en.pdf

ETUC (European Trade Union Confederation) (2016) 'ETUC on Semester package'. Available at: www.etuc.org/en/pressrelease/etuc-semester-package

ETUCE (European Trade Union Committee for Education) (2016a) *The state of funding in education, teachers' working conditions, social dialogue and trade union rights in Western European countries*, Brussels: ETUCE.

ETUCE (2016b) *The state of funding in education, teachers' working conditions, social dialogue and trade union rights in Central and Eastern European countries*, Brussels: ETUCE.

ETUCE (2017) *Practical guide for an effective involvement of education trade unions in the European Semester on education and training*, Brussels: ETUCE.

ETUCE (2018) 'European Semester'. Available at: www.csee-etuce.org/en/policy-issues/31-trade-and-economic-governance/economic-governance/71-european-semester-country-specific-recommendations

European Commission (2010) 'Europe 2020: A European strategy for smart, sustainable and inclusive growth'. Available at: http://ec.europa.eu/eu2020/pdf/COMPLET%20EN%20BARROSO%20%20%20007%20-%20Europe%202020%20-%20EN%20version.pdf

European Commission (2015) 'The EU's economic governance explained'. Available at: http://ec.europa.eu/rapid/press-release_MEMO-15-6071_en.pdf

European Commission (2016) 'A new start for social dialogue'. Available at: http://ec.europa.eu/social/BlobServlet?docId=16099&langId=en

European Commission (2017) 'European pillar of social rights'. Available at: https://ec.europa.eu/commission/priorities/deeper-and-fairer-economic-and-monetary-union/european-pillar-social-rights_en

European Commission (2018) 'Speakings by Commissioner Thyssen on the 2018 European Semester country reports'. Available at: http://europa.eu/rapid/press-release_SPEECH-18-1684_en.htm

Grahl, J. (2012) 'The first European Semester: An incoherent strategy', paper presented at the PERG workshop 'Europe in Crisis', Kingston University.

Gros, D. and Alcidi, C. (2015) 'Economic policy coordination in the euro area under the European Semester', CEPS Special Report. Available at: www.ceps.eu/publications/economic-policy-coordination-euro-area-under-european-semester

Holford, J. and Mohorčič Špolar, V. (2012) 'Neoliberal and inclusive themes in European lifelong learning policy', in S. Riddell, J. Markowitsch and E. Weedon (eds) *Lifelong learning in Europe: Equity and efficiency in the balance*, Bristol: The Policy Press, pp 39–61.

Jessop, B. (2017) 'The organic crisis of the British state: Putting Brexit in its place', *Globalizations*, 14: 133–41.

Lawn, M. (2006) 'Soft governance and the learning spaces of Europe', *Comparative European Politics*, 4: 272–88.

Lawn, M. and Grek, S. (2012) *Europeanizing education: Governing a new policy space*, Oxford: Symposium Books.

Peña-Casas, R., Sabato, S., Lisi, V. and Agostini, C. (2015) *The European Semester and modernisation of public administration*, Brussels: European Social Observatory.

Sabato, S. and Vanhercke, B., with Spasova, S. (2017) *Listened to, but not heard? Social partners' multilevel involvement in the European Semester*, Brussels: European Social Observatory.

Stevenson, H., Hagger-Vaughan, L., Milner, A. and Winchip, E. (2017) *Education and training policy in the European Semester: Public investment, public policy, social dialogue and privatisation patterns across Europe*, Brussels: ETUCE.

Zeitlin, J. and Vanhercke, B. (2018) 'Socializing the European Semester: EU social and economic policy co-ordination in crisis and beyond', *Journal of European Public Policy*, 25: 149–74.

15

Rethinking adult education for active participatory citizenship and resistance in Europe

George K. Zarifis

Introduction

There is only one meaningful mission for adult education – for all education that matters perhaps – and that is to empower learners towards making meaning of the world and their condition and to emancipate them from all that oppresses them. This is not a new concept, but the role of adult education as a medium for empowerment and emancipation has been challenged in the late 20th century by global policies. These have elevated distorted notions of freedom and autonomy as self-actualisation through competitiveness, with a focus on learning outcomes and investment in marketable skills. Many of these policies were openly received by the European Union (EU), which developed its own agenda for adult education that eventually led to a series of benchmarks and measuring tools, all focused on 'investing in human resources' (European Commission, 2000: 12).

It took ten years, with a series of terrorist attacks in major European cities, a lasting economic crisis with severe social repercussions, the influx of a large number of war refugees and economic migrants, and the opportunistic rise of the Far Right, for the policy rhetoric to shift towards the need for an education that encourages empowerment and emancipation. This rhetoric was encompassed in the term 'active citizenship'. The term was endorsed in the European Council and European Commission's joint report about the 'new priorities for European cooperation in education and training' (Official Journal of the European Union, 2015), but also in the Paris Declaration on 'promoting citizenship and the common values of freedom, tolerance and non-discrimination through education' (EU Ministries of Education, 2015). In European policy documents, however, active citizenship is interpreted as specific skills, attitudes and knowledge (that is, measured learning outcomes) that can be acquired through education. The EU's political aim is to create feelings of belonging, participation and democracy through *social activities and learning*. Growing ethnic and religious diversity in Europe, however, poses both opportunities and challenges to European policymakers and societies. It is expected that this diversity will continue to increase. At the same time, recent studies (Van Driel et al, 2016) show that intolerance and social exclusion are increasing, with some migrant groups feeling alienated. This is leading to incidences of social unrest. So, how can adult education prepare societies for dealing with these phenomena?

EU rhetoric states: 'education and training can help to prevent and tackle poverty and social exclusion, promote mutual respect and build a foundation for an open and democratic society on which active citizenship rests' (Official Journal of the European Union, 2015: 3). It also suggests that 'education and training provide individuals with the knowledge, skills and competences that enable them to grow and to influence their situations, by broadening their perspectives, equipping [sic] people favourably for their future lives, laying the foundations for active citizenship and democratic values, and promoting inclusion, equity and equality' (Official Journal of the European Union, 2015: 4). The policy rhetoric was only triggered in response to the terrorist attacks in France and Denmark in 2015, which recalled similar atrocities in Europe in the recent past.

Research also shows that the fundamental problem of European adult education is its failure to meet the needs of the least educated or otherwise socially vulnerable population (Schraad-Tischler and Kroll, 2014). Although the term 'vulnerable' is a contested one because vulnerability is essentially part of the human condition, adult education needs to readdress and recapture its role as a means for resistance to social discrimination and social disempowerment.

The question is: what can adult education do to reconstitute its meaningful purpose? The answer certainly comes with a cost, both for the field of adult education, and for those who work in it. Resisting the neoliberal debate as the new role for adult education is difficult as many have embraced practices (not unwillingly since much of what has been organised since 2000 is EU-funded) that largely endorse, rather than defend against, the neoliberal notions of qualifications, competence-based curricula, institutional reputation and expert labour. How easy can it be to resist what has been politically and socially normalised over the last 20 years? In addition, how can the 'new mission' for European adult education be anchored to a concept that is as challenging for policymakers as it is for institutions responsible for education? Policymaking has its own targets for citizenship, but are these consistent with pedagogical and democratic values that allow individuals to be excluded from active participation in decision-making? The crucial question is: how can the priorities for a resistant adult education that targets empowerment for emancipation through promoting active citizenship be achieved?

Unfortunately, many of the suggestions that are included in the existing policy agenda (European Commission, 1998) provide little help to achieve what the rhetoric prescribes because access to learning opportunities and further learning remain socially and spatially divided across the EU. In many cases, education systems in member states make things *worse* – through unequal funding and less enriching experiences of learning for different target groups. Socio-economic background, disability, ethnic or migrant status, gender, geographic location, and other factors still affect adults' educational opportunities, learning experiences and educational outcomes strongly. Complete social groups or subsets of the population persistently achieve less well in education – often despite the presence of policy initiatives that are designed to redress these inequities. Furthermore, the integration of refugees and asylum seekers into education and training is a crucial step towards their social inclusion, employability, professional and personal fulfilment, and, of course, active citizenship.

I will now explore the relevance of active participatory citizenship to the notions of empowerment and emancipation as '*agents de résistance*' to what has largely distorted the meaningful mission of adult education: neoliberalism. My argument is partly based on the preliminary findings from the Horizon 2020 EU-funded project EduMAP[1] (Nr 693388), which focuses on adult education among young adults at risk of social exclusion, with particular attention to fostering active citizenship among vulnerable young people.

Adult education for empowerment and resistance and active participatory citizenship

The power of resistance to neoliberal values in adult education is essentially positioned with those who actively and directly participate in it: learners, educators and organisers. It largely relies on the level of readiness for change through empowerment, particularly in educators and learners, and depends on the learning matter and the type of the programme in which they all participate and interact. It is commonly expressed through learning environments where participatory dialogue is exercised and reflective methods of learning are employed.

Nevertheless, this resistance is not easily visible or recognisable. It is normally resistance '*sub silentio*' – in silence, not expressed but implied – with no immediate social benefit since it passes unnoticed except by those who share the experience. This type of resistance relates to what Hollander and Einwohner (2004: 538) define as *opposition* in that actors challenge, subvert or intentionally reject dominant discourses in some way. It is about the conscious questioning of dominant discourses of power.

The concept of 'active citizenship' is used across European countries with a different emphasis because the way in which the term is used reflects the policy priorities of the country. For instance, there is a growing focus on political participation in France and Germany, while in Britain, there is a greater focus on community activities (Hoskins et al, 2012: 23–4). In France, values like liberty, equality, fraternity, human rights, tolerance, rule of law and citizen duties are explicitly stressed, while support for the development of democratic competences (among citizens and denizens) is highlighted in Germany (Nosko and Szeger, 2013). A tendency to increase social cohesion through community activities can also be seen in the ways in which active citizenship is discussed in Southern European countries. In Spain, respecting others, showing tolerance and cooperation and solidarity among people and groups are central values (Hoskins and Kerr, 2012). The actual political, social and economic situations are related to policy discussions. For instance, in Greece, active citizenship is currently highly valued because of social problems related to the economic crisis and the growth of Extreme Right forces (Karakatsani, 2013).

Promoting active citizenship through education is one of the European Commission's strategies for increasing social cohesion and reducing the democratic deficit across Europe (Mascherini et al, 2009: 5). It is expected that adult education will enable people to voice their opinions in a democratic way and thus increase their trust in the political system. The importance of strengthening democratic citizenship through education has been underscored by the recommendation on key competences for lifelong learning (European Commission, DG Education and Culture, 2006), which suggests that civic competence should be based on the knowledge of social and political concepts and structures and a commitment to active and democratic participation. The neoliberal shift, however, leaves little space for developing practices that go beyond the rhetoric of developing competences, rather than acknowledging the need for adult education practices that are enriched by diversity and the wide range of learning contexts and communicative practices.

While adult education has historically been an important means for providing people with a broader, more humane education, in many European countries, adult education has recently become reduced to employability or 'learning for earning'. According to Werquin (2010: 8), the labour market is the focal point for current concerns, which means that the system for recognising non-formal and informal learning outcomes and the financial support on which it depends are conditioned by the overall economic situation. These concerns have been strengthened by the 2008 crisis and 'unemployment', 'skills', 'competitiveness', 'employability', 'labour market integration' and 'productivity' are now terms often featured in official statements.

More recently, young people have been targeted through initiatives to encourage active citizenship through community involvement and volunteering. The crucial question is whether these initiatives encourage learning that fosters active citizenship or whether their aim is to channel a person's political agency into the reproduction of the existing socio-political order. Brooks and Holford (2009: 21) suggest that we should consider the extent to which individuals are participants not only in states and other territorial entities, but also in discursive networks of contested information and knowledge. This approach would draw upon young people's own political concerns and recognise their potential for establishing new forms of solidarity. Currently, however, the objectives of lifelong learning have the effect of making individuals less dependent upon the state, or transforming learning into a desirable consumer commodity, and have thus been used for mobilising people to help themselves, rather than providing services to them. Registration fees, for example, represent the share of the costs that is borne by adults themselves. Cost is an important factor in Greece, for example, as people with modest qualifications are also those on low incomes. For them, the cost is money but also time (opportunity cost) (Werquin, 2010: 58). This tendency for mobilising people to help themselves asks for more reflective practices by adult educators in order to adjust their role to the current social and cultural diversity. It also requires broader outreach as the majority of young adults *not participating in education* are those who are on the brink of social exclusion or poverty, or with diverse ethno-cultural backgrounds. A capacity for political, social and economic participation is a necessary, but not a sufficient, condition for active citizenship. Thus, in addition to improving the skills and knowledge needed for active participation, the transformation of the learner's identification and engagement must be part of the agenda.

In discussing adult education as a means to achieve active citizenship, it is important to examine the educational implications of relevant theories on citizenship. I conceptualise active citizenship as membership of a politico-legal community that serves as a forum for *political, social and economic participation* (Milana, 2008). In Europe, in addition to the right to vote, there are other means of political participation open to legally resident individuals. In practice, however, citizenship often entails exclusion. Research (see Mascherini et al, 2009) has shown that social exclusion and alienation are real problems among representatives of minority groups.

In exploring the links between adult education and active citizenship, three different interrelationships can be identified: learning *about* citizenship; learning *through* citizenship; and learning *for* citizenship (Kalekin-Fishman et al, 2007: 28–32). Learning about citizenship is the traditional task of the subject of civics in formal adult education settings. This learning is primarily about citizenship as *status*, and focuses mainly on the individual. Conceptualised as preparatory learning, it is relatively formal and top-down in its delivery. Learning through citizenship may involve incidental learning arising from a range of different contexts, but it is more likely to involve an element of conscious reflection and discussion on different experiences of citizenship in everyday life. The focus can be on both the individual and the collective, and it is developmental in its approach towards citizenship as a *practice*.

Learning for citizenship is appropriate for adult education as it offers the prospect of linking formal and informal learning, linking individual and collective citizenship, and making dynamic connections between citizenship as status and citizenship as practice. Relevant evidence collected in the EduMAP project from adult educators[2] who work with young adults in educational and support programmes shows that adult educators have a concrete view of active citizenship related to the competences of decision-making, collaborative learning and critical thinking, with reference to social participation, support and solidarity. Some of them emphasised that it is painful to see fellow citizens becoming poor, unemployed or homeless, but what is even scarier is that many young adults just get used to this reality. Adult educators in Greece and Portugal claim that active citizenship is about *resisting* this reality through targeted actions that affect decision-making at local and regional levels first and the national level later.

Vulnerability: an issue for adult educators as resistance mediators

In order to resist the neoliberal rhetoric on marketable skills and educational instrumentality, adult education needs to reshape curriculum contents, educational initiatives and pedagogies in ways that are acceptable to a wide range of cultural codes and communicative practices. Educators must not only take account of diverse cultural backgrounds, but also actively involve adult learners in educational initiatives that will take account of the differing needs of minority groups. Consequently, adult education could be regarded as a means of bridging the gap between hegemonic and peripheral cultures, but a crucial issue remains: what kind of educational activities are needed to encourage active citizenship among social groups that are discriminated against so that it will be able to overcome barriers to political, social and economic participation for people at risk of social exclusion (Bagnall, 2010)?

Research evidence shows that the fundamental problem of the European adult education system is its failure to meet the needs of the least educated or otherwise vulnerable population. While adult education has problems in meeting the educational needs of vulnerable groups, it offers good educational opportunities to those who are already highly educated, or, at its best, to those who are 'the most disadvantaged of the advantaged' (for example, a person with good qualifications but a weak labour market position) or 'the most advantaged of the disadvantaged', such as individuals with low educational levels in a good socio-economic situation (Burls and Recknagel, 2013). In the research conducted for EduMAP with adult educators, policymakers and vulnerable young adults, it is evident that resistance is largely associated with accepting and naturalising certain policy-dominant concepts like 'vulnerability'. The concept of vulnerability seems to collect a variety of interpretations. Some young adult learners attribute to vulnerability characteristics that are not compatible with their own condition and therefore refuse to identify themselves as vulnerable. They believe that vulnerability relates more to youth, or being a refugee, homeless, physically challenged and so on. One learner told us that:

> 'I don't consider myself as vulnerable. I have support from my family on anything I do. Even for being here in this programme, I received help from my mother, who is a lawyer.... A vulnerable person is normally someone with no help or support at all. Being totally alone, abandoned or being a refugee without a visible future ahead or maybe being crippled [sic] in a wheelchair, although these people are receiving benefits so they are not as vulnerable then.' (Interview IT_GP1_Stu4_M_171018, translation from Italian)

For educators, the term 'vulnerability' refers to the condition of disempowerment that many adults experience due to abrupt life changes or transitions. This condition is normally associated with the development of psychological pressure and/or mood disorders that can cause extreme and persistent feelings of sadness, hopelessness and worthlessness. As one of the instructors suggests:

> 'I notice that more and more of those young adults participating in our programmes express negative feelings, both for the social and political situation as well as for themselves. They do not directly refer to vulnerability as a condition that may define their own situation; they want to appear positive and optimistic, but during our counselling sessions, negative feelings resurface. It is when they realize that the future they are facing is bleak and they cannot expect much.... Vulnerability is a hard hit by reality I suppose.' (Interview GR_GP5_Edu2_F_171220, translation from Greek)

The term 'vulnerability' was frequently used during the interviews, but what is defined in either policy or academic terms as vulnerability is not accepted by young adults. Resisting the acceptance and naturalisation of dominant policy concepts is part of a Freireian approach to educational processes, which empowers learners in meaning-making processes through coding and decoding the meaning of terms. This essentially asks for reflective practices that also resist understanding active citizenship as a competence that is measurable through its learning outcomes. Resistance to dominant forms of curriculum development and delivery are also prioritised by adult educators. Many respondents felt that an exciting, varied and interactive learning delivery style is important in engaging young adults, but educators need to realise the limitations and their own incapacities. As one educator noted:

> 'Citizenship has to be learned like any other skill. However, most effective learning will not take place through the given curriculum, but through positive experiences of participation.... Providers, but also we, the instructors, might do well to consider our own list of citizenship skills.... The curriculum, pedagogy and approach to the programme could then be reconstructed with the aim of developing

these skills.' (Interview GR_GP5_Edu3_M_171203, translation from Greek)

In the light of current policy initiatives, as well as theoretical approaches and relevant research in the field in Europe, the following implications for adult educators and training practitioners as resistance mediators are suggested:

- *Respect for others can be taught.* From an early age, there is a need to correct misconceptions and provide opportunities for genuine intercultural experiences. Particularly for active citizenship, many respondents suggest that the focus is more on the development of cognitive skills and knowledge. However, the underlying assumption of programmes aiming to foster active citizenship should be opened up to scrutiny:

  'we must always ask what it is that people are being encouraged to participate in. Is it about marketable skills? No! Is it about becoming better as a person? Yes! How can this be achieved? By questioning what is considered a given, to challenge what is dominant. Essentially, to reverse … the process of reproducing stereotypes.' (Interview PT_GP1_Edu3_F_170618, translation from Portuguese)

- *Adult education programmes need to create conditions for inter-ethnic cooperation and foster tolerance.* Simply bringing adults from different backgrounds together is not sufficient to reduce prejudice and develop positive intercultural relations. Many educators and learners stress that adult education needs to create the conditions for all learners and teaching staff to develop intercultural competence.
- *The way in which adult education operates makes a difference.* In particular, adult education settings with strong and dynamic ties to the local community have great potential for promoting cohesion. They create a sustainable positive atmosphere in adult education settings, as well as a stronger sense of belonging. As a Cypriot adult educator argued:

  'Unless I have reason otherwise, I give as much flexibility as I can to accommodate their schedule. I believe the adult learner wants to be in this class, missing class is a stressor. But, sometimes, there are other priorities they just have to attend to, so they may be a few minutes late, or they have to

> leave early, or they have to miss a class. They are adults, they assume the responsibility but I try to be as accommodating and reasonable as I can.' (InterviewCY_GP1_Edu1_M_170618, adapted translation from Greek)

- *Use effective methods for creating inclusive programmes.* Most European countries still tend to use traditional teaching methods, although methods such as project-based learning, cooperative learning and peer education are becoming more common. These methods have demonstrated their value in combating intolerance as activities that involve learners dialoguing with each other and the instructor. Beliefs, assumptions, attitudes and perspectives are challenged and examined in the classroom where dialogue is encouraged.
- *Adult teachers and educators need diversity training.* The intercultural competence of adult educators in Europe needs to be strengthened. The majority of adult educators who participated in the EduMAP research suggested that they also feel weak and vulnerable when it comes to performing in learning environments with diverse audiences.
- *Adult education practice could benefit more from third-sector know-how.* Local and international non-governmental organisations (NGOs) with specific expertise in the field can enhance the expertise in adult education settings but are underutilised in both formal and non-formal adult education. As a Greek adult educator stressed:

> 'Life is about relationships; so community is important to learning. I think there is, in that community, accountability. [The students] know one another and know their strengths and weaknesses … [so] they begin to care about each other as students, but also as a person. Hopefully, [students] are developing some deep relationships over time so that when life happens, maybe they can step in and support and encourage.' (Interview GR_GP3_Edu4_F_171019, translation from Greek)

Conclusion

Learning for active citizenship offers a broad platform for resistance where three overlapping dimensions can be distinguished: learning for multicultural citizenship; learning for inclusive citizenship; and learning for participatory citizenship. To this end, adult education policies and practices should be acceptable to a wide range of ways of living and communicative practices. The increasing availability of digital media and communication, in particular, opens up many innovative avenues for young people to practise their citizenship in multiple ways, but they also pose new challenges for adult educators. These challenges relate both to their practice roles and to their personal and professional development as resistance agents, and involve the promotion of social, economic and political aspects of active citizenship. Furthermore, multiple characteristics of citizenship and contexts where citizenship can be learned should be recognised in adult education practices. The complexity of vulnerability should be recognised in designing and delivering adult education programmes. Vulnerability should be considered and recognised as 'a situation of risk', rather than 'a label' applied to specific groups at risk of social exclusion. Consideration of the issues that might make people vulnerable (for example, gender, age, disability and so on), rather than labelling specific groups as vulnerable, should be taken into account as a prerequisite of effective resistance in adult education. Importantly, efforts are needed to include young women in active societal participation through adult education.

EduMAP's preliminary results show that European adult education as a means for resistance, although desired, is still far from happening because adult education has not fully embraced the empowerment and emancipation of the individual through learning how to think and reflect critically (Crowther, 2004). Adult education must resist the governing policy language and prevent the regurgitation of the messages of a dominant political culture that, despite its value-filled rhetoric, allows value-free practices. Adult education for active participatory citizenship can operate as a platform towards organising programmes that will operate as resistance agents to the neoliberal callings. There are many challenges to be faced in the process because education for active citizenship was created by the EU to counteract deficits in the integration process, where the goal was to increase the political conscience of citizens and their identification with the EU, and to strengthen social cohesion and European solidarity. Research has shown (ECORYS, 2015) that the majority of EU-funded projects keep a close connection with labour market policy with an objective of employability, and only a minority of existing projects are dedicated to the objective of active citizenship as such.

Nevertheless, active citizenship cannot be encapsulated in a set of competences to be acquired once and for all. Beyond the conceptualisation of multiple dimensions of citizenship, the elaboration of education for active participation needs to be based on a theoretical grasp of the role of learners' cultural backgrounds. This is particularly evident in the research results that were conducted as part of the EduMAP project, which explores the policies and practices needed in the field of adult education to include young adults at risk of social exclusion in active participatory citizenship in Europe. Preliminary results from the EduMAP project show that social exclusion and alienation are real problems among socially disadvantaged adults. Learning in adult education settings, while essential, plays only a minimal role in addressing the needs of socially disadvantaged adults. The new role for adult educators as resistance agents in Europe is therefore primarily to ensure a safe, judgement-free learning space for all adults, a learning space that is oriented towards basic human ethics, recognises the values of diversity and respect for differences, and *predominantly integrates social reaction in the learning process*. Being aware that one's own culture may shape one's reactions will then operate as pedagogical inspiration for many and, consequently, be the basis for an entirely new set of educational traditions, procedures and routines that will eventually promote and support active participatory citizenship.

Notes

1 More details on EduMAP are available at: http://blogs.uta.fi/edumap/. EduMAP (No. 693388) is funded under the EU's Horizon 2020 Research and Innovation Programme. The opinions of the author do not represent those of the European Commission or the EduMAP Consortium.

2 The information was collected through interviews conducted during the period between June 2017 and December 2017 with 32 adult educators from Greece, Cyprus, Malta, Italy and Portugal as part of the research conducted in the EduMAP project.

References

Bagnall, R. (2010) 'Citizenship and belonging as a moral imperative for lifelong learning', *International Journal of Lifelong Education*, 29(4): 449–60.

Brooks, R. and Holford, J. (2009) 'Citizenship, learning, education: Themes and issues', *Citizenship Studies*, 13(2): 85–103.

Burls, K. and Recknagel, G. (2013) *Approaches to active citizens learning: A review of policy and practice 2010–2013*, Lincoln: Take Part Research Cluster.

Crowther, J. (2004) '"In and against" lifelong learning: Flexibility and the corrosion of character', *International Journal of Lifelong Education*, 23(2): 125–36.

ECORYS (Economic Consultancy and Research Services) (2015) 'Interim evaluation of the Europe for Citizens Programme 2007–13', final report, Birmingham, ECORYS. Available at: http://ec.europa.eu/citizenship/pdf/doc1227_en.pdf (accessed 1 June 2018).

EU (European Union) Ministries of Education (2015) 'Declaration on promoting citizenship and the common values of freedom, tolerance and non-discrimination through education', informal meeting of European Union education ministers. Available at: http://ec.europa.eu/assets/eac/education/news/2015/documents/citizenship-education-declaration_en.pdf (accessed 1 June 2018).

European Commission (1998) *Education and active citizenship in the European Union*, Luxembourg: Office for Official Publications of the European Communities. Available at: https://publications.europa.eu/en/publication-detail/-/publication/b33ea18c-355e-4fa5-bee6-cc07194831ad (accessed 1 June 2018).

European Commission (2000) *A memorandum on lifelong learning*, Commission staff working paper (SEC 2000, 1832), Brussels: European Commission. Available at: http://arhiv.acs.si/dokumenti/Memorandum_on_Lifelong_Learning.pdf (accessed 1 June 2018).

European Commission, DG Education and Culture (2006) 'The key competences for lifelong learning – A European framework', *Journal of the European Union*, 30 December, L394.

Hollander, J.A. and Einwohner, R.L. (2004) 'Conceptualizing resistance', *Sociological Forum*, 19(4): 533–54.

Hoskins, B. and Kerr, D. (2012) 'Participatory citizenship in the European Union Institute of Education: Final study summary and policy recommendations'. Available at: http://ec.europa.eu/citizenship/pdf/report_4_final_study_summary_and_policy_recommendations_.pdf (accessed 1 June 2018).

Hoskins, B., Abs, H., Han, C., Kerr, D. and Veugelers, W. (2012) *Contextual analysis report. Participatory citizenship in the European Union. Institute of Education*, Report 1, Brussels: European Commission, Europe for Citizens Programme.

Kalekin-Fishman, D., Tsitselikis, K. and Pitkänen, P. (2007) 'Theorizing multiple citizenship', in D. Kalekin-Fishman and P. Pitkänen (eds) *Multiple citizenship as a challenge to European nation-states*, Rotterdam: Sense Publishers, pp 1–38.

Karakatsani, D. (2013) 'Higher education, participation and active learning in Greece', in P. Cunningham (ed) *Identities and citizenship education: Controversy, crisis and challenges. Selected papers from the fifteenth Conference of Children's Identity and Citizenship in Europe Academic Network*, London: CiCe, pp 194–204.

Mascherini, M., Manca, A.R. and Hoskins, B. (2009) *The characterization of active citizenship in Europe*, Luxemburg: Institute for the Protection and Security of the Citizen.

Milana, M. (2008) 'Is the European (active) citizenship ideal fostering inclusion within the Union? A critical review', *European Journal of Education*, 43(2): 207–16.

Nosko, A. and Szeger, K. (2013) 'Active citizenship can change your country for the better', *Open Society Foundations*, February 25. Available at: https://www.opensocietyfoundations.org/voices/active-citizenship-can-change-your-country-better (accessed 1 June 2018).

Official Journal of the European Union (2015) 'Joint report of the Council and the Commission on the implementation of the strategic framework for European cooperation in education and training (ET 2020), new priorities for European cooperation in education and training (2015/C 417/04)', C 417/25. Available at: http://eur-lex.europa.eu/legal-content/EN/TXT/?uri=celex:52015XG1215%2802%29 (accessed 1 June 2018).

Schraad-Tischler, D. and Kroll, C. (2014) 'Social justice in the EU – A cross-national comparison. Social Inclusion Monitor Europe (SIM)', index report. Available at: http://news.sgi-network.org/uploads/tx_amsgistudies/Social-Justice-in-the-EU-2014.pdf (accessed 1 June 2018).

Van Driel, B., Darmody, M. and Kerzil, J. (2016) *Education policies and practices to foster tolerance, respect for diversity and civic responsibility in children and young people in the EU*, NESET II report, Luxembourg: Publications Office of the European Union. Available at: http://nesetweb.eu/wp-content/uploads/2015/08/NESET2_AR3.pdf (accessed 1 June 2018).

Werquin, P. (2010) *Recognition of non-formal and informal learning: Country practices*, Paris: OECD. Available at: www.oecd.org/education/skills-beyond-school/44600408.pdf (accessed 1 June 2018).

16

Leaving no one behind: bringing equity and inclusion back into education

Carlos Vargas-Tamez

Introduction

In the past three decades, the international community has witnessed two simultaneous, albeit contradictory, developments in education. On the one hand, the formation and pursuit of various global education agendas, which establish commitments and goals for all countries, instil educational priorities and aim at promoting values and ideals of social progress and justice, equality, peace, sustainability, and human rights.

On the other hand, a set of globally converging discourses on education that flag opposing views has emerged and been consolidated around the world. Embedded in a neoliberal imaginary, these discourses have narrowed down the purpose of education so as to prioritise its economic function, namely, economic growth and employability, over some equally important objectives like social cohesion and participation. As a result, the very notions of equity and inclusion have been rearticulated under utilitarian principles that entangle equity with quality and excellence in the outcomes of education, thus diluting more robust understandings of equity and inclusion as social justice in which inequality in education is explained by structural factors like widespread poverty, marginalisation and cumulative disadvantage.

Taking equity and inclusion as points of departure, this chapter posits that these foundational principles have implications in terms of the conceptualisation and formulation of education policies, strategies and the governance and financing of education for the most vulnerable populations. In so doing, it explores how participatory policymaking processes may foster dialogue among different groups, allowing for the recognition of difference and diversity and the representation of marginalised groups and their world views, needs, wants and aspirations.

Different conceptualisations of equity and inclusion

Definitions of equity and inclusion vary according to different philosophical traditions. Their conceptualisation has been strongly associated with the development of theories of social justice, ranging from utilitarianism to contractualism. The former identifies justice (the morally right action) with the satisfaction of desire and the search for happiness as ultimate goods. As such, under utilitarianism, the right action is the one that produces the most good. As explained by Jeremy Bentham (2000: 14):

> By the principle of utility is meant that principle which approves or disapproves of every action whatsoever according to the tendency it appears to have to augment or diminish the happiness of the party whose interest is in question: or, what is the same thing in other words to promote or to oppose that happiness.

The problem with this view of justice is the subjective nature of pleasure and happiness. Under utilitarianism, what counts is the satisfaction of desires but not so much what the desires are for or what effects these may have. Utilitarians, holding high regard for liberty and freedom, are mostly concerned with individual utility and interpret the good of society as constituted by the advantages enjoyed by individuals, by the maximisation of the levels of satisfaction. Another passage in Bentham's *Principles of morals and legislation* confirms that 'The community is a fictitious body' and that 'the interest of the community is the sum of the interests of the several members who compose it' (Bentham, 2000: 15).

By contrast, John Rawls, among others, introduced a social and collective dimension to the idea of justice and sees 'fairness' as a fundamental aim of equity. He argues that a basic goal of every policy should be one of equality: 'as far as possible the "good things" of life should be shared equally: education and career opportunities, welfare services, leisure and so on' (Rawls, cited in Blakemore and Griggs, 2007: 24). His idea of social justice is grounded on two foundational principles:

> First: each person is to have an equal right to the most extensive scheme of equal basic liberties compatible with a similar scheme of liberties for others.
>
> Second: social and economic inequalities are to be arranged so that they are both (a) reasonably expected to be to

> everyone's advantage, and (b) attached to positions and offices open to all. (Rawls, 1999: 53)

The first principle (the principle of equal liberty) encapsulates the basic liberties and fundamental freedoms that are highly esteemed by utilitarianism, and underscores the need for equal treatment as a fundamental characteristic of a just society (Sidelil, 2011). In this formulation, individuals build their conceptions of what is good with due respect of the liberties of others. 'The principles of right, and so of justice, put limits on which satisfactions have value; they impose restrictions on what are reasonable conceptions of one's good' (Rawls, 1999: 27). The second principle (the difference principle) opens the possibility for – deliberate – inequalities that may produce societal welfare. Examples of such unequal, yet egalitarian, measures are those based on merit (for example, meritocracy) but also those aimed at redressing historic disadvantage (for example, affirmative action).

The difference between utilitarianism and justice as fairness is that in the latter, the concept of right is prior to that of the good, while in utilitarianism, the maximisation of the good is the overriding parameter. At the core of this distinction lies a profound difference in the conceptions of society between both traditions. While utilitarianism is imprinted by a rather individualistic formulation of desires and their efficient fulfilment and maximisation, justice as fairness addresses societal and collective concerns.

From the main tenets of the philosophical traditions explained earlier, it is possible to identify some current conceptualisations of equity in education that are akin to utilitarianism and others that are closer to a view of rights, to justice as fairness. These distinctions are important as both principles are used as policy orientations and their interpretations have different implications for education.

Equity as a utilitarian construction

Over the past two decades, an understanding of equity in education has been formed around a rearticulated concept of fairness that subsumes the former under the overarching principle of economic growth. Under this rearticulation, equity is reconfigured and assembled with the pursuit of quality and excellence in education, as measured by school and learner performance (Sellar and Lingard, 2014), in a belief that such learning outcomes will result in better employment, income and, ultimately, economic growth. A good example of this view of equity is large-scale assessments, particularly the Organisation for

Economic Co-operation and Development's (OECD's) Programme for International Student Assessment (PISA), which interprets equity as 'fairness and inclusion': 'equity in education means that personal or social circumstances such as gender, ethnic origin or family background, are not obstacles to achieving educational potential (fairness) and that all individuals reach at least a basic minimum level of skills (inclusion)' (OECD, 2012: 9). From this perspective, inclusion does not mean being able to access an education that adapts to the needs of all learners or that education is made inclusive, but ensuring a basic minimum standard of education, while fairness is construed not as justice or as right, but as an outcome, that is, ensuring that personal and social circumstances do not interfere with educational potential, and this, in turn, is conceived as the learning outcomes prescribed in a test.

While connecting equity with performance links the latter to personal and social circumstances, the emphasis is placed on in-school factors as enablers in overcoming socio-economic constraints, hence shifting the responsibility of equity from systemic and contextual factors to the deeds of teachers, parents and learners. This reduced view of equity is problematic for two reasons: on the one hand, it decontextualises equity, taking for granted issues of social and cultural capital, the reproduction of inequality, and cumulative disadvantage; while, on the other, it legitimates education governance technologies based on performativity and comparison, what Nikolas Rose (1991) termed 'governing by numbers'.

This understanding of equity as fairness and inclusion resembles the idea of equity in utilitarianism in that all that matters is not how we arrive at good educational outcomes (whether teaching to the test or addressing the underlying causes of social inequality), but the desired good (performance) is achieved and maximised. The policy effects of such an understanding of equity are also utilitarian as they hide from view the structural and socio-economic factors behind inequality and miss the effective measures to dismount it:

> The result is that inequities in schooling are constructed as a problem of teacher quality.... Equity is thus rearticulated as a matter of improving teacher (and perhaps teaching) quality, rather than reducing growing social inequalities that are associated with the production of gaps in educational outcomes between more and less advantaged groups. (Sellar and Lingard, 2014: 10)

The utilitarian outlook of equity has gained considerable currency around the world as it has been influenced by international practices of standardised testing and international formulations that prioritise within-school factors in the explanation and undertaking of equity in education. One such formulation is that of 'the learning crisis', which has been recollected by various international organisations. For example, in its latest *World development report*, the World Bank (2018: 3) claims that 'schooling without learning is a wasted opportunity ... a great injustice', and that the 'learning crisis is a moral crisis'. The report alerts us to a 'learning crisis' consisting of three dimensions, one of which is poor learning outcomes. The emphasis on learning outcomes confirms 'an empirical shift away from philosophical discourses about social justice to a reliance on more data driven practices of equity ... this has weakened the influence of conceptual-discursive accounts of what constitutes social justice in schooling' (Lingard and Savage, 2014: 712). Consistent with this imaginary, the policy responses ideated for equity are utilitarian in nature. This explains why the World Bank (2018) suggests that to assess learning, measuring and tracking should be 'serious goals' in order to act on evidence (which again relies on measurement of learning as guidance on how to remedy learning deficits) and to align actors.

Indeed, there is an economic preoccupation with underperformance and with underachievement, which is consistent with a utilitarian view of both education and equity. This conceptualisation of equity, fairness and inclusion is consistent with the neoliberal imaginary of education in which equity matters because it is 'economically efficient' (OECD, 2012: 14) because 'educational failure ... imposes high costs on society [and because] poorly educated people limit economies' capacity to produce, grow and innovate' (OECD, 2012: 3). This economic formulation has been taken up by the International Commission for Financing Global Education Opportunity (Education Commission), whose 'Learning generation' report (Education Commission, 2016a: 13) claims that 'the growing skills gap will stunt economic growth, with far-reaching social and political repercussions'.

Perhaps the most detrimental consequence of this notion of equity and inclusion is that the policy solutions conceived to promote equity do not counter inequality. Even if improving learning outcomes may have good consequences in the future in terms of educational achievement and, possibly, upward social mobility at the individual level (let us remember here that the sum of individual inclusion does not make an inclusive society), there are social and structural factors challenging the possibility of breaking patterns of disadvantage in education today.

Ultimately, the argument of the learning crisis confounds the causes with the consequences of a lack of learning, like unemployment, poverty, discrimination, gender inequality and violence. This misperception is aided by the fact that equity and inclusion are rearticulated and assembled across a number of related concepts like excellence, autonomy and efficiency that are associated with a neoliberal approach to politics (Rizvi and Lingard, 2011). From a review of the literature and the policy positions of certain countries and intergovernmental organisations (IGOs), it is clear that equity and inclusion have become functions of economic growth instead of ends in themselves. Both objectives are reformulated into utilitarian notions of well-being in which social equity is valued inasmuch as it provides a better framework for economic growth (Vargas, 2017).

Equity and social justice

Since the policy ideals of equity and inclusion can only be understood in reference to their relationship to other values, if we aim to problematise and politicise inequality in education, equity may be better articulated through a notion of social justice. For that purpose, Nancy Fraser's (2009) threefold concept of social justice – redistribution, recognition and representation – may be useful to shed light on the possible implications of promoting equity in education, including the redistribution of learning opportunities among the most marginalised groups, the promotion of their participation in all matters concerning their lives and well-being, and a recognition of their diversity and of the structural reasons behind their exclusion and marginalisation. In what follows, it is argued that the international community's 2030 Agenda for Sustainable Development, and particularly Sustainable Development Goal (SDG) 4 – Education 2030, provides an invaluable opportunity to frame equity and inclusion in this direction.

Equity and inclusion as guiding principles of SDG 4 – Education 2030

The 2030 Agenda for Sustainable Development, adopted by the international community in 2015, set out an action plan for people, planet and prosperity to be reached by 2030. Composed of 17 SDGs aiming at eliminating poverty and hunger, reducing inequalities, strengthening universal peace and freedom, and promoting cooperation and sustainability, the 2030 Agenda conceives of education as a key goal that may help in the achievement of all other goals. Encapsulated in SDG 4, the goal aims to 'ensure inclusive and equitable quality education and promote lifelong learning opportunities for all' by 2030, and includes ten targets to achieve such ambitions.

From its formulation, it is clear that equity and inclusion are important drivers for SDG 4 but also goals in themselves. In the 2015 Incheon Declaration, member states committed to 'addressing all forms of exclusion and marginalization, disparities and inequalities in access, participation and learning outcomes', and to 'making the necessary changes in education policies and focusing efforts on the most disadvantaged … to ensure that no one is left behind' (UNESCO, 2016a: 7). The Declaration conceives of 'inclusion and equity in and through education [as] the cornerstone of a transformative education agenda' and asserts that 'no education target should be considered met unless met by all' (UNESCO, 2016a: 7).

The policy intention of leaving no one behind and the commitment to reach the needs of the furthest behind first permeates the 2030 Agenda and holds promise to bring the world's poorest and most marginalised groups to the forefront of political decision-making and to redress their historical subordinate condition. The first step to do this is the identification of who the vulnerable groups are, as well as the source of their vulnerability. The 2030 Agenda and SDG 4 identify 'children, youth, persons with disabilities, people living with HIV/AIDS, older persons, indigenous peoples, refugees and internally displaced persons and migrants' (United Nations, 2015: para 23) as those whose development should be prioritised. The pledge of leaving none of these groups behind included the commitment to take further effective measures and actions to remove obstacles and constraints, strengthen support, and meet their special needs. For this to materialise, it is necessary to arrive at non-utilitarian, humanistic notions of equity and inclusion, and to unpack their implications in terms of the conceptualisation and formulation of education policies and strategies, the governance and financing of education, the identification of obstacles in the way, and the review and monitoring of educational development.

Participatory policymaking

According to the United Nations Educational, Scientific and Cultural Organization (UNESCO, 2017b: 18), 'a focus on equity implies inclusive policy dialogue that allows for diverse constituencies to have greater voice in decision-making processes and ensure the legitimacy of national education policy choices'. This is particularly true for vulnerable groups given the fact that the benefits and burdens of any given policy tend to be distributed among different target groups according to their political power and how they are socially esteemed. In the case of vulnerable groups, they have traditionally been construed as objects of charity instead of rights-holders who can and should take part in decision-making processes concerning their lives and opportunities (Vargas, 2014). This is especially the case when it comes to education: vulnerable groups are often considered not knowledgeable enough, or as not having the skills or experience, to be policy partners; they have thus been traditionally ill-served by public policy.

A focus on equity must ensure the representation of vulnerable groups and their participation in decision-making. For the state, this means an obligation: to engage in participatory processes in the definition, implementation and evaluation of education policies; to guarantee a safe and open public space to discuss, dissent and agree on the best courses of action; and to integrate different views to give equal voice to all stakeholders. Such processes aim at fostering dialogue, allowing for the recognition of difference and diversity and the representation of marginalised groups.

These participatory mechanisms may shed light on the factors that contribute to marginalisation as experienced by the vulnerable groups themselves. These include laws, policies and institutional arrangements that may reinforce social barriers and discriminatory behaviours. The state must thus engage in deconstructing institutional and cultural frameworks that perpetuate disadvantage.

The participation of marginalised populations in the identification of the obstacles they face may result in better and more nuanced knowledge for the strategies aiming at redressing disadvantage and ensuring equity and inclusion. The construction of such strategies requires finding the intersection – and coherence – of education, social and economic policies so that they may move forward in the same direction, fostering equity and inclusion in all policies instead of implementing palliative social measures for vulnerable groups while economic policy keeps reproducing disadvantage. This is perhaps the largest challenge, which calls for a reform of economic policies so that they are driven by equity concerns and not efficiency, by solidarity instead of competition, by redistribution instead of pure growth, and by social justice and affirmative action instead of simplistic meritocratic claims that hide from view the structural causes of social inequality and threaten to reproduce it.

Tracking progress in equity and inclusion

It is paramount to track the progress of equity and inclusion in education. At the moment, the global and thematic indicators to monitor the progress of SDG 4 (see UNESCO, 2016a) include issues like equal access, enrolment ratios, gender parity and participation rates, but there are no specific indicators that show how marginalised groups are being prioritised.

To this effect, civil society organisations are lobbying for governments to provide evidence that no one is left behind in the implementation of the 2030 Agenda for Sustainable Development. For example, Bond (2018) has proposed that governments identify their marginalised populations, develop a 'leave no one behind' strategy and begin its implementation by September 2018 (the first 1,000 days of the SDGs). Also, the Overseas Development Institute and Save the Children have proposed that 'all Voluntary National Reviews (VNRs) should contain a section dedicated to "leave no one behind" and that UN guidelines for VNRs should include specific guidance for how countries report progress on the pledge' (Bond, 2018: 35). This calls for more reliable disaggregated data to monitor progress towards SDG 4 (UNESCO, 2017b), albeit a disaggregation that goes beyond traditional markers of inequality like marital status, religion or lesbian, gay, bisexual, trans and intersex (LGBTI) status, and that might be more relevant in certain localities rather than others.

Funding education equitably

'The ambition of the SDG 4 – Education 2030 agenda to expand access to learning opportunities for all throughout life places great pressure on public funding of education' (UNESCO, 2017b: 17). According to UNESCO's (2015) Global Education Monitoring Report, the annual total cost of achieving universal pre-primary, primary and secondary education in low- and lower-middle-income countries is projected to more than double between 2015 and 2030, and to triple in low-income countries. A recent policy paper (UNESCO, 2017c) confirms that domestic expenditure in low- and lower-middle-income countries cannot cover the cost of reaching SDG 4 and that external funding, especially foreign aid, is called on to supplement domestic financing.

However, today, development aid for education is lower than it was in 2009 (UNESCO, 2016b).

The fall of official development assistance (ODA) is just one illustration of the sense of equity shared across countries; another example is the funding mechanisms that condition resources to the attainment of certain learning outcomes (for instance, results-based financing schemes). However, beyond external sources, national governments are also failing to comply with the international financing agreements of allocating between 4 per cent and 6 per cent of gross domestic product (GDP), or between 15 per cent and 20 per cent of public expenditure, to education.

An equity outlook on financing, however, places an emphasis not only on increasing funds, but also on improving the use of existing financial resources, both in the international development arena and in national accounts. Transparency and accountability mechanisms are needed to assess not only effectiveness, but also fairness, in the distribution of public funds and ODA; more and better data are needed to monitor how funds are being targeted at those furthest behind.

When it comes to assessing the use of funds, the main preoccupation has been with the performance of education systems and their efficiency, mainly understood as value for money and assessed by learning outcomes; however, these assessments should contemplate evidence of their efficiency in reducing inequality as well:

> resources allocated to education should be used in a more equitable and targeted manner. Disadvantaged children, youth and adults, as well as women and girls and people in conflict-affected areas, typically have the greatest education needs and financing should therefore be targeted towards them. (UNESCO, 2017b: 22)

In terms of expanding domestic funding, an equity concern has been raised concerning tax systems that are asymmetrically taxing individuals by means of value added tax (VAT) or goods and services tax (GST), which affect the poorest indiscriminately, and neglecting direct taxes on income, profits, assets and capital gains (Education Commission, 2016b).

Tax systems are also enabling the evasion and avoidance of fiscal obligations by large – often transnational – corporations by means of tax heavens, tax incentives, tax exemptions and tax relief formulae. National governments are losing precious resources to these schemes. According to the Education Commission (2016b: iv): 'Globally, revenues losses due to multinational corporate tax manipulation is estimated (including by International Monetary Fund researchers) at or above USD $600 billion annually (for all countries, not just lower income ones). Revenue losses on income taxes due to undeclared offshore wealth, meanwhile, are estimated to approach $200 billion.' Hence, civil society voices have called for tax justice and progressive domestic tax systems to fund the SDGs, and SDG 4 in particular, as education is itself – potentially – a great equaliser.

Conclusion

This chapter has argued that social justice and equity are being rearticulated with utilitarian notions of quality and excellence, and that this has given way to limited concepts of equity and inclusion, as well as to the transformation of 'education into a field of measurement and comparison' (Lingard and Savage, 2014: 712). This neoliberal interpretation of equity has caused education systems to focus on learning outcomes and in-school factors rather than structural inequality and cumulative disadvantage, thus missing the mark in addressing inequality.

The zest for efficiency, propounded by neoliberalism, also jeopardises the policy intentions of equity and inclusion contained in SDG 4 – Education 2030. Given the Agenda's breath and ambition, the need to report progress, and the scarcity of resources dedicated to education, there is a risk that – for the sake of efficiency – governments may prioritise those areas and social groups within easy reach (cherry-picking) and that donors may privilege 'programmes which appear to reach the largest quantifiable number of beneficiaries, rather than reaching the most marginalised people thereby undermining commitments to "leave no one behind"' (Bond, 2018: 25). In both cases, efficiency and 'value for money' as policy logics are in conflict with equity and inclusion as they may reproduce disadvantage by continuing to favour the privileged few (Matthew effect) and to exclude those most in need.

The consequences of neoliberalism call for subverting this educational discourse and to mainstream equity and inclusion as understood from a social justice perspective. To this effect, there is a wide array of possible resistance practices, beginning with the deconstruction of privilege in socio-economic, cultural and political terms. This entails questioning: the institutionalisation of disadvantage that deprives subordinate groups of their legitimate rights; the ideologies justifying these forms of domination; and the rituals and practices that regulate the possibilities of subaltern groups and individuals to dissent and contest official narratives of – and alternatives to – equality (Scott, 1990).

For education to fulfil its promise, to break with inequality and to advance social justice, a non-utilitarian conceptualisation of equity and inclusion is indispensable, one that may re-examine the discourse of meritocracy in societies that distribute opportunities to develop merit unequally, and that may propose affirmative actions to eliminate the barriers that keep vulnerable learners out of quality education programmes. The renewed impetus for equity and inclusion in SDG 4 represents an invaluable opportunity to counter neoliberalism in education, to rethink its purpose and to construe learning and education as common goods (UNESCO, 2015), leading to a collective, shared responsibility for the well-being of people and the planet in order to ensure its sustainability and to make of it a more just and egalitarian place for all.

References

Bentham, J. (2000) *An introduction to the principles of morals and legislation*, Ontario: Batoche Books.

Blakemore, K. and Griggs, E. (eds) (2007) *Social policy: An introduction* (3rd edn), Maidenhead: Open University Press.

Bond (2018) *Leave no one behind: How the development community is realising the pledge*, London: Bond.

Education Commission (2016a) 'The learning generation. Investing in education for a changing world'. Available at: http://report.educationcommission.org/wpcontent/uploads/2016/09/Learning_Generation_Full_Report.pdf

Education Commission (2016b) 'Global taxation', background paper on financing education and the other Sustainable Development Goals for the Learning Generation. Available at: www.taxjustice.net/wp-content/uploads/2016/11/Global-Taxation-Financing-Education.pdf

Fraser, N. (2009) *Scales of justice. Reimagining political space in a globalizing world*, New York, NY: Columbia University Press.

Lingard, B. and Savage, G. (2014) 'Re-articulating social justice as equity in schooling policy: The effects of testing and data infrastructure', *British Journal of Sociology of Education*, 35(5): 710–30.

OECD (Organisation for Economic Co-operation and Development) (2012) *Equity and quality in education. Supporting disadvantaged students and schools*, Paris: OECD Publishing.

Rawls, J. (1999) *A theory of justice (revised edition)*, Cambridge, MA: Harvard University Press.

Rizvi, F. (2017) 'Globalization and the neoliberal imaginary of educational reform', UNESCO's Education Research and Foresight Working Papers Series, No. 20, pp 1–13.

Rizvi, F. and Lingard, B. (2011) 'Social equity and the assemblage of values in Australian higher education', *Cambridge Journal of Education*, 41(1): 5–22.

Rose, N. (1991) 'Governing by numbers: Figuring out democracy', *Accounting, Organizations and Society*, 16(7): 673–92.

Scott, J.C. (1990) *Domination and the arts of resistance. Hidden transcripts*, New Haven, CT: Yale University Press.

Sellar, S. and Lingard, B. (2014) 'Equity in Australian schooling: The absent presence of socioeconomic context', in S. Gannon and W. Sawyer (eds) *Contemporary issues of equity in education*, Newcastle upon Tyne: Cambridge Scholars Publishing.

Sidelil, L.T. (2011) 'Equity and quality assurance policies in higher education: The case of Ethiopian higher education', master's thesis, Bilbao, University of Deusto.

UNESCO (2015) 'Pricing the right to education: The cost of reaching new targets by 2030', Education for All Global Monitoring Report, Policy Paper 18.

UNESCO (2016a) *Education 2030 Incheon Declaration and Framework for Action for the implementation of Sustainable Development Goal 4*, Paris: UNESCO.

UNESCO (2016b) *Global Education Monitoring Report. Education for people and planet: Creating sustainable futures for all*, Paris: UNESCO.

UNESCO (2017a) *A guide for ensuring inclusion and equity in education*, Paris: UNESCO.

UNESCO (2017b) *Unpacking Sustainable Development Goal 4 – Education 2030 guide*, Paris: UNESCO.

UNESCO (2017c) 'Aid to education is stagnating and not going to countries most in need', Global Education Monitoring Report Policy Paper 31.

United Nations (2015) 'Transforming our world: The 2030 agenda for sustainable development', A/RES/70/1. Available at: https://sustainabledevelopment.un.org/content/documents/21252030%20Agenda%20for%20Sustainable%20Development%20web.pdf

Vargas, C. (2014) 'Democratising education policy making or legitimizing discourse? An analysis of the new Lifelong Learning Law in the Basque Country', *Encyclopaedia Journal of Phenomenology in Education*, 18(40): 87–103.

Vargas, C. (2017) 'Lifelong learning from a social justice perspective', UNESCO's Education Research and Foresight Working Paper, No. 21, pp 1–13.

World Bank (2018) *World development report. Learning to realize education's promise*, Washington, DC: World Bank Publishing.

Afterword: resources of hope

Mary Hamilton and Lyn Tett

The aim of this book, as explained in the Introduction, is to demonstrate not only the urgent challenges from neoliberalism facing educationalists, but also a range of positive responses to these challenges. We have taken Raymond Williams (1989) notion of 'resources of hope' to draw together the rich variety of responses offered by contributors to the book and to identify what Milana and Rapanà call 'interstices for resistance' – points where it is possible to intervene to disrupt the dominant neoliberal regime and to help emergent, more emancipatory, cultures to take root. The notion of hope is explicitly referred to by several contributors as central to affirming identity and emboldening action.

Some of these resources are directly relevant to educational practitioners, suggesting strategies that can be used in teaching or other aspects of institutional practice. Some are resources that can guide educational researchers in designing and carrying out 'resistant' research that foregrounds alternatives to neoliberal values. Some are principles and rules of thumb that can be used in both practice and research.

Many involve collaboration with others, with the aim of pooling resources and widening the spaces for action. Such collaborations can be formalised through organised public events and networks, but the contributors to this book also assert the value of persisting with what may seem like mundane, everyday, acts of resistance that are based on seeing and seizing opportunities to do and say things differently. Such acts are, they argue, the bedrock for fostering wider change. In the following, we identify ten key ideas gathered from across the chapters that contribute to such changes:

1. Many chapters make the point that a core aspect of resistance in a difficult or hostile environment is to find ways *to create dialogic, emancipatory spaces* that are affirming, positive and culturally sensitive for those participating in them. Identifying and forcing open such spaces requires sustained effort and strong commitment. In practice, this can be done via pedagogy and curriculum (Desai et al), and making opportunities for the professional exchange of experiences, opinions, learning, collective action and mutual aid (as in Quinn and Bates, with their Radical Librarians Collective, and Hursh

et al's parents and teachers in the opt-out movement in the US). As Hamilton shows for the aftermath of the higher education staff strikes in the UK, it is not just the collective action itself that gets results, but the process of developing this action that builds knowledge useful for resistance. Sometimes, these spaces exist but are not used, as Stevenson et al argue in relation to the European Semester. While European Union (EU) rules allow trade unions to be part of decision-making bodies, they rarely take up these opportunities, perhaps because the spaces on offer are not recognised as potential forums for useful action. Vargas-Tamez makes the same point when identifying the United Nations' (UN's) Sustainable Development Goals as levers for positive action. It is a matter of looking for the potential in existing places, and perhaps working to revision these.

2. *Prioritising learner perspectives.* Desai et al argue that in order to undermine institutionalised disadvantage and instil hope for equitable and diverse outcomes, we need to change 'the centre of gravity of whose perspectives count' within curriculum and pedagogy. Duckworth and Smith draw on Bourdieu to argue for the importance of overturning negative classifications of learners that lead to 'symbolic violence'. Their transformative pedagogy rests on the assumption that all learners have equal potential to benefit from education and that teachers can learn from students – affirming the experience and knowledge that they bring into the classroom. We need to revision students as agentic subjects and citizens with rights. McKee et al show how even early-years children can be seen as 'pedagogical informants' who can help practitioners see classroom activities in new ways and guide their decisions about curriculum and method. Milana and Rapanà concur with their account of repositioning older learners as active knowledge producers and economic contributors (for example, through their work in voluntary organisations). Older people are not simply consumers and ageing is seen as a time of positive change and cultural production rather than one of inevitable decline.
3. *Harnessing communication technologies* to amplify local and submerged voices and to model citizenship within educational practice. Duckworth and Smith set up a website to enable the digital sharing of learner stories in further education. They publicised this through social media to enable others to gain inspiration from positive case studies and to create networks of like-minded supporters, thereby building what they call 'resistance capital'. Similarly, Hursh et al report on how US parents and teachers organising to opt out of

standardised testing in schools create and circulate digital resources from local action for others to use. A local dialogic, emancipatory space has much more power if it can be shared as a model and replicated or extended across many community settings. Zarifis proposes using digital media for young economically deprived adults to practise their citizenship within adult education.

4. *Explicit sharing of core values* among practitioners enables them to resist negative changes and to counter neoliberal values of commodification and competition. Allatt and Tett give an example of this in relation to Scottish adult literacy workers, who, in many ways, lack power working as they do in a fragmented and under-resourced field of education but are still able to assert their values as a professional community. Informal opportunities for professional learning can strengthen these values and make them explicit. Yasukawa and Osmond use the activity theorists' concept of 'knotworking' to show this as a process that can generate emergent culture and a sense of vocational commitment, reinforced through professional associations. The chapters by Hamilton and by Quinn and Bates on higher education show how underpinning professional values make everyday tactics meaningful and can be effectively supported by both disciplinary networks and trade union action.
5. *Fostering creativity* both directly with learners and in dealing with the institutional demands of policy. Thomson and Hall discuss creativity in terms of countering the 'dullness' of narrow, assessment-driven curricula through new interdisciplinary partnerships between teachers, visual artists and writers. Desai et al see this narrowness as crucially damaging to the identities and potential of marginalised groups and argue that it can and must be overcome by incorporating performance and artistic activities inspired by indigenous knowledges into the curriculum. Likewise, McKee et al show how respecting young children's perspectives inevitably shifts the curriculum and teaching towards multiple modes of expression. They advocate for alternative approaches to professional development by using classroom spaces and technologies differently in order to foster participation and respect. Playful, joyful pedagogies change the dynamic between teachers, children and peers. At the institutional level, creativity involves resourcefulness in reinterpreting policy discourses. Zarifis, for example, repurposes the idea of 'integration' and uses it to prioritise political consciousness and citizenship education in his work with disadvantaged adults. Vargas-Tamez asserts that at the global level, narrow concepts and policy discourses lead to limited outcomes and quality in education and reinforce

privilege. Thériault shows how youth practitioners in Québec act as mediators between policy and front-line work, working with the gap between policy and learners' perspectives. They find ways to compromise in order to obtain the resources they need, looking out for and seizing opportunities to do things differently.

6. *Collaborating with new groups* who share similar values, including international colleagues and organisations. Yasukawa and Osmond cite the importance of making links with adult education and literacy work internationally in countries where essential core values are still in evidence. This helps to show the need for different kinds of policy and to understand the dynamics of change across different contexts. Stevenson et al warn of the importance of staying connected to civil society so that educators do not get co-opted into dysfunctional system values. For discursive shifts to happen, a wider range of people need to be assembled around the policy tables, creating an enlarged policy space for working on designs for new forms of education.
7. It is important to use both *horizontal (peer alliances) and vertical (institutional) strategies* to pressure for change, combining strategies from all interested participants – students, support staff, parents and citizens. Hursh et al exemplify this approach in their work with the parents' opt-out movement in the US. Finnegan suggests that tactical workarounds become more meaningful when combined with a good knowledge of how institutional structures work and an awareness of realistic possibilities for change. It is important to develop understandings of how soft power operates, making a technocratic expert system open and transparent so that you can act to intervene if appropriate. This resonates with Hamilton's observations about piercing the obscurity of university governance.
8. Developing and encouraging a '*knowledge commons*' using and strengthening possibilities for open access to information by resisting paywalls and the domination of large-scale publishing companies. As argued both by Finnegan and by Quinn and Bates, it is urgent to keep libraries open as physically ungated and welcoming spaces – not just in universities, but in public libraries too. Quinn and Bates show how a horizontal alliance between library workers and supporters can offer solidarity, space for discussion, mutual aid nationally and support for everyday workplace acts of resistance.
9. Encouraging both learners and professionals to take *shared responsibility* for promoting education as a common good rather than assuming that it is for someone else or some institutional force to change the neoliberal status quo. Both Stevenson et al and Zarifis argue this in relation to participation in and understanding of EU

policy; Vargas-Tamez takes up the same point in relation to the UN's Sustainable Development Goals. This involves encouraging forms of educational provision that are based on active citizenship and inclusive values (as in Cort and Larson's promotion of popular education).

10. The final key point – and perhaps the core contribution of this book – is about the possibilities of *using educational research itself as a resource* for hope and for making change. Since many contributors are researchers as well as experienced practitioners, they have developed strong arguments about this that complement the practice-oriented strategies outlined earlier. First, they assert the importance of *documenting local experience and valuing participant perspectives in* investigating research problems, whether participants are young people (as in Thériault), children (as in McKee et al), literacy students (as in Duckworth and Smith) or older adults (as in Milana and Rapanà). *Offering alternative concepts and analyses of issues* can help people make new meaning of their experiences and to understand that discourses have material social outcomes (Vargas-Tamez and Desai et al). This can also be achieved through research that *makes institutional systems and spaces of governance transparent* through offering information about less visible aspects and dynamics of governance (as in Stevenson, as well as Hamilton). Cort and Larson, in their work on the disappearance of popular education in Danish policy, show how *researching history* can recover lost or submerged knowledges, help maintain and strengthen 'residual cultures', and identify continuities in change, as evidenced through the actions and statements of certain ministers and officials. Historical research can reconnect us with core alternative values and show the continuity of these values into the present.

Reference

Williams, R. (1989) *Resources of hope*, London: Verso

Index

Note: Page numbers in *italics* refer to figures and tables.

J

K

L

M